FRANCESCO PETRARCH

CANZONIERE

FRANCESCO PETRARCH

CANZONIERE

Edited by Thomas Campbell

Edited by Cassidy Hughes

CRESCENT MOON

CRESCENT MOON PUBLISHING
P.O. Box 1312, Maidstone
Kent, ME14 5XU
Great Britain
ww.crmoon.com

First published 1879. This edition 2017.

Printed and bound in the U.S.A.
Set in Book Antiqua 10 on 14pt.
Designed by Radiance Graphics.

British Library Cataloguing in Publication data

ISBN-13 9781861715999

CONTENTS

A NOTE ON THE TEXT

The poems and translations are from Francesco Petrarch, *The Sonnets, Triumphs and Other Poems of Petrarch*, edited by Thomas Campbell, and published by George Bell & Sons, London, 1879.

Other elements of the edition of *The Sonnets, Triumphs and Other Poems of Petrarch*, such as the *Triumphs* and the *Life of the Poet*, are not included.

Two translations by George MacDonald of two Petrarch sonnets have been included from *Rampoli* (1905).

Portraits of Francesco Petrarch
(this page and over)

Giorgio Vasari, Six Tuscan Poets, 1544, Minneapolis

Boccaccio, Vision of Petrarch, 1467, Glasgow

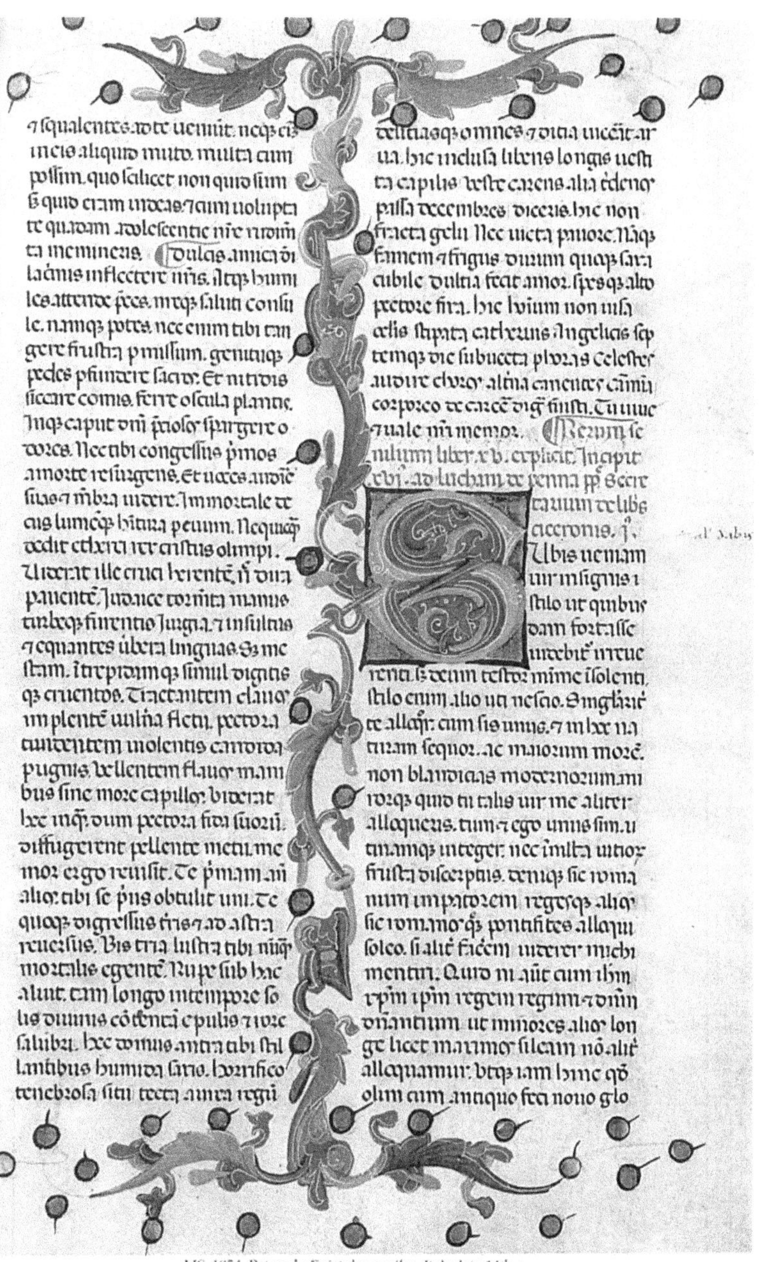

MS 1954 Petrarch: Epistolae seniles. Italy, late 14th c.

Francesco Petrarch, a page from his letters, 14th century

Francesco Petrarch
by Justo de Gante,
15th century (left).

PREFACE

By Thomas Campbell

The present translation of Petrarch completes the Illustrated Library series of the Italian Poets emphatically distinguished as "I Quattro Poeti Italiani."

It is rather a singular fact that, while the other three Poets of this world-famed series – Dante, Ariosto, and Tasso – have each found several translators, no complete version of the fourth, and in Italy the most popular, has hitherto been presented to the English reader. This lacune becomes the more remarkable when we consider the great influence which Petrarch has undoubtedly exercised on our poetry from the time of Chaucer downwards.

The plan of the present volume has been to select from all the known versions those most distinguished for fidelity and rhythm. Of the more favourite poems, as many as three or four are occasionally given; while of others, and those by no means few, it has been difficult to find even one. Indeed, many must have remained entirely unrepresented but for the spirited efforts of Major Macgregor, who has recently translated nearly the whole, and that with great closeness both as to matter and form. To this gentleman we have to return our especial thanks for his liberal permission to make free use of his labours.

Among the translators will be found Chaucer, Spenser, Sir Thomas Wyatt, Anna Hume, Sir John Harington, Basil Kennett, Anne

Bannerman, Drummond of Hawthornden, R. Molesworth, Hugh Boyd, Lord Woodhouselee, the Rev. Francis Wrangham, the Rev. Dr. Nott, Dr. Morehead, Lady Dacre, Lord Charlemont, Capel Lofft, John Penn, Charlotte Smith, Mrs. Wrottesley, Miss Wollaston, J.H. J.H. Merivale, the Rev. W. Shepherd, and Leigh Hunt, besides many anonymous.

The order of arrangement is that adopted by Marsand and other recent editors; but to prevent any difficulty in identification, the Italian first lines have been given throughout, and repeated in an alphabetical index.

York Street, Covent Garden,
June 28, 1869.

INTRODUCTION

By Cassidy Hughes

Francesco Petrarch (Francesco Petrarca, 1304-1374) is the supreme poet of love in the Western tradition, alongside poets such as Sappho and William Shakespeare. Francesco Petrarch is also the Renaissance artist and humanist par excellence. Petrarchism is termed the longest poetic tradition in the Occident, and Petrarch has influenced poets such as Maurice Scève, Sir Thomas Wyatt, Torquato Tasso, Edmund Spenser, Michael Drayton, Joachim Du Bellay, Pierre de Ronsard, Rainer Maria Rilke and Robert Graves, among hundreds of others.

Francesco Petrarch is also called the first modernist: his poetic persona is an early modern version of one of those now familiar alienated, bourgeois, modern outsiders, the kind found in the work of Jean-Paul Sartre, Knut Hamsun, André Gide, Albert Camus and Arthur Rimbaud. Articles and magazines and quarterlies and journals abound which deal with Petrarch and aspects of his poetry, philosophy and rhetoric.[1]

Francesco Petrarch is a poet's poet, an artist who tried to make art in the purest fashion, who burned brightly for his art. He is one of the first

1 *Convivium, Journal of the History of Ideas, Modern Language Notes, Studies in Philology. Giornala storico del la letteratura itallana, Pacific Coast Philology, Italian Philological Quarterly, Cultura Neolatina, Forum Italicum, Dante Studies, Yearbook of Italian Studies, Lettere Italiane, Italian Quarterly, Italianistica, Italia medioevale et umanistica, Enciclopedia Dantesca, Diacritics, Journal of Medieval and Renaissance Studies, Romance Notes* and *Renaissance and Reformation.*

poets to exalt the individual in the way we recognize as modern, and Petrarch's ruthless self-analysis seems wholly in tune with that of, say, Arthur Rimbaud, Julia Kristeva, Lawrence Durrell or Virginia Woolf.

But it is as a love poet that Francesco Petrarch is celebrated – as a love poet rather than a rhetorician, humanist or philosopher (although his work in those areas is very important). Petrarch's *Canzoniere*, often also known as the *Rime Sparse*, lies at the heart of his achievement: it comprises 366 poems about love, written in Italian and worked on right up until Petrarch's death in 1374. In the *Canzoniere*, there are hundreds of sonnets, 29 *canzoni*, 7 *ballate*, 9 *sestine* and 4 *madrigali*. Petrarch's other major works included *Secretum, Triumphs, Africa, De Vita Solitaria*, verse epistles, biographies, allegorical ecologues and hundreds of letters.

Love rules, and Francesco Petrarch is so popular partly because of his love poetry, because he writes so well about love, because he flatters the reader's received notions of love, because most critics (the people who exalt Petrarch in critical writings) are male, and Petrarch's philosophy of love is masculinist and patriarchal. Petrarch celebrates mainly masculine ideas of love, sex, seduction and romance. He trades on desire, and desire is at the heart of Western culture (in movies, pop songs, advertizing, novels, magazines, radio shows, TV sit corms, fashion, etc). The desire is for the unattainable – variously imagined to be the distant but beautiful woman, the Holy Grail, the ideal love, heaven, world peace, an end to poverty, etc.

The focus of the quest in Francesco Petrarch's *Rime Sparse* is Laura de Sade, the beloved woman (she was probably Laura de Noves, wife of the Count Hugues de Sade. As modern commentators can't resist pointing out, Laura's husband was an ancestor of the Marquis de Sade, further embedding Petrarch in the *avant garde* and progressive literary tradition of Europe).

Francesco Petrarch emerges as the poet who is the apotheosis of courtly love, and his *Canzoniere* is the supreme example of the troubadour ethic. At the same time, the *Rime Sparse* is a decadent text, falling into self-parody and too sweetly refined artifice. The power of Petrarch's work is even so undeniable.

BIBLIOGRAPHY

F. Ames-Lewis & M. Rogers, eds. *Concepts of Beauty in Renaissance Art*, Scolar Press, London, 1998

T. Bahti. "Petrarch and the Scene of Writing: A Reading of *Rime* CXXIX", *Yale Italian Studies*, 1, 1980

– . *Ends of the Lyric: Direction and Consequence in Western Poetry*, Johns Hopkins University Press, Baltimore, MD, 1996

T. Barolini. "The Making of a Lyric Sequence: Time and Narrative in Petrarch's *Rerum vulgarium fragmenta*", *Modern Language Notes*, 104, 1989

A. Bernardo, ed. *Francesco Petrarca*, Albany, NY, 1980

– . "The importance of the non-love poems in Petrarch's *Cazoniere*", *Italica*, 27, 1950

– . "Petrarch's attitude towards Dante", *Proceedings of the Modern Language Association*, 70, 1955

– . "Petrarch and the Art of Literature", in Molinaro, 1973

– . *Petrarch, Laura, and the 'Triumphs'*, Albany, NY, 1974

– . & A.L. Pellegrini, eds. *Dante, Petrarch, Boccaccio, Medieval and Renaissance Texts and Studies*, Binghamton, 1983

E. Bigi. "La rima del Petrarca", *Studi petrarcheschi*, 7, 1961

– . "La ballate del Petrarca", *Giornale storico della letteratura italiana*, 151, 1974

– . "Alcuni aspetti dello stile del *Canzoniere* petrarchesco", *Dal Petrarca al Leopardi*, Milan, 1954

M. Bishop. *Petrarch and His World*, Indiana University Press Bloomington, London, 1963

E.L. Boggs. "Cino and Petrarca", *Modern Language Notes*, 94, 1979

U. Bosc. *Francesco Petrarca*, Bari, 1961

C.B. Bouchard. *"Strong of Body, Brave and Noble": Chivalry and Society in Medieval France*, Cornell University Press, Ithaca, NY, 1998

M. O'Rouke Boyle. *Petrarch's Genius: Pentimento and Prophecy*, University of California Press, Berkeley, CA, 1991

G. Braden. "Love and Fame: The Petrarchan Career", in Smith, 1986

J. Brenkman. "Writing, Desire, Dialectic in Petrarch's *Rime* 23", *Pacific Coast Philology*, 9, 1974

G.A. Cesareo. *Su le 'poesie volgari' del Petrarca*, Rocca San Casciano, 1898

F.L. Cheyette. *Ermengard of Narbonne and the World of the Troubadors*, Cornell University Press, Ithaca, NY, 2001

E. Chiappelli. *Studi sui linguaggio del Petrarca: la canzone della visioni*, Florence, 1971

G. Cipolla. "Labyrinthine Imagery in Petrarch", *Italica*, 54, 1977

R.J. Clements. "Préhistoire de l'aura de Pétraque", in *Varianti e altra linguistica*, 193-9, Einaudi, Turin, 1970

G. Contini. "Anti-Petrarchism of the Pléiade", *Modern Philology*, 39, 1942

Convegno Internazionale Francesco Petrarca, Rome, 1976

K. Cool. "The Petrarchan Landscape as Palimpsest", *Journal of Medieval and Renaissance*

Studies, 11, 1981

M. Cottino-Jones. "The Myth of Apollo and Daphne in Petrarch's *Canzoniere*", in Scaglione, 1975

D. Dtuschke. "The Anniversary Poems in Petrarch's *Canzoniere*", *Italica*, 58, 1981

– . *Francesco Petrarca: Canzone XXIII From First to Final Version*, Ravenna, 1977

R.M. Durling. "Petrarch's 'Giovene donna sotto un verde lauro'", *Modern Language Notes*, 86, 1971

L. Enterline. "Embodied Voices: Petrarch Reading (Himself Reading) Ovid", in Finucci, 1994

P. Erickson & C. Hulse, eds. *Early Modern Visual Culture*, University of Pennsylvania Press, Philadelphia, PA, 2000

F. Figurelli. "L'architettura del sonetto in Francesco Petrarca", *Studi petrarcheschi*, 7, 1961

V. Finucci & R.M. Schawrtz, eds. *Desire in the Renaissance: Literature and Psychoanalysis*, Princeton University Press, Princeton, NJ, 1994

K. Foster. *Petrarch: Poet and Humanist*, Edinburgh, 1984

W. Franke. *Dante's Interpretive Journey*, Chicago University Press, Chicago, IL, 1996

J. Freccero. "The Fig Tree and the Laurel: Petrarch's Poetics", *Diacritics*, Spring, 1975

G. Genot. "Petrarque et la scene du regard", *Journal of Medieval and Renaissance Studies*, 2, 1972

E. Gianturco. "The Double Gift: Inner Vision and Pictorial Sense in Petrarch", *Renaissance and Reformation*, 8, 1972

B. Gold *et al*, eds. *Sex and Gender in Medieval and Renaissance Texts: The Latin Tradition*, State University of New York Press, Albany, NY, 1997

C. Grössinger. *Picturing Women in Late Mediaeval Art*, Manchester University Press, Manchester, 1997

P. Hainsworth. *Petrarch the Poet: An Introduction to the 'Rerum Vulgarium Fragmente'*, Routledge, London, 1988

E. Harvey, ed. *Sensible Flesh: On Touch in Early Modern Culture*, University of Pennsylvania Press, Philadelphia, PA, 2002

E. Jager. *The Book of the Heart*, University Press of Chicago, Chicago, IL, 2000

F.J. Jones. "Laura's date of birth and the calendrical system implicit in the *Cazoniere*", *Italianistica*, 1, 1983

– . "Arguments in favour of a calendrical structure for Petrarch's *Canzoniere*", *Modern Language Review*, 79, 1984

– . "Further evidence of the identity of Petrarch's Laura", *Italian Studies*, 39, 1984

H.A. Mathes. "Petrarch's Tranquillo Porto'", *Italica*, 26, 1949

W.J. Kennedy. "Petrarchan Textuality", in Brownlee, 1989

G. Mazzotta. "Petrarch's Song 126", in Caws, 1986

– . "The *Canzoniere* and the Language of the Self", *Studies in Philology*, 75, 1978

– . ed. *The World of Petrarch*, Duke University Press, Durham, NC, 1993

E. Parker & D. Quint, eds. *Literary Theory/ Renaissance Texts*, Johns Hopkins University Press, Baltimore, MD, 1986

M. Perugi. *Trovatori a Valchiusa: un frammento della cultura provenzale del Petrarca*, Studi sul Petrarca, 18, Antenore, Padua, 1985

F. Petrarch. *Petrarch's Lyric Poems; the Rime Sparse and other Lyrics*, tr. Robert M. Durling, Harvard University Pr4ess, Cambridge, MA, 1978

– . *Petrarch and Petrarchism*, tr. Stephen Minta, Manchester University Press, Manchester, 1980

– . *Selected Poems*, ed. T. Gwynfor Griffith & P.R.J. Hainsworth, Manchester University Press, Manchester, 1971

– . *Selected Poems*, tr. Anthony Mortimer, University of Alabama Press, Alabama, 1977

– . *Selections From the 'Canonziere' and Other Works*, tr. Mark Musa, Oxford University Press, Oxford, 1985

J. Petrie. Pe*trarch:* P. Possiedi: "Petrarca Petrosco", *Forum italicum*, 8, 1974

A.E. Quaglio. *Francesco Petrarca*, Milan, 1967
M.S. Regan. "Petrarch's Courtly and Christian Vocabularies: Language in *Canzoniere* 61-63", *Romance Notes*, 15, 1974
F. Rigolot. "Nature and Function of Paronomasia in the *Canzoniere*", *Italian Quarterly*, 18, 1974
T. Roche. "The Calendrical Structure of Petrarch's *Canzoniere*", *Studies in Philology*, 7, 1974
– . *Petrarch and the English Sonnet Sequences*, AMS Press, New York, 1989
N. Rosenberg. "Petrarch's Limping: The Foot Unequal to the Eye", *Modern Language Notes*, 77, 1962
I. Scarano, ed. *Francesco Petrarca*, Naples, 1972
E. Scarry, ed. *Fins de Siècle: English Poetry in 1590, 1690, 1790., 1890, 1990*, Johns Hopkins University Press, Baltimore, MD, 1995
F. Schalk, ed. *Petrarca 1304-1374: Beitrage zu Werk und Wirkung*, Frankfurt, 1975
E.M Selinger. *What is it then between us?: Traditions of Love in American Poetry*, Cornell University Press, Ithaca, NY, 1998
M. Shapiro. *Hieroglyph of Time: The Petrarchan Sestina*, Minneapolis, MN, 1980
J.H. Smith, ed. *Pragmatism's Freud: The Moral Disposition of Psychoanalysis*, Johns Hopkins University Press, Baltimore, MD, 1986
B.T. Sozzi. *Petrarca*, Palermo, 1963
S. Sturm-Maddox. "Petrarch's Serpent in the Grass: The Fall as Subtext in the *Rime Sparse*", *Journal of Medieval and Renaissance Studies*, 13, 1983
– . "Petrarch's Siren", *Italian Quarterly*, 103, 1986
J. Tilden. "Spiritual Conflict in Petrarch's *Canzoniere*", in F. Schalk
M. Turchi. "Il centenario del Petrarca e la critica", *Italianistica*, 7, 1978
G. Velli. "La memoria poetica del Petrarca", *Italia medievale e umanistica*, 19, 1976
– . "La metafora del Petrarca", in Goldin, 1980
M. Waller. *Petrarch's Poetics and Literary History*, Amherst, MA, 1980
E.H. Wilkins. *Petrarch at Vaucluse*, Chicago University Press, Chicago, IL, 1958
– . *The Making of the 'Canzoniere' and other Petrarchan Studies*, Rome, 1951
– . *Life of Petrarch*, Chicago University Press, Chicago, IL, 1961
– . *Studies in the Life and Works of Petrarch*, Harvard University Press, Cambridge, MA, 1955
– . *Petrarch's Eight Years in Milan*, Harvard University Press, Cambridge, MA, 1958
– . *Petrarch's Later Years*, Harvard University Press, Cambridge, MA, 1959
– . *Petrarch's Correspondence*, Harvard University Press, Cambridge, MA, 1960
E. Williamson. "A Consideration of 'Virgine bella'", *Italica*, 29, 1952

PART ONE

TO LAURA IN LIFE

SONNET I.

Voi, ch' ascoltate in rime sparse il suono.

HE CONFESSES THE VANITY OF HIS PASSION

Ye who in rhymes dispersed the echoes hear
Of those sad sighs with which my heart I fed
When early youth my mazy wanderings led,
Fondly diverse from what I now appear,
Fluttering 'twixt frantic hope and frantic fear,
From those by whom my various style is read,
I hope, if e'er their hearts for love have bled,
Not only pardon, but perhaps a tear.
But now I clearly see that of mankind
Long time I was the tale: whence bitter thought
And self-reproach with frequent blushes teem;
While of my frenzy, shame the fruit I find,
And sad repentance, and the proof, dear-bought,
That the world's joy is but a flitting dream.

Lord Charlemont.

O ye, who list in scatter'd verse the sound
Of all those sighs with which my heart I fed,
When I, by youthful error first misled,
Unlike my present self in heart was found;
Who list the plaints, the reasonings that abound
Throughout my song, by hopes, and vain griefs bred;
If e'er true love its influence o'er ye shed,
Oh! let your pity be with pardon crown'd.
But now full well I see how to the crowd
For length of time I proved a public jest:
E'en by myself my folly is allow'd:
And of my vanity the fruit is shame,
Repentance, and a knowledge strong imprest,
That worldly pleasure is a passing dream.

Dr Nott

Ye, who may listen to each idle strain
Bearing those sighs, on which my heart was fed
In life's first morn, by youthful error led,
(Far other then from what I now remain!)
That thus in varying numbers I complain,
Numbers of sorrow vain and vain hope bred,
If any in love's lore be practisèd,
His pardon, – e'en his pity I may obtain:
But now aware that to mankind my name
Too long has been a bye-word and a scorn,
I blush before my own severer thought;
Of my past wanderings the sole fruit is shame,
And deep repentance, of the knowledge born
That all we value in this world is naught.

Lady Dacre.

SONNET II.

Per far una leggiadra sua vendetta.

HOW HE BECAME THE VICTIM OF LOVE.

For many a crime at once to make me smart,
And a delicious vengeance to obtain,
Love secretly took up his bow again,
As one who acts the cunning coward's part;
My courage had retired within my heart,
There to defend the pass bright eyes might gain;
When his dread archery was pour'd amain
Where blunted erst had fallen every dart.
Scared at the sudden brisk attack, I found
Nor time, nor vigour to repel the foe
With weapons suited to the direful need;
No kind protection of rough rising ground,
Where from defeat I might securely speed,
Which fain I would e'en now, but ah, no method know!

Dr Nott

One sweet and signal vengeance to obtain
To punish in a day my life's long crime,
As one who, bent on harm, waits place and time,
Love craftily took up his bow again.
My virtue had retired to watch my heart,
Thence of weak eyes the danger to repell,
When momently a mortal blow there fell
Where blunted hitherto dropt every dart.
And thus, o'erpower'd in that first attack,
She had nor vigour left enough, nor room
Even to arm her for my pressing need,
Nor to the steep and painful mountain back
To draw me, safe and scathless from that doom,
Whence, though alas! too weak, she fain had freed.

Robert Macgregor.

SONNET III.

Era 'l giorno ch' al sol si scoloraro.

HE BLAMES LOVE FOR WOUNDING HIM ON A HOLY DAY (GOOD FRIDAY).

'Twas on the morn, when heaven its blessed ray
In pity to its suffering master veil'd,
First did I, Lady, to your beauty yield,
Of your victorious eyes th' unguarded prey.
Ah! little reck'd I that, on such a day,
Needed against Love's arrows any shield;
And trod, securely trod, the fatal field:
Whence, with the world's, began my heart's dismay.
On every side Love found his victim bare,
And through mine eyes transfix'd my throbbing heart;
Those eyes, which now with constant sorrows flow:
But poor the triumph of his boasted art,
Who thus could pierce a naked youth, nor dare
To you in armour mail'd even to display his bow!

Francis Wrangham.

'Twas on the blessed morning when the sun
In pity to our Maker hid his light,
That, unawares, the captive I was won,
Lady, of your bright eyes which chain'd me quite;
That seem'd to me no time against the blows
Of love to make defence, to frame relief:
Secure and unsuspecting, thus my woes
Date their commencement from the common grief.
Love found me feeble then and fenceless all,
Open the way and easy to my heart
Through eyes, where since my sorrows ebb and flow:
But therein was, methinks, his triumph small,
On me, in that weak state, to strike his dart,
Yet hide from you so strong his very bow.

Robert Macgregor.

SONNET IV.

Quel ch' infinita providenza ed arte.

HE CELEBRATES THE BIRTHPLACE OF LAURA.

He that with wisdom, goodness, power divine,
Did ample Nature's perfect book design,
Adorn'd this beauteous world, and those above,
Kindled fierce Mars, and soften'd milder Jove:
When seen on earth the shadows to fulfill
Of the less volume which conceal'd his will,
Took John and Peter from their homely care,
And made them pillars of his temple fair.
Nor in imperial Rome would He be born,
Whom servile Judah yet received with scorn:
E'en Bethlehem could her infant King disown,
And the rude manger was his early throne.
Victorious sufferings did his pomp display,
Nor other chariot or triumphal way.
At once by Heaven's example and decree,
Such honour waits on such humility.

Basil Kennet.

The High Eternal, in whose works supreme
The Master's vast creative power hath spoke:
At whose command each circling sphere awoke,
Jove mildly rose, and Mars with fiercer beam:
To earth He came, to ratify the scheme
Reveal'd to us through prophecy's dark cloak,
To sound redemption, speak man's fallen yoke:
He chose the humblest for that heavenly theme.
But He conferr'd not on imperial Rome
His birth's renown; He chose a lowlier sky, –
To stand, through Him, the proudest spot on earth!
And now doth shine within its humble home
A star, that doth each other so outvie,
That grateful nature hails its lovely birth.

Miss Wollaston.

Who show'd such infinite providence and skill
In his eternal government divine,
Who launch'd the spheres, gave sun and moon to shine,
And brightest wonders the dark void to fill;
On earth who came the Scriptures to maintain,
Which for long years the truth had buried yet,
Took John and Peter from the fisher's net
And gave to each his part in the heavenly reign.
He for his birth fair Rome preferr'd not then,
But lowly Bethlehem; thus o'er proudest state
He ever loves humility to raise.
Now rises from small spot like sun again,
Whom Nature hails, the place grows bright and great
Which birth so heavenly to our earth displays.

Robert Macgregor.

SONNET V.

Quand' io movo i sospiri a chiamar voi.

HE PLAYS UPON THE NAME LAURETA OR LAURA.

In sighs when I outbreathe your cherish'd name,
That name which love has writ upon my heart,
LAUd instantly upon my doting tongue,
At the first thought of its sweet sound, is heard;
Your REgal state, which I encounter next,
Doubles my valour in that high emprize:
But TAcit ends the word; your praise to tell
Is fitting load for better backs than mine.
Thus all who call you, by the name itself,
Are taught at once to LAUd and to REvere,
O worthy of all reverence and esteem!
Save that perchance Apollo may disdain
That mortal tongue of his immortal boughs
Should ever so presume as e'en to speak.

Anonymous

SONNET VI.

Sì traviato è 'l folle mio desio.

OF HIS FOOLISH PASSION FOR LAURA.

So wayward now my will, and so unwise,
To follow her who turns from me in flight,
And, from love's fetters free herself and light,
Before my slow and shackled motion flies,
That less it lists, the more my sighs and cries
Would point where passes the safe path and right,
Nor aught avails to check or to excite,
For Love's own nature curb and spur defies.
Thus, when perforce the bridle he has won,
And helpless at his mercy I remain,
Against my will he speeds me to mine end
'Neath yon cold laurel, whose false boughs upon
Hangs the harsh fruit, which, tasted, spreads the pain
I sought to stay, and mars where it should mend.

Robert Macgregor.

My tameless will doth recklessly pursue
Her, who, unshackled by love's heavy chain,
Flies swiftly from its chase, whilst I in vain
My fetter'd journey pantingly renew;
The safer track I offer to its view,
But hopeless is my power to restrain,
It rides regardless of the spur or rein;
Love makes it scorn the hand that would subdue.
The triumph won, the bridle all its own,
Without one curb I stand within its power,
And my destruction helplessly presage:
It guides me to that laurel, ever known,
To all who seek the healing of its flower,
To aggravate the wound it should assuage.

Miss Wollaston.

SONNET VII.

La gola e 'l sonno e l' oziose piume.

TO A FRIEND, ENCOURAGING HIM TO PURSUE POETRY.

Torn is each virtue from its earthly throne
By sloth, intemperance, and voluptuous ease;
E'en nature deviates from her wonted ways,
Too much the slave of vicious custom grown.
Far hence is every light celestial gone,
That guides mankind through life's perplexing maze;
And those, whom Helicon's sweet waters please,
From mocking crowds receive contempt alone.
Who now would laurel, myrtle-wreaths obtain?
Let want, let shame, Philosophy attend!
Cries the base world, intent on sordid gain.
What though thy favourite path be trod by few;
Let it but urge thee more, dear gentle friend!
Thy great design of glory to pursue.

Anonymous

Intemperance, slumber, and the slothful down
Have chased each virtue from this world away;
Hence is our nature nearly led astray
From its due course, by habitude o'erthrown;
Those kindly lights of heaven so dim are grown,
Which shed o'er human life instruction's ray;
That him with scornful wonder they survey,
Who would draw forth the stream of Helicon.
"Whom doth the laurel please, or myrtle now?
Naked and poor, Philosophy, art thou!"
The worthless crowd, intent on lucre, cries.
Few on thy chosen road will thee attend;
Yet let it more incite thee, gentle friend,
To prosecute thy high-conceived emprize.

Dr Nott

SONNET VIII.

A piè de' colli ove la bella vesta.

HE FEIGNS AN ADDRESS FROM SOME BIRDS WHICH HE HAD PRESENTED.

Beneath the verdant hills – where the fair vest
Of earthly mould first took the Lady dear,
Who him that sends us, feather'd captives, here
Awakens often from his tearful rest –
Lived we in freedom and in quiet, blest
With everything which life below might cheer,
No foe suspecting, harass'd by no fear
That aught our wanderings ever could molest;
But snatch'd from that serener life, and thrown
To the low wretched state we here endure,
One comfort, short of death, survives alone:
Vengeance upon our captor full and sure!
Who, slave himself at others' power, remains
Pent in worse prison, bound by sterner chains.

Robert Macgregor.

Beneath those very hills, where beauty threw
Her mantle first o'er that earth-moulded fair,
Who oft from sleep, while shedding many a tear,
Awakens him that sends us unto you,
Our lives in peacefulness and freedom flew,
E'en as all creatures wish who hold life dear;
Nor deem'd we aught could in its course come near,
Whence to our wanderings danger might accrue.
But from the wretched state to which we're brought,
Leaving another with sereneness fraught,
Nay, e'en from death, one comfort we obtain;
That vengeance follows him who sent us here;
Another's utmost thraldom doomed to bear,
Bound he now lies with a still stronger chain.

Dr Nott

SONNET IX.

Quando 'l pianeta che distingue l' ore.

WITH A PRESENT OF FRUIT IN SPRING.

When the great planet which directs the hours
To dwell with Taurus from the North is borne,
Such virtue rays from each enkindled horn,
Rare beauty instantly all nature dowers;
Nor this alone, which meets our sight, that flowers
Richly the upland and the vale adorn,
But Earth's cold womb, else lustreless and lorn,
Is quick and warm with vivifying powers,
Till herbs and fruits, like these I send, are rife.
– So she, a sun amid her fellow fair,
Shedding the rays of her bright eyes on me,
Thoughts, acts, and words of love wakes into life –
But, ah! for me is no new Spring, nor e'er,
Smile they on whom she will, again can be.

Robert Macgregor.

When Taurus in his house doth Phœbus keep,
There pours so bright a virtue from his crest
That Nature wakes, and stands in beauty drest,
The flow'ring meadows start with joy from sleep:
Nor they alone rejoice – earth's bosom deep
(Though not one beam illumes her night of rest)
Responsive smiles, and from her fruitful breast
Gives forth her treasures for her sons to reap.
Thus she, who dwells amid her sex a sun,
Shedding upon my soul her eyes' full light,
Each thought creates, each deed, each word of love:
But though my heart's proud mastery she hath won
Alas! within me dwells eternal night:
My spirit ne'er Spring's genial breath doth prove.

Miss Wollaston.

SONNET X.

Gloriosa Colonna, in cui s' appoggia.

TO STEFANO COLONNA THE ELDER, INVITING HIM TO THE COUNTRY.

Glorious Colonna! still the strength and stay
Of our best hopes, and the great Latin name
Whom power could never from the true right way
Seduce by flattery or by terror tame:
No palace, theatres, nor arches here,
But, in their stead, the fir, the beech, and pine
On the green sward, with the fair mountain near
Paced to and fro by poet friend of thine;
Thus unto heaven the soul from earth is caught;
While Philomel, who sweetly to the shade
The livelong night her desolate lot complains,
Fills the soft heart with many an amorous thought:
– Ah! why is so rare good imperfect made
While severed from us still my lord remains.

Robert Macgregor.

Glorious Colonna! thou, the Latins' hope,
The proud supporter of our lofty name,
Thou hold'st thy path of virtue still the same,
Amid the thunderings of Rome's Jove – the Pope.
Not here do human structures interlope
The fir to rival, or the pine-tree's claim,
The soul may revel in poetic flame
Upon yon mountain's green and gentle slope.
And thus from earth to heaven the spirit soars,
Whilst Philomel her tale of woe repeats
Amid the sympathising shades of night,
Thus through man's breast love's current sweetly pours:
Yet still thine absence half the joy defeats, –
Alas! my friend, why dim such radiant light?

Miss Wollaston.

BALLATA I.

Lassare il velo o per sole o per ombra.

PERCEIVING HIS PASSION, LAURA'S SEVERITY INCREASES.

Never thy veil, in sun or in the shade,
Lady, a moment I have seen
Quitted, since of my heart the queen
Mine eyes confessing thee my heart betray'd
While my enamour'd thoughts I kept conceal'd.
Those fond vain hopes by which I die,
In thy sweet features kindness beam'd:
Changed was the gentle language of thine eye
Soon as my foolish heart itself reveal'd;
And all that mildness which I changeless deem'd –
All, all withdrawn which most my soul esteem'd.
Yet still the veil I must obey,
Which, whatsoe'er the aspect of the day,
Thine eyes' fair radiance hides, my life to overshade.

Capel Lofft.

Wherefore, my unkind fair one, say,
Whether the sun fierce darts his ray,
Or whether gloom o'erspreads the sky,
That envious veil is ne'er thrown by;
Though well you read my heart, and knew
How much I long'd your charms to view?
While I conceal'd each tender thought,
That my fond mind's destruction wrought,
Your face with pity sweetly shone;
But, when love made my passion known,
Your sunny locks were seen no more,
Nor smiled your eyes as heretofore;
Behind a jealous cloud retired
Those beauties which I most admired.
And shall a veil thus rule my fate?
O cruel veil, that whether heat
Or cold be felt, art doom'd to prove
Fatal to me, shadowing the lights I love!

Dr Nott

SONNET XI.

Se la mia vita dall' aspro tormento.

HE HOPES THAT TIME WILL RENDER HER MORE MERCIFUL.

If o'er each bitter pang, each hidden throe
Sadly triumphant I my years drag on,
Till even the radiance of those eyes is gone,
Lady, which star-like now illume thy brow;
And silver'd are those locks of golden glow,
And wreaths and robes of green aside are thrown,
And from thy cheek those hues of beauty flown,
Which check'd so long the utterance of my woe,
Haply my bolder tongue may then reveal
The bosom'd annals of my heart's fierce fire,
The martyr-throbs that now in night I veil:
And should the chill Time frown on young Desire.
Still, still some late remorse that breast may feel,
And heave a tardy sigh – ere love with life expire.

Francis Wrangham.

Lady, if grace to me so long be lent
From love's sharp tyranny and trials keen,
Ere my last days, in life's far vale, are seen,
To know of thy bright eyes the lustre spent,
The fine gold of thy hair with silver sprent,
Neglected the gay wreaths and robes of green,
Pale, too, and thin the face which made me, e'en
'Gainst injury, slow and timid to lament:
Then will I, for such boldness love would give,
Lay bare my secret heart, in martyr's fire
Years, days, and hours that yet has known to live;
And, though the time then suit not fair desire,
At least there may arrive to my long grief,
Too late of tender sighs the poor relief.

Robert Macgregor.

SONNET XII.

Quando fra l' altre donne ad ora ad ora.

THE BEAUTY OF LAURA LEADS HIM TO THE CONTEMPLATION OF THE SUPREME GOOD.

Throned on her angel brow, when Love displays
His radiant form among all other fair,
Far as eclipsed their choicest charms appear,
I feel beyond its wont my passion blaze.
And still I bless the day, the hour, the place,
When first so high mine eyes I dared to rear;
And say, "Fond heart, thy gratitude declare,
That then thou had'st the privilege to gaze.
'Twas she inspired the tender thought of love,
Which points to heaven, and teaches to despise
The earthly vanities that others prize:
She gave the soul's light grace, which to the skies
Bids thee straight onward in the right path move;
Whence buoy'd by hope e'en, now I soar to worlds above."

Francis Wrangham.

When Love, whose proper throne is that sweet face,
At times escorts her 'mid the sisters fair,
As their each beauty is than hers less rare,
So swells in me the fond desire apace.
I bless the hour, the season and the place,
So high and heavenward when my eyes could dare;
And say: "My heart! in grateful memory bear
This lofty honour and surpassing grace:
From her descends the tender truthful thought,
Which follow'd, bliss supreme shall thee repay,
Who spurn'st the vanities that win the crowd:
From her that gentle graceful love is caught,
To heaven which leads thee by the right-hand way,
And crowns e'en here with hopes both pure and proud."

Robert Macgregor.

BALLATA II.

Occhi miei lassi, mentre ch' io vi giro.

HE INVITES HIS EYES TO FEAST THEMSELVES ON LAURA.

My wearied eyes! while looking thus
On that fair fatal face to us,
Be wise, be brief, for – hence my sighs –
Already Love our bliss denies.
Death only can the amorous track
Shut from my thoughts which leads them back
To the sweet port of all their weal;
But lesser objects may conceal
Our light from you, that meaner far
In virtue and perfection are.
Wherefore, poor eyes! ere yet appears,
Already nigh, the time of tears,
Now, after long privation past,
Look, and some comfort take at last.

Robert Macgregor.

SONNET XIII.

Io mi rivolgo indietro a ciascun passo.

ON QUITTING LAURA.

With weary frame which painfully I bear,
I look behind me at each onward pace,
And then take comfort from your native air,
Which following fans my melancholy face;
The far way, my frail life, the cherish'd fair
Whom thus I leave, as then my thoughts retrace,
I fix my feet in silent pale despair,
And on the earth my tearful eyes abase.
At times a doubt, too, rises on my woes,
"How ever can this weak and wasted frame
Live from life's spirit and one source afar?"
Love's answer soon the truth forgotten shows –
"This high pure privilege true lovers claim,
Who from mere human feelings franchised are!"

Robert Macgregor.

I look behind each step I onward trace,
Scarce able to support my wearied frame,
Ah, wretched me! I pantingly exclaim,
And from her atmosphere new strength embrace;
I think on her I leave – my heart's best grace –
My lengthen'd journey – life's capricious flame –
I pause in withering fear, with purpose tame,
Whilst down my cheek tears quick each other chase.
My doubting heart thus questions in my grief:
"Whence comes it that existence thou canst know
When from thy spirit thou dost dwell entire?"
Love, holy Love, my heart then answers brief:
"Such privilege I do on all bestow
Who feed my flame with nought of earthly fire!"

Miss Wollaston.

SONNET XIV.

Movesi 'l vecchierel canuto e bianco.

HE COMPARES HIMSELF TO A PILGRIM.

The palmer bent, with locks of silver gray,
Quits the sweet spot where he has pass'd his years,
Quits his poor family, whose anxious fears
Paint the loved father fainting on his way;
And trembling, on his aged limbs slow borne,
In these last days that close his earthly course,
He, in his soul's strong purpose, finds new force,
Though weak with age, though by long travel worn:
Thus reaching Rome, led on by pious love,
He seeks the image of that Saviour Lord
Whom soon he hopes to meet in bliss above:
So, oft in other forms I seek to trace
Some charm, that to my heart may yet afford
A faint resemblance of thy matchless grace.

Lady Dacre.

As parts the aged pilgrim, worn and gray,
From the dear spot his life where he had spent,
From his poor family by sorrow rent,
Whose love still fears him fainting in decay:
Thence dragging heavily, in life's last day,
His suffering frame, on pious journey bent,
Pricking with earnest prayers his good intent,
Though bow'd with years, and weary with the way,
He reaches Rome, still following his desire
The likeness of his Lord on earth to see,
Whom yet he hopes in heaven above to meet;
So I, too, seek, nor in the fond quest tire,
Lady, in other fair if aught there be
That faintly may recall thy beauties sweet.

Robert Macgregor.

SONNET XV.

Piovonmi amare lagrime dal viso.

HIS STATE WHEN LAURA IS PRESENT, AND WHEN SHE DEPARTS.

Down my cheeks bitter tears incessant rain,
And my heart struggles with convulsive sighs,
When, Laura, upon you I turn my eyes,
For whom the world's allurements I disdain,
But when I see that gentle smile again,
That modest, sweet, and tender smile, arise,
It pours on every sense a blest surprise;
Lost in delight is all my torturing pain.
Too soon this heavenly transport sinks and dies:
When all thy soothing charms my fate removes
At thy departure from my ravish'd view.
To that sole refuge its firm faith approves
My spirit from my ravish'd bosom flies,
And wing'd with fond remembrance follows you.

Capel Lofft.

Tears, bitter tears adown my pale cheek rain,
Bursts from mine anguish'd breast a storm of sighs,
Whene'er on you I turn my passionate eyes,
For whom alone this bright world I disdain.
True! to my ardent wishes and old pain
That mild sweet smile a peaceful balm supplies,
Rescues me from the martyr fire that tries,
Rapt and intent on you whilst I remain;
Thus in your presence – but my spirits freeze
When, ushering with fond acts a warm adieu,
My fatal stars from life's quench'd heaven decay.
My soul released at last with Love's apt keys
But issues from my heart to follow you,
Nor tears itself without much thought away.

Robert Macgregor.

SONNET XVI.

Quand' io son tutto volto in quella parte.

HE FLIES, BUT PASSION PURSUES HIM.

When I reflect and turn me to that part
Whence my sweet lady beam'd in purest light,
And in my inmost thought remains that light
Which burns me and consumes in every part,
I, who yet dread lest from my heart it part
And see at hand the end of this my light,
Go lonely, like a man deprived of light,
Ignorant where to go; whence to depart.
Thus flee I from the stroke which lays me dead,
Yet flee not with such speed but that desire
Follows, companion of my flight alone.
Silent I go: – but these my words, though dead,
Others would cause to weep – this I desire,
That I may weep and waste myself alone.

Capel Lofft.

When all my mind I turn to the one part
Where sheds my lady's face its beauteous light,
And lingers in my loving thought the light
That burns and racks within me ev'ry part,
I from my heart who fear that it may part,
And see the near end of my single light,
Go, as a blind man, groping without light,
Who knows not where yet presses to depart.
Thus from the blows which ever wish me dead
I flee, but not so swiftly that desire
Ceases to come, as is its wont, with me.
Silent I move: for accents of the dead
Would melt the general age: and I desire
That sighs and tears should only fall from me.

Robert Macgregor.

SONNET XVII.

Son animali al mondo di sì altera.

HE COMPARES HIMSELF TO A MOTH.

Creatures there are in life of such keen sight
That no defence they need from noonday sun,
And others dazzled by excess of light
Who issue not abroad till day is done,
And, with weak fondness, some because 'tis bright,
Who in the death-flame for enjoyment run,
Thus proving theirs a different virtue quite –
Alas! of this last kind myself am one;
For, of this fair the splendour to regard,
I am but weak and ill – against late hours
And darkness gath'ring round – myself to ward.
Wherefore, with tearful eyes of failing powers,
My destiny condemns me still to turn
Where following faster I but fiercer burn.

Robert Macgregor.

SONNET XVIII.

Vergognando talor ch' ancor si taccia.

THE PRAISES OF LAURA TRANSCEND HIS POETIC POWERS.

Ashamed sometimes thy beauties should remain
As yet unsung, sweet lady, in my rhyme;
When first I saw thee I recall the time,
Pleasing as none shall ever please again.
But no fit polish can my verse attain,
Not mine is strength to try the task sublime:
My genius, measuring its power to climb,
From such attempt doth prudently refrain.
Full oft I oped my lips to chant thy name;
Then in mid utterance the lay was lost:
But say what muse can dare so bold a flight?
Full oft I strove in measure to indite;
But ah, the pen, the hand, the vein I boast,
At once were vanquish'd by the mighty theme!

Dr Nott

Ashamed at times that I am silent, yet,
Lady, though your rare beauties prompt my rhyme,
When first I saw thee I recall the time
Such as again no other can be met.
But, with such burthen on my shoulders set.
My mind, its frailty feeling, cannot climb,
And shrinks alike from polish'd and sublime,
While my vain utterance frozen terrors let.
Often already have I sought to sing,
But midway in my breast the voice was stay'd,
For ah! so high what praise may ever spring?
And oft have I the tender verse essay'd,
But still in vain; pen, hand, and intellect
In the first effort conquer'd are and check'd.

Robert Macgregor.

SONNET XIX.

Mille fiate, o dolce mia guerrera.

HIS HEART, REJECTED BY LAURA, WILL PERISH, UNLESS SHE RELENT.

A thousand times, sweet warrior, have I tried,
Proffering my heart to thee, some peace to gain
From those bright eyes, but still, alas! in vain,
To such low level stoops not thy chaste pride.
If others seek the love thus thrown aside,
Vain were their hopes and labours to obtain;
The heart thou spurnest I alike disdain,
To thee displeasing, 'tis by me denied.
But if, discarded thus, it find not thee
Its joyless exile willing to befriend,
Alone, untaught at others' will to wend,
Soon from life's weary burden will it flee.
How heavy then the guilt to both, but more
To thee, for thee it did the most adore.

Robert Macgregor.

A thousand times, sweet warrior, to obtain
Peace with those beauteous eyes I've vainly tried,
Proffering my heart; but with that lofty pride
To bend your looks so lowly you refrain:
Expects a stranger fair that heart to gain,
In frail, fallacious hopes will she confide:
It never more to me can be allied;
Since what you scorn, dear lady, I disdain.
In its sad exile if no aid you lend
Banish'd by me; and it can neither stay
Alone, nor yet another's call obey;
Its vital course must hasten to its end:
Ah me, how guilty then we both should prove,
But guilty you the most, for you it most doth love.

Dr Nott

SESTINA I.

A qualunque animale alberga in terra.

NIGHT BRINGS HIM NO REST. HE IS THE PREY OF DESPAIR.

To every animal that dwells on earth,
Except to those which have in hate the sun,
Their time of labour is while lasts the day;
But when high heaven relumes its thousand stars,
This seeks his hut, and that its native wood,
Each finds repose, at least until the dawn.

But I, when fresh and fair begins the dawn
To chase the lingering shades that cloak'd the earth,
Wakening the animals in every wood,
No truce to sorrow find while rolls the sun;
And, when again I see the glistening stars,
Still wander, weeping, wishing for the day.

When sober evening chases the bright day,
And this our darkness makes for others dawn,
Pensive I look upon the cruel stars
Which framed me of such pliant passionate earth,
And curse the day that e'er I saw the sun,
Which makes me native seem of wildest wood.
And yet methinks was ne'er in any wood,

So wild a denizen, by night or day,
As she whom thus I blame in shade and sun:
Me night's first sleep o'ercomes not, nor the dawn,
For though in mortal coil I tread the earth,
My firm and fond desire is from the stars.
Ere up to you I turn, O lustrous stars,
Or downwards in love's labyrinthine wood,

Leaving my fleshly frame in mouldering earth,
Could I but pity find in her, one day
Would many years redeem, and to the dawn

With bliss enrich me from the setting sun!
Oh! might I be with her where sinks the sun,
No other eyes upon us but the stars,

Alone, one sweet night, ended by no dawn,
Nor she again transfigured in green wood,
To cheat my clasping arms, as on the day,
When Phœbus vainly follow'd her on earth.
I shall lie low in earth, in crumbling wood.
And clustering stars shall gem the noon of day,
Ere on so sweet a dawn shall rise that sun.

Robert Macgregor.

Each creature on whose wakeful eyes
The bright sun pours his golden fire,
By day a destined toil pursues;
And, when heaven's lamps illume the skies,
All to some haunt for rest retire,
Till a fresh dawn that toil renews.
But I, when a new morn doth rise,
Chasing from earth its murky shades,
While ring the forests with delight,
Find no remission of my sighs;
And, soon as night her mantle spreads,
I weep, and wish returning light
Again when eve bids day retreat,
O'er other climes to dart its rays;
Pensive those cruel stars I view,
Which influence thus my amorous fate;
And imprecate that beauty's blaze,
Which o'er my form such wildness threw.
No forest surely in its glooms
Nurtures a savage so unkind
As she who bids these sorrows flow:
Me, nor the dawn nor sleep o'ercomes;
For, though of mortal mould, my mind
Feels more than passion's mortal glow.
Ere up to you, bright orbs, I fly,
Or to Love's bower speed down my way,
While here my mouldering limbs remain;
Let me her pity once espy;
Thus, rich in bliss, one little day
Shall recompense whole years of pain.
Be Laura mine at set of sun;
Let heaven's fires only mark our loves,
And the day ne'er its light renew;
My fond embrace may she not shun;
Nor Phœbus-like, through laurel groves,
May I a nymph transform'd pursue!
But I shall cast this mortal veil on earth,
And stars shall gild the noon, ere such bright scenes have birth.

Dr Nott

CANZONE I.

Nel dolce tempo della prima etade.

HIS SUFFERINGS SINCE HE BECAME THE SLAVE OF LOVE.

In the sweet season when my life was new,
Which saw the birth, and still the being sees
Of the fierce passion for my ill that grew,
Fain would I sing – my sorrow to appease –
How then I lived, in liberty, at ease,
While o'er my heart held slighted Love no sway;
And how, at length, by too high scorn, for aye,
I sank his slave, and what befell me then,
Whereby to all a warning I remain;
Although my sharpest pain
Be elsewhere written, so that many a pen
Is tired already, and, in every vale,
The echo of my heavy sighs is rife,
Some credence forcing of my anguish'd life;
And, as her wont, if here my memory fail,
Be my long martyrdom its saving plea,
And the one thought which so its torment made,
As every feeling else to throw in shade,
And make me of myself forgetful be –
Ruling life's inmost core, its bare rind left for me.

Long years and many had pass'd o'er my head,
Since, in Love's first assault, was dealt my wound,
And from my brow its youthful air had fled,
While cold and cautious thoughts my heart around
Had made it almost adamantine ground,
To loosen which hard passion gave no rest:
No sorrow yet with tears had bathed my breast,
Nor broke my sleep: and what was not in mine
A miracle to me in others seem'd.
Life's sure test death is deem'd,
As cloudless eve best proves the past day fine;
Ah me! the tyrant whom I sing, descried

Ere long his error, that, till then, his dart
Not yet beneath the gown had pierced my heart,
And brought a puissant lady as his guide,
'Gainst whom of small or no avail has been
Genius, or force, to strive or supplicate.
These two transform'd me to my present state,
Making of breathing man a laurel green,
Which loses not its leaves though wintry blasts be keen.

What my amaze, when first I fully learn'd
The wondrous change upon my person done,
And saw my thin hairs to those green leaves turn'd
(Whence yet for them a crown I might have won);
My feet wherewith I stood, and moved, and run –
Thus to the soul the subject members bow –
Become two roots upon the shore, not now
Of fabled Peneus, but a stream as proud,
And stiffen'd to a branch my either arm!
Nor less was my alarm,
When next my frame white down was seen to shroud,
While, 'neath the deadly leven, shatter'd lay
My first green hope that soar'd, too proud, in air,
Because, in sooth, I knew not when nor where
I left my latter state; but, night and day,
Where it was struck, alone, in tears, I went,
Still seeking it alwhere, and in the wave;
And, for its fatal fall, while able, gave
My tongue no respite from its one lament,
For the sad snowy swan both form and language lent.

Thus that loved wave – my mortal speech put by
For birdlike song – I track'd with constant feet,
Still asking mercy with a stranger cry;
But ne'er in tones so tender, nor so sweet,
Knew I my amorous sorrow to repeat,
As might her hard and cruel bosom melt:
Judge, still if memory sting, what then I felt!
But ah! not now the past, it rather needs
Of her my lovely and inveterate foe
The present power to show,
Though such she be all language as exceeds.

She with a glance who rules us as her own,
Opening my breast my heart in hand to take,
Thus said to me: "Of this no mention make."
I saw her then, in alter'd air, alone,
So that I recognised her not – O shame
Be on my truant mind and faithless sight!
And when the truth I told her in sore fright,
She soon resumed her old accustom'd frame,
While, desperate and half dead, a hard rock mine became.

As spoke she, o'er her mien such feeling stirr'd,
That from the solid rock, with lively fear,
"Haply I am not what you deem," I heard;
And then methought, "If she but help me here,
No life can ever weary be, or drear;
To make me weep, return, my banish'd Lord!"
I know not how, but thence, the power restored,
Blaming no other than myself, I went,
And, nor alive, nor dead, the long day past.
But, because time flies fast,
And the pen answers ill my good intent,
Full many a thing long written in my mind
I here omit; and only mention such
Whereat who hears them now will marvel much.
Death so his hand around my vitals twined,
Not silence from its grasp my heart could save,
Or succour to its outraged virtue bring:
As speech to me was a forbidden thing,
To paper and to ink my griefs I gave –
Life, not my own, is lost through you who dig my grave.

I fondly thought before her eyes, at length,
Though low and lost, some mercy to obtain;
And this the hope which lent my spirit strength.
Sometimes humility o'ercomes disdain,
Sometimes inflames it to worse spite again;
This knew I, who so long was left in night,
That from such prayers had disappear'd my light;
Till I, who sought her still, nor found, alas!
Even her shade, nor of her feet a sign,
Outwearied and supine,

As one who midway sleeps, upon the grass
Threw me, and there, accusing the brief ray,
Of bitter tears I loosed the prison'd flood,
To flow and fall, to them as seem'd it good.
Ne'er vanish'd snow before the sun away,
As then to melt apace it me befell,
Till, 'neath a spreading beech a fountain swell'd;
Long in that change my humid course I held, –
Who ever saw from Man a true fount well?
And yet, though strange it sound, things known and sure I tell.

The soul from God its nobler nature gains
(For none save He such favour could bestow)
And like our Maker its high state retains,
To pardon who is never tired, nor slow,
If but with humble heart and suppliant show,
For mercy for past sins to Him we bend;
And if, against his wont, He seem to lend,
Awhile, a cold ear to our earnest prayers,
'Tis that right fear the sinner more may fill;
For he repents but ill
His old crime for another who prepares.
Thus, when my lady, while her bosom yearn'd
With pity, deign'd to look on me, and knew
That equal with my fault its penance grew,
To my old state and shape I soon return'd.
But nought there is on earth in which the wise
May trust, for, wearying braving her afresh,
To rugged stone she changed my quivering flesh.
So that, in their old strain, my broken cries
In vain ask'd death, or told her one name to deaf skies.

A sad and wandering shade, I next recall,
Through many a distant and deserted glen,
That long I mourn'd my indissoluble thrall.
At length my malady seem'd ended, when
I to my earthly frame return'd again,
Haply but greater grief therein to feel;
Still following my desire with such fond zeal
That once (beneath the proud sun's fiercest blaze,
Returning from the chase, as was my wont)

Naked, where gush'd a font,
My fair and fatal tyrant met my gaze;
I whom nought else could pleasure, paused to look,
While, touch'd with shame as natural as intense,
Herself to hide or punish my offence,
She o'er my face the crystal waters shook
– I still speak true, though truth may seem a lie –
Instantly from my proper person torn,
A solitary stag, I felt me borne
In wingèd terrors the dark forest through,
As still of my own dogs the rushing storm I flew
My song! I never was that cloud of gold
Which once descended in such precious rain,
Easing awhile with bliss Jove's amorous pain;
I was a flame, kindled by one bright eye,
I was the bird which gladly soar'd on high,
Exalting her whose praise in song I wake;
Nor, for new fancies, knew I to forsake
My first fond laurel, 'neath whose welcome shade
Ever from my firm heart all meaner pleasures fade.

Robert Macgregor.

SONNET XX.

Se l' onorata fronde, che prescrive.

TO STRAMAZZO OF PERUGIA, WHO INVITED HIM TO WRITE POETRY.

If the world-honour'd leaf, whose green defies
The wrath of Heaven when thunders mighty Jove,
Had not to me prohibited the crown
Which wreathes of wont the gifted poet's brow,
I were a friend of these your idols too,
Whom our vile age so shamelessly ignores:
But that sore insult keeps me now aloof
From the first patron of the olive bough:
For Ethiop earth beneath its tropic sun
Ne'er burn'd with such fierce heat, as I with rage
At losing thing so comely and beloved.
Resort then to some calmer fuller fount,
For of all moisture mine is drain'd and dry,
Save that which falleth from mine eyes in tears.

Robert Macgregor.

SONNET XXI.

Amor piangeva, ed io con lui talvolta.

HE CONGRATULATES BOCCACCIO ON HIS RETURN TO THE RIGHT PATH.

Love grieved, and I with him at times, to see
By what strange practices and cunning art,
You still continued from his fetters free,
From whom my feet were never far apart.
Since to the right way brought by God's decree,
Lifting my hands to heaven with pious heart,
I thank Him for his love and grace, for He
The soul-prayer of the just will never thwart:
And if, returning to the amorous strife,
Its fair desire to teach us to deny,
Hollows and hillocks in thy path abound,
'Tis but to prove to us with thorns how rife
The narrow way, the ascent how hard and high,
Where with true virtue man at last is crown'd.

Robert Macgregor.

SONNET XXII.

Più di me lieta non si vede a terra.

ON THE SAME SUBJECT.

Than me more joyful never reach'd the shore
A vessel, by the winds long tost and tried,
Whose crew, late hopeless on the waters wide,
To a good God their thanks, now prostrate, pour;
Nor captive from his dungeon ever tore,
Around whose neck the noose of death was tied,
More glad than me, that weapon laid aside
Which to my lord hostility long bore.
All ye who honour love in poet strain,
To the good minstrel of the amorous lay
Return due praise, though once he went astray;
For greater glory is, in Heaven's blest reign,
Over one sinner saved, and higher praise,
Than e'en for ninety-nine of perfect ways.

Robert Macgregor.

SONNET XXIII.

Il successor di Carlo, che la chioma.

ON THE MOVEMENT OF THE EMPEROR AGAINST THE INFIDELS, AND THE RETURN OF THE POPE TO ROME.

The high successor of our Charles,[2] whose hair
The crown of his great ancestor adorns,
Already has ta'en arms, to bruise the horns
Of Babylon, and all her name who bear;
Christ's holy vicar with the honour'd load
Of keys and cloak, returning to his home,
Shall see Bologna and our noble Rome,
If no ill fortune bar his further road.
Best to your meek and high-born lamb belongs
To beat the fierce wolf down: so may it be
With all who loyalty and love deny.
Console at length your waiting country's wrongs,
And Rome's, who longs once more her spouse to see,
And gird for Christ the good sword on thy thigh.

Robert Macgregor.

2 Charlemagne.

CANZONE II.

O aspettata in ciel, beata e bella.

IN SUPPORT OF THE PROPOSED CRUSADE AGAINST THE INFIDELS.

O spirit wish'd and waited for in heaven,
That wearest gracefully our human clay,
Not as with loading sin and earthly stain,
Who lov'st our Lord's high bidding to obey, –
Henceforth to thee the way is plain and even
By which from hence to bliss we may attain.
To waft o'er yonder main
Thy bark, that bids the world adieu for aye
To seek a better strand,
The western winds their ready wings expand;
Which, through the dangers of that dusky way,
Where all deplore the first infringed command,
Will guide her safe, from primal bondage free,
Reckless to stop or stay,
To that true East, where she desires to be.

Haply the faithful vows, and zealous prayers,
And pious tears by holy mortals shed,
Have come before the mercy-seat above:
Yet vows of ours but little can bestead,
Nor human orison such merit bears
As heavenly justice from its course can move.
But He, the King whom angels serve and love,
His gracious eyes hath turn'd upon the land
Where on the cross He died;
And a new Charlemagne hath qualified
To work the vengeance that on high was plann'd,
For whose delay so long hath Europe sigh'd.
Such mighty aid He brings his faithful spouse,
That at its sound the pride
Of Babylon with trembling terror bows.

All dwellers 'twixt the hills and wild Garonne,
The Rhodanus, and Rhine, and briny wave,
Are banded under red-cross banners brave;
And all who honour'd guerdon fain would have
From Pyrenees to the utmost west, are gone,
Leaving Iberia lorn of warriors keen,
And Britain, with the islands that are seen
Between the columns and the starry wain,
(Even to that land where shone
The far-famed lore of sacred Helicon,)
Diverse in language, weapon, garb and strain,
Of valour true, with pious zeal rush on.
What cause, what love, to this compared may be?
What spouse, or infant train
E'er kindled such a righteous enmity?

There is a portion of the world that lies
Far distant from the sun's all-cheering ray,
For ever wrapt in ice and gelid snows;
There under cloudy skies, in stinted day,
A people dwell, whose heart their clime outvies
By nature framed stern foemen of repose.
Now new devotion in their bosom glows,
With Gothic fury now they grasp the sword.
Turk, Arab, and Chaldee,
With all between us and that sanguine sea,
Who trust in idol-gods, and slight the Lord,
Thou know'st how soon their feeble strength would yield;
A naked race, fearful and indolent,
Unused the brand to wield,
Whose distant aim upon the wind is sent.

Now is the time to shake the ancient yoke
From off our necks, and rend the veil aside
That long in darkness hath involved our eyes;
Let all whom Heaven with genius hath supplied,
And all who great Apollo's name invoke,
With fiery eloquence point out the prize,
With tongue and pen call on the brave to rise;
If Orpheus and Amphion, legends old,
No marvel cause in thee,

It were small wonder if Ausonia see
Collecting at thy call her children bold,
Lifting the spear of Jesus joyfully.
Nor, if our ancient mother judge aright,
Doth her rich page unfold
Such noble cause in any former fight.

Thou who hast scann'd, to heap a treasure fair,
Story of ancient day and modern time,
Soaring with earthly frame to heaven sublime,
Thou know'st, from Mars' bold son, her ruler prime,
To great Augustus, he whose waving hair
Was thrice in triumph wreathed with laurel green,
How Rome hath of her blood still lavish been
To right the woes of many an injured land;
And shall she now be slow,
Her gratitude, her piety to show?
In Christian zeal to buckle on the brand,
For Mary's glorious Son to deal the blow?
What ills the impious foeman must betide
Who trust in mortal hand,
If Christ himself lead on the adverse side!

And turn thy thoughts to Xerxes' rash emprize,
Who dared, in haste to tread our Europe's shore,
Insult the sea with bridge, and strange caprice;
And thou shalt see for husbands then no more
The Persian matrons robed in mournful guise,
And dyed with blood the seas of Salamis,
Nor sole example this:
(The ruin of that Eastern king's design),
That tells of victory nigh:
See Marathon, and stern Thermopylæ,
Closed by those few, and chieftain leonine,
And thousand deeds that blaze in history.
Then bow in thankfulness both heart and knee
Before his holy shrine,
Who such bright guerdon hath reserved for thee.

Thou shalt see Italy and that honour'd shore,
O song! a land debarr'd and hid from me

By neither flood nor hill!
But love alone, whose power hath virtue still
To witch, though all his wiles be vanity,
Nor Nature to avoid the snare hath skill.
Go, bid thy sisters hush their jealous fears,
For other loves there be
Than that blind boy, who causeth smiles and tears.

Miss *** (Foscolo's Essay).

O thou, in heaven expected, bright and blest,
Spirit! who, from the common frailty free
Of human kind, in human form art drest,
God's handmaid, dutiful and dear to thee
Henceforth the pathway easy lies and plain,
By which, from earth, we bless eternal gain:
Lo! at the wish, to waft thy venturous prore
From the blind world it fain would leave behind
And seek that better shore,
Springs the sweet comfort of the western wind,
Which safe amid this dark and dangerous vale,
Where we our own, the primal sin deplore,
Right on shall guide her, from her old chains freed,
And, without let or fail,
Where havens her best hope, to the true East shall lead.

Haply the suppliant tears of pious men,
Their earnest vows and loving prayers at last
Unto the throne of heavenly grace have past;
Yet, breathed by human helplessness, ah! when
Had purest orison the skill and force
To bend eternal justice from its course?
But He, heaven's bounteous ruler from on high,
On the sad sacred spot, where erst He bled,
Will turn his pitying eye,
And through the spirit of our new Charles spread
Thirst of that vengeance, whose too long delay
From general Europe wakes the bitter sigh;
To his loved spouse such aid will He convey,
That, his dread voice to hear,
Proud Babylon shall shrink assail'd with secret fear.

All, by the gay Garonne, the kingly Rhine,
Between the blue Rhone and salt sea who dwell,
All in whose bosoms worth and honour swell,
Eagerly haste the Christian cross to join;
Spain of her warlike sons, from the far west
Unto the Pyrenee, pours forth her best:
Britannia and the Islands, which are found
Northward from Calpe, studding Ocean's breast,
E'en to that land renown'd

In the rich lore of sacred Helicon,
Various in arms and language, garb and guise,
With pious fury urge the bold emprize.
What love was e'er so just, so worthy, known?
Or when did holier flame
Kindle the mind of man to a more noble aim?

Far in the hardy north a land there lies,
Buried in thick-ribb'd ice and constant snows,
Where scant the days and clouded are the skies,
And seldom the bright sun his glad warmth throws;
There, enemy of peace by nature, springs
A people to whom death no terror brings;
If these, with new devotedness, we see
In Gothic fury baring the keen glaive,
Turk, Arab, and Chaldee!
All, who, between us and the Red Sea wave,
To heathen gods bow the idolatrous knee,
Arm and advance! we heed not your blind rage;
A naked race, timid in act, and slow,
Unskill'd the war to wage,
Whose far aim on the wind contrives a coward blow.

Now is the hour to free from the old yoke
Our gallèd necks, to rend the veil away
Too long permitted our dull sight to cloak:
Now too, should all whose breasts the heavenly ray
Of genius lights, exert its powers sublime,
And or in bold harangue, or burning rhyme,
Point the proud prize and fan the generous flame.
If Orpheus and Amphion credit claim,
Legends of distant time,
Less marvel 'twere, if, at thy earnest call,
Italia, with her children, should awake,
And wield the willing lance for Christ's dear sake.
Our ancient mother, read she right, in all
Her fortune's history ne'er
A cause of combat knew so glorious and so fair!

Thou, whose keen mind has every theme explored,
And truest ore from Time's rich treasury won,

On earthly pinion who hast heavenward soar'd,
Well knowest, from her founder, Mars' bold son,
To great Augustus, he, whose brow around
Thrice was the laurel green in triumph bound,
How Rome was ever lavish of her blood,
The right to vindicate, the weak redress;
And now, when gratitude,
When piety appeal, shall she do less
To avenge the injury and end the scorn
By blessed Mary's glorious offspring borne?
What fear we, while the heathen for success
Confide in human powers,
If, on the adverse side, be Christ, and his side ours?

Turn, too, when Xerxes our free shores to tread
Rush'd in hot haste, and dream'd the perilous main
With scourge and fetter to chastise and chain,
– What see'st? Wild wailing o'er their husbands dead,
Persia's pale matrons wrapt in weeds of woe,
And red with gore the gulf of Salamis!
To prove our triumph certain, to foreshow
The utter ruin of our Eastern foe,
No single instance this;
Miltiades and Marathon recall,
See, with his patriot few, Leonidas
Closing, Thermopylæ, thy bloody pass!
Like them to dare and do, to God let all
With heart and knee bow down,
Who for our arms and age has kept this great renown.

Thou shalt see Italy, that honour'd land,
Which from my eyes, O Song! nor seas, streams, heights,
So long have barr'd and bann'd,
But love alone, who with his haughty lights
The more allures me as he worse excites,
Till nature fails against his constant wiles.
Go then, and join thy comrades; not alone
Beneath fair female zone
Dwells Love, who, at his will, moves us to tears or smiles.

Robert Macgregor.

CANZONE III.

Verdi panni, sanguigni, oscuri o persi.

WHETHER OR NOT HE SHOULD CEASE TO LOVE LAURA.

Green robes and red, purple, or brown, or gray
No lady ever wore,
Nor hair of gold in sunny tresses twined,
So beautiful as she, who spoils my mind
Of judgment, and from freedom's lofty path
So draws me with her that I may not bear
Any less heavy yoke.

And if indeed at times – for wisdom fails
Where martyrdom breeds doubt –
The soul should ever arm it to complain
Suddenly from each reinless rude desire
Her smile recalls, and razes from my heart
Every rash enterprise, while all disdain
Is soften'd in her sight.

For all that I have ever borne for love,
And still am doom'd to bear,
Till she who wounded it shall heal my heart,
Rejecting homage e'en while she invites,
Be vengeance done! but let not pride nor ire
'Gainst my humility the lovely pass
By which I enter'd bar.

The hour and day wherein I oped my eyes
On the bright black and white,
Which drive me thence where eager love impell'd
Where of that life which now my sorrow makes
New roots, and she in whom our age is proud,
Whom to behold without a tender awe
Needs heart of lead or wood.

The tear then from these eyes that frequent falls –

HE thus my pale cheek bathes
Who planted first within my fenceless flank
Love's shaft – diverts me not from my desire;
And in just part the proper sentence falls;
For her my spirit sighs, and worthy she
To staunch its secret wounds.

Spring from within me these conflicting thoughts,
To weary, wound myself,
Each a sure sword against its master turn'd:
Nor do I pray her to be therefore freed,
For less direct to heaven all other paths,
And to that glorious kingdom none can soar
Certes in sounder bark.

Benignant stars their bright companionship
Gave to the fortunate side
When came that fair birth on our nether world,
Its sole star since, who, as the laurel leaf,
The worth of honour fresh and fragrant keeps,
Where lightnings play not, nor ungrateful winds
Ever o'ersway its head.

Well know I that the hope to paint in verse
Her praises would but tire
The worthiest hand that e'er put forth its pen:
Who, in all Memory's richest cells, e'er saw
Such angel virtue so rare beauty shrined,
As in those eyes, twin symbols of all worth,
Sweet keys of my gone heart?
Lady, wherever shines the sun, than you
Love has no dearer pledge.

Robert Macgregor.

SESTINA II

Giovane donna sott' un verde lauro.

THOUGH DESPAIRING OF PITY, HE VOWS TO LOVE HER UNTO DEATH.

A youthful lady 'neath a laurel green
Was seated, fairer, colder than the snow
On which no sun has shone for many years:
Her sweet speech, her bright face, and flowing hair
So pleased, she yet is present to my eyes,
And aye must be, whatever fate prevail.

These my fond thoughts of her shall fade and fail
When foliage ceases on the laurel green;
Nor calm can be my heart, nor check'd these eyes
Until the fire shall freeze, or burns the snow:
Easier upon my head to count each hair
Than, ere that day shall dawn, the parting years.

But, since time flies, and roll the rapid years,
And death may, in the midst, of life, assail,
With full brown locks, or scant and silver hair,
I still the shade of that sweet laurel green
Follow, through fiercest sun and deepest snow,
Till the last day shall close my weary eyes.

Oh! never sure were seen such brilliant eyes,
In this our age or in the older years,
Which mould and melt me, as the sun melts snow,
Into a stream of tears adown the vale,
Watering the hard roots of that laurel green,
Whose boughs are diamonds and gold whose hair.

I fear that Time my mien may change and hair,
Ere, with true pity touch'd, shall greet my eyes
My idol imaged in that laurel green:
For, unless memory err, through seven long years

Till now, full many a shore has heard my wail,
By night, at noon, in summer and in snow.

Thus fire within, without the cold, cold snow,
Alone, with these my thoughts and her bright hair,
Alway and everywhere I bear my ail,
Haply to find some mercy in the eyes
Of unborn nations and far future years,
If so long flourishes our laurel green.

The gold and topaz of the sun on snow
Are shamed by the bright hair above those eyes,
Searing the short green of my life's vain years.

Robert Macgregor.

SONNET XXIV.

Quest' anima gentil che si diparte.

ON LAURA DANGEROUSLY ILL.

That graceful soul, in mercy call'd away
Before her time to bid the world farewell,
If welcomed as she ought in the realms of day,
In heaven's most blessèd regions sure shall dwell.
There between Mars and Venus if she stay,
Her sight the brightness of the sun will quell,
Because, her infinite beauty to survey,
The spirits of the blest will round her swell.
If she decide upon the fourth fair nest
Each of the three to dwindle will begin,
And she alone the fame of beauty win,
Nor e'en in the fifth circle may she rest;
Thence higher if she soar, I surely trust
Jove with all other stars in darkness will be thrust.

Robert Macgregor.

SONNET XXV.

Quanto più m' avvicino al giorno estremo.

HE CONSOLES HIMSELF THAT HIS LIFE IS ADVANCING TO ITS CLOSE.

Near and more near as life's last period draws,
Which oft is hurried on by human woe,
I see the passing hours more swiftly flow,
And all my hopes in disappointment close.
And to my heart I say, amidst its throes,
"Not long shall we discourse of love below;
For this my earthly load, like new-fall'n snow
Fast melting, soon shall leave us to repose.
With it will sink in dust each towering hope,
Cherish'd so long within my faithful breast;
No more shall we resent, fear, smile, complain:
Then shall we clearly trace why some are blest,
Through deepest misery raised to Fortune's top,
And why so many sighs so oft are heaved in vain."

Francis Wrangham.

The nearer I approach my life's last day,
The certain day that limits human woe,
I better mark, in Time's swift silent flow,
How the fond hopes he brought all pass'd away.
Of love no longer – to myself I say –
We now may commune, for, as virgin snow,
The hard and heavy load we drag below
Dissolves and dies, ere rest in heaven repay.
And prostrate with it must each fair hope lie
Which here beguiled us and betray'd so long,
And joy, grief, fear and pride alike shall cease:
And then too shall we see with clearer eye
How oft we trod in weary ways and wrong,
And why so long in vain we sigh'd for peace.

Robert Macgregor.

SONNET XXVI.

Già fiammeggiava l' amorosa stella.

LAURA, WHO IS ILL, APPEARS TO HIM IN A DREAM, AND ASSURES HIM *THAT SHE STILL LIVES.*

Throughout the orient now began to flame
The star of love; while o'er the northern sky
That, which has oft raised Juno's jealousy,
Pour'd forth its beauteous scintillating beam:
Beside her kindled hearth the housewife dame,
Half-dress'd, and slipshod, 'gan her distaff ply:
And now the wonted hour of woe drew nigh,
That wakes to tears the lover from his dream:
When my sweet hope unto my mind appear'd,
Not in the custom'd way unto my sight;
For grief had bathed my lids, and sleep had weigh'd;
Ah me, how changed that form by love endear'd!
"Why lose thy fortitude?" methought she said,
"These eyes not yet from thee withdraw their light."

Dr Nott

Already in the east the amorous star
Illumined heaven, while from her northern height
Great Juno's rival through the dusky night
Her beamy radiance shot. Returning care
Had roused th' industrious hag, with footstep bare,
And loins ungirt, the sleeping fire to light;
And lovers thrill'd that season of despight,
Which wont renew their tears, and wake despair.
When my soul's hope, now on the verge of fate,
(Not by th' accustomed way; for that in sleep
Was closed, and moist with griefs,) attain'd my heart.
Alas, how changed! "Servant, no longer weep,"
She seem'd to say; "resume thy wonted state:
Not yet thine eyes from mine are doom'd to part."

Lord Charlemont.

Already, in the east, the star of love
Was flaming, and that other in the north,
Which Juno's jealousy is wont to move,
Its beautiful and lustrous rays shot forth;
Barefooted and half clad, the housewife old
Had stirr'd her fire, and set herself to weave;
Each tender heart the thoughtful time controll'd
Which evermore the lover wakes to grieve,
When my fond hope, already at life's last,
Came to my heart, not by the wonted way,
Where sleep its seal, its dew where sorrow cast –
Alas! how changed – and said, or seem'd to say,
"Sight of these eyes not yet does Heaven refuse,
Then wherefore should thy tost heart courage lose?"

Robert Macgregor.

SONNET XXVII.

Apollo, s' ancor vive il bel desio.

HE COMPARES HER TO A LAUREL, WHICH HE SUPPLICATES APOLLO TO DEFEND.

O Phœbus, if that fond desire remains,
Which fired thy breast near the Thessalian wave;
If those bright tresses, which such pleasure gave,
Through lapse of years thy memory not disdains;
From sluggish frosts, from rude inclement rains.
Which last the while thy beams our region leave,
That honour'd sacred tree from peril save,
Whose name of dear accordance waked our pains!
And, by that amorous hope which soothed thy care,
What time expectant thou wert doom'd to sigh
Dispel those vapours which disturb our sky!
So shall we both behold our favorite fair
With wonder, seated on the grassy mead,
And forming with her arms herself a shade.

Dr Nott

If live the fair desire, Apollo, yet
Which fired thy spirit once on Peneus' shore,
And if the bright hair loved so well of yore
In lapse of years thou dost not now forget,
From the long frost, from seasons rude and keen,
Which last while hides itself thy kindling brow,
Defend this consecrate and honour'd bough,
Which snared thee erst, whose slave I since have been.
And, by the virtue of the love so dear
Which soothed, sustain'd thee in that early strife,
Our air from raw and lowering vapours clear:
So shall we see our lady, to new life
Restored, her seat upon the greensward take,
Where her own graceful arms a sweet shade o'er her make.

Robert Macgregor.

SONNET XXVIII.

Solo e pensoso i più deserti campi.

HE SEEKS SOLITUDE, BUT LOVE FOLLOWS HIM EVERYWHERE.

Alone, and lost in thought, the desert glade
Measuring I roam with ling'ring steps and slow;
And still a watchful glance around me throw,
Anxious to shun the print of human tread:
No other means I find, no surer aid
From the world's prying eye to hide my woe:
So well my wild disorder'd gestures show,
And love lorn looks, the fire within me bred,
That well I deem each mountain, wood and plain,
And river knows, what I from man conceal,
What dreary hues my life's fond prospects dim.
Yet whate'er wild or savage paths I've ta'en,
Where'er I wander, love attends me still,
Soft whisp'ring to my soul, and I to him.

Anonymous, Ox., 1795.

Alone, and pensive, near some desert shore,
Far from the haunts of men I love to stray,
And, cautiously, my distant path explore
Where never human footsteps mark'd the way.
Thus from the public gaze I strive to fly,
And to the winds alone my griefs impart;
While in my hollow cheek and haggard eye
Appears the fire that burns my inmost heart.
But ah, in vain to distant scenes I go;
No solitude my troubled thoughts allays.
Methinks e'en things inanimate must know
The flame that on my soul in secret preys;
Whilst Love, unconquer'd, with resistless sway
Still hovers round my path, still meets me on my way.

J.B. Taylor.

Alone and pensive, the deserted plain,
With tardy pace and sad, I wander by;
And mine eyes o'er it rove, intent to fly
Where distant shores no trace of man retain;
No help save this I find, some cave to gain
Where never may intrude man's curious eye,
Lest on my brow, a stranger long to joy,
He read the secret fire which makes my pain
For here, methinks, the mountain and the flood,
Valley and forest the strange temper know
Of my sad life conceal'd from others' sight –
Yet where, where shall I find so wild a wood,
A way so rough that there Love cannot go
Communing with me the long day and night?

Robert Macgregor.

SONNET XXIX.

S' io credessi per morte essere scarco.

HE PRAYS FOR DEATH, BUT IN VAIN.

Had I believed that Death could set me free
From the anxious amorous thoughts my peace that mar,
With these my own hands which yet stainless are,
Life had I loosed, long hateful grown to me.
Yet, for I fear 'twould but a passage be
From grief to grief, from old to other war,
Hither the dark shades my escape that bar,
I still remain, nor hope relief to see.
High time it surely is that he had sped
The fatal arrow from his pitiless bow,
In others' blood so often bathed and red;
And I of Love and Death have pray'd it so –
He listens not, but leaves me here half dead.
Nor cares to call me to himself below.

Robert Macgregor.

Oh! had I deem'd that Death had freed my soul
From Love's tormenting, overwhelming thought,
To crush its aching burthen I had sought,
My wearied life had hasten'd to its goal;
My shivering bark yet fear'd another shoal,
To find one tempest with another bought,
Thus poised 'twixt earth and heaven I dwell as naught,
Not daring to assume my life's control.
But sure 'tis time that Death's relentless bow
Had wing'd that fatal arrow to my heart,
So often bathed in life's dark crimson tide:
But though I crave he would this boon bestow,
He to my cheek his impress doth impart,
And yet o'erlooks me in his fearful stride.

Miss Wollaston.

CANZONE IV.

Si è debile il filo a cui s' attene.

HE GRIEVES IN ABSENCE FROM LAURA.

The thread on which my weary life depends
So fragile is and weak,
If none kind succour lends,
Soon 'neath the painful burden will it break;
Since doom'd to take my sad farewell of her,
In whom begins and ends
My bliss, one hope, to stir
My sinking spirit from its black despair,
Whispers, "Though lost awhile
That form so dear and fair,
Sad soul! the trial bear,
For thee e'en yet the sun may brightly shine,
And days more happy smile,
Once more the lost loved treasure may be thine."
This thought awhile sustains me, but again
To fail me and forsake in worse excess of pain.

Time flies apace: the silent hours and swift
So urge his journey on,
Short span to me is left
Even to think how quick to death I run;
Scarce, in the orient heaven, yon mountain crest
Smiles in the sun's first ray,
When, in the adverse west,
His long round run, we see his light decay
So small of life the space,
So frail and clogg'd with woe,
To mortal man below,
That, when I find me from that beauteous face
Thus torn by fate's decree,
Unable at a wish with her to be,
So poor the profit that old comforts give,
I know not how I brook in such a state to live.

Each place offends, save where alone I see
Those eyes so sweet and bright,
Which still shall bear the key
Of the soft thoughts I hide from other sight;
And, though hard exile harder weighs on me,
Whatever mood betide,
I ask no theme beside,
For all is hateful that I since have seen.
What rivers and what heights,
What shores and seas between
Me rise and those twin lights,
Which made the storm and blackness of my days
One beautiful serene,
To which tormented Memory still strays:
Free as my life then pass'd from every care,
So hard and heavy seems my present lot to bear.

Alas! self-parleying thus, I but renew
The warm wish in my mind,
Which first within it grew
The day I left my better half behind:
If by long absence love is quench'd, then who
Guides me to the old bait,
Whence all my sorrows date?
Why rather not my lips in silence seal'd?
By finest crystal ne'er
Were hidden tints reveal'd
So faithfully and fair,
As my sad spirit naked lays and bare
Its every secret part,
And the wild sweetness thrilling in my heart,
Through eyes which, restlessly, o'erfraught with tears,
Seek her whose sight alone with instant gladness cheers.

Strange pleasure! – yet so often that within
The human heart to reign
Is found – to woo and win
Each new brief toy that men most sigh to gain:
And I am one from sadness who relief
So draw, as if it still

My study were to fill
These eyes with softness, and this heart with grief:
As weighs with me in chief
Nay rather with sole force,
The language and the light
Of those dear eyes to urge me on that course,
So where its fullest source
Long sorrow finds, I fix my often sight,
And thus my heart and eyes like sufferers be,
Which in love's path have been twin pioneers to me.

The golden tresses which should make, I ween,
The sun with envy pine;
And the sweet look serene,
Where love's own rays so bright and burning shine,
That, ere its time, they make my strength decline,
Each wise and truthful word,
Rare in the world, which late
She smiling gave, no more are seen or heard.
But this of all my fate
Is hardest to endure,
That here I am denied
The gentle greeting, angel-like and pure,
Which still to virtue's side
Inclined my heart with modest magic lure;
So that, in sooth, I nothing hope again
Of comfort more than this, how best to bear my pain.

And – with fit ecstacy my loss to mourn –
The soft hand's snowy charm,
The finely-rounded arm,
The winning ways, by turns, that quiet scorn,
Chaste anger, proud humility adorn,
The fair young breast that shrined
Intellect pure and high,
Are now all hid the rugged Alp behind.
My trust were vain to try
And see her ere I die,
For, though awhile he dare
Such dreams indulge, Hope ne'er can constant be,
But falls back in despair

Her, whom Heaven honours, there again to see,
Where virtue, courtesy in her best mix,
And where so oft I pray my future home to fix.

My Song! if thou shalt see,
Our common lady in that dear retreat,
We both may hope that she
Will stretch to thee her fair and fav'ring hand,
Whence I so far am bann'd;
– Touch, touch it not, but, reverent at her feet,
Tell her I will be there with earliest speed,
A man of flesh and blood, or else a spirit freed.

Robert Macgregor.

SONNET XXX.

Orso, e' non furon mai fiumi nè stagni.

HE COMPLAINS OF THE VEIL AND HAND OF LAURA, THAT THEY DEPRIVE HIM OF THE SIGHT OF HER EYES.

Orso, my friend, was never stream, nor lake,
Nor sea in whose broad lap all rivers fall,
Nor shadow of high hill, or wood, or wall,
Nor heaven-obscuring clouds which torrents make,
Nor other obstacles my grief so wake,
Whatever most that lovely face may pall,
As hiding the bright eyes which me enthrall,
That veil which bids my heart "Now burn or break,"
And, whether by humility or pride,
Their glance, extinguishing mine every joy,
Conducts me prematurely to my tomb:
Also my soul by one fair hand is tried,
Cunning and careful ever to annoy,
'Gainst my poor eyes a rock that has become.

Robert Macgregor.

SONNET XXXI.

Io temo sì de' begli occhi l' assalto.

HE EXCUSES HIMSELF FOR HAVING SO LONG DELAYED TO VISIT HER.

So much I fear to encounter her bright eye.
Alway in which my death and Love reside,
That, as a child the rod, its glance I fly,
Though long the time has been since first I tried;
And ever since, so wearisome or high,
No place has been where strong will has not hied,
Her shunning, at whose sight my senses die,
And, cold as marble, I am laid aside:
Wherefore if I return to see you late,
Sure 'tis no fault, unworthy of excuse,
That from my death awhile I held aloof:
At all to turn to what men shun, their fate,
And from such fear my harass'd heart to loose,
Of its true faith are ample pledge and proof.

Robert Macgregor.

SONNET XXXII.

S' amore o morte non dà qualche stroppio.

HE ASKS FROM A FRIEND THE LOAN OF THE WORKS OF ST. AUGUSTINE.

If Love or Death no obstacle entwine
With the new web which here my fingers fold,
And if I 'scape from beauty's tyrant hold
While natural truth with truth reveal'd I join,
Perchance a work so double will be mine
Between our modern style and language old,
That (timidly I speak, with hope though bold)
Even to Rome its growing fame may shine:
But, since, our labour to perfèct at last
Some of the blessed threads are absent yet
Which our dear father plentifully met,
Wherefore to me thy hands so close and fast
Against their use? Be prompt of aid and free,
And rich our harvest of fair things shall be.

Robert Macgregor.

SONNET XXXIII

Quando dal proprio sito si rimove.

WHEN LAURA DEPARTS, THE HEAVENS GROW DARK WITH STORMS.

When from its proper soil the tree is moved
Which Phœbus loved erewhile in human form,
Grim Vulcan at his labour sighs and sweats,
Renewing ever the dread bolts of Jove,
Who thunders now, now speaks in snow and rain,
Nor Julius honoureth than Janus more:
Earth moans, and far from us the sun retires
Since his dear mistress here no more is seen.
Then Mars and Saturn, cruel stars, resume
Their hostile rage: Orion arm'd with clouds
The helm and sails of storm-tost seamen breaks.
To Neptune and to Juno and to us
Vext Æolus proves his power, and makes us feel
How parts the fair face angels long expect.

Robert Macgregor.

SONNET XXXIV.

Ma poi che 'l dolce riso umile e piano.

HER RETURN GLADDENS THE EARTH AND CALMS THE SKY.

But when her sweet smile, modest and benign,
No longer hides from us its beauties rare,
At the spent forge his stout and sinewy arms
Plieth that old Sicilian smith in vain,
For from the hands of Jove his bolts are taken
Temper'd in Ætna to extremest proof;
And his cold sister by degrees grows calm
And genial in Apollo's kindling beams.
Moves from the rosy west a summer breath,
Which safe and easy wafts the seaward bark,
And wakes the sweet flowers in each grassy mead.
Malignant stars on every side depart,
Dispersed before that bright enchanting face,
For which already many tears are shed.

Robert Macgregor.

SONNET XXXV.

Il figliuol di Latona avea già nove.

THE GRIEF OF PHŒBUS AT THE LOSS OF HIS LOVE.

Nine times already had Latona's son
Look'd from the highest balcony of heaven
For her, who whilom waked his sighs in vain,
And sighs as vain now wakes in other breasts;
Then seeking wearily, nor knowing where
She dwelt, or far or near, and why delay'd,
He show'd himself to us as one, insane
For grief, who cannot find some loved lost thing:
And thus, for clouds of sorrow held aloof,
Saw not the fair face turn, which, if I live,
In many a page shall praised and honour'd be,
The misery of her loss so changed her mien
That her bright eyes were dimm'd, for once, with tears,
Thereon its former gloom the air resumed.

Robert Macgregor.

SONNET XXXVI.

Quel che 'n Tessaglia ebbe le man sì pronte.

SOME HAVE WEPT FOR THEIR WORST ENEMIES, BUT LAURA DEIGNS HIM NOT A SINGLE TEAR.

He who for empire at Pharsalia threw,
Reddening its beauteous plain with civil gore,
As Pompey's corse his conquering soldiers bore,
Wept when the well-known features met his view:
The shepherd youth, who fierce Goliath slew,
Had long rebellious children to deplore,
And bent, in generous grief, the brave Saul o'er
His shame and fall when proud Gilboa knew:
But you, whose cheek with pity never paled,
Who still have shields at hand to guard you well
Against Love's bow, which shoots its darts in vain,
Behold me by a thousand deaths assail'd,
And yet no tears of thine compassion tell,
But in those bright eyes anger and disdain.

Robert Macgregor.

SONNET XXXVII.

Il mio avversario, in cui veder solete.

LAURA AT HER LOOKING-GLASS.

My foe, in whom you see your own bright eyes,
Adored by Love and Heaven with honour due,
With beauties not its own enamours you,
Sweeter and happier than in mortal guise.
Me, by its counsel, lady, from your breast,
My chosen cherish'd home, your scorn expell'd
In wretched banishment, perchance not held
Worthy to dwell where you alone should rest.
But were I fasten'd there with strongest keys,
That mirror should not make you, at my cost,
Severe and proud yourself alone to please.
Remember how Narcissus erst was lost!
His course and thine to one conclusion lead,
Of flower so fair though worthless here the mead.

Robert Macgregor.

My mirror'd foe reflects, alas! so fair
Those eyes which Heaven and Love have honour'd too!
Yet not his charms thou dost enamour'd view,
But all thine own, and they beyond compare:
O lady! thou hast chased me at its prayer
From thy heart's throne, where I so fondly grew;
O wretched exile! though too well I knew
A reign with thee I were unfit to share.
But were I ever fix'd thy bosom's mate,
A flattering mirror should not me supplant,
And make thee scorn me in thy self-delight;
Thou surely must recall Narcissus' fate,
But if like him thy doom should thee enchant,
What mead were worthy of a flower so bright?

Miss Wollaston.

SONNET XXXVIII.

L' oro e le perle, e i fior vermigli e i bianchi.

HE INVEIGHS AGAINST LAURA'S MIRROR, BECAUSE IT MAKES HER FORGET HIM.

Those golden tresses, teeth of pearly white,
Those cheeks' fair roses blooming to decay,
Do in their beauty to my soul convey
The poison'd arrows from my aching sight.
Thus sad and briefly must my days take flight,
For life with woe not long on earth will stay;
But more I blame that mirror's flattering sway,
Which thou hast wearied with thy self-delight.
Its power my bosom's sovereign too hath still'd,
Who pray'd thee in my suit – now he is mute,
Since thou art captured by thyself alone:
Death's seeds it hath within my heart instill'd,
For Lethe's stream its form doth constitute,
And makes thee lose each image but thine own.

Miss Wollaston.

The gold and pearls, the lily and the rose
Which weak and dry in winter wont to be,
Are rank and poisonous arrow-shafts to me,
As my sore-stricken bosom aptly shows:
Thus all my days now sadly shortly close,
For seldom with great grief long years agree;
But in that fatal glass most blame I see,
That weary with your oft self-liking grows.
It on my lord placed silence, when my suit
He would have urged, but, seeing your desire
End in yourself alone, he soon was mute.
'Twas fashion'd in hell's wave and o'er its fire,
And tinted in eternal Lethe: thence
The spring and secret of my death commence.

Robert Macgregor.

SONNET XXXIX.

Io sentia dentr' al cor già venir meno.

HE DESIRES AGAIN TO GAZE ON THE EYES Of LAURA.

I now perceived that from within me fled
Those spirits to which you their being lend;
And since by nature's dictates to defend
Themselves from death all animals are made,
The reins I loosed, with which Desire I stay'd,
And sent him on his way without a friend;
There whither day and night my course he'd bend,
Though still from thence by me reluctant led.
And me ashamed and slow along he drew
To see your eyes their matchless influence shower,
Which much I shun, afraid to give you pain.
Yet for myself this once I'll live; such power
Has o'er this wayward life one look from you: –
Then die, unless Desire prevails again.

Anonymous, Ox., 1795.

Because the powers that take their life from you
Already had I felt within decay,
And because Nature, death to shield or slay,
Arms every animal with instinct true,
To my long-curb'd desire the rein I threw,
And turn'd it in the old forgotten way,
Where fondly it invites me night and day,
Though 'gainst its will, another I pursue.
And thus it led me back, ashamed and slow,
To see those eyes with love's own lustre rife
Which I am watchful never to offend:
Thus may I live perchance awhile below;
One glance of yours such power has o'er my life
Which sure, if I oppose desire, shall end.

Robert Macgregor.

SONNET XL.

Se mai foco per foco non si spense.

HIS HEART IS ALL IN FLAMES, BUT HIS TONGUE IS MUTE, IN HER PRESENCE.

If fire was never yet by fire subdued,
If never flood fell dry by frequent rain,
But, like to like, if each by other gain,
And contraries are often mutual food;
Love, who our thoughts controllest in each mood,
Through whom two bodies thus one soul sustain,
How, why in her, with such unusual strain
Make the want less by wishes long renewed?
Perchance, as falleth the broad Nile from high,
Deafening with his great voice all nature round,
And as the sun still dazzles the fix'd eye,
So with itself desire in discord found
Loses in its impetuous object force,
As the too frequent spur oft checks the course.

Robert Macgregor.

SONNET XLI.

Perch' io t' abbia guardato di menzogna.

IN HER PRESENCE HE CAN NEITHER SPEAK, WEEP, NOR SIGH.

Although from falsehood I did thee restrain
With all my power, and paid thee honour due,
Ungrateful tongue; yet never did accrue
Honour from thee, but shame, and fierce disdain:
Most art thou cold, when most I want the strain
Thy aid should lend while I for pity sue;
And all thy utterance is imperfect too,
When thou dost speak, and as the dreamer's vain.
Ye too, sad tears, throughout each lingering night
Upon me wait, when I alone would stay;
But, needed by my peace, you take your flight:
And, all so prompt anguish and grief t' impart,
Ye sighs, then slow, and broken breathe your way:
My looks alone truly reveal my heart.

Dr Nott

With all my power, lest falsehood should invade,
I guarded thee and still thy honour sought,
Ungrateful tongue! who honour ne'er hast brought,
But still my care with rage and shame repaid:
For, though to me most requisite, thine aid,
When mercy I would ask, availeth nought,
Still cold and mute, and e'en to words if wrought
They seem as sounds in sleep by dreamers made.
And ye, sad tears, o' nights, when I would fain
Be left alone, my sure companions, flow,
But, summon'd for my peace, ye soon depart:
Ye too, mine anguish'd sighs, so prompt to pain,
Then breathe before her brokenly and slow,
And my face only speaks my suffering heart.

Robert Macgregor.

CANZONE V.

Nella stagion che 'l ciel rapido inchina.

NIGHT BRINGS REPOSE TO OTHERS, BUT NOT TO HIM.

In that still season, when the rapid sun
Drives down the west, and daylight flies to greet
Nations that haply wait his kindling flame;
In some strange land, alone, her weary feet
The time-worn pilgrim finds, with toil fordone,
Yet but the more speeds on her languid frame;
Her solitude the same,
When night has closed around;
Yet has the wanderer found
A deep though short forgetfulness at last
Of every woe, and every labour past.
But ah! my grief, that with each moment grows,
As fast, and yet more fast,
Day urges on, is heaviest at its close.

When Phœbus rolls his everlasting wheels
To give night room; and from encircling wood,
Broader and broader yet descends the shade;
The labourer arms him for his evening trade,
And all the weight his burthen'd heart conceals
Lightens with glad discourse or descant rude;
Then spreads his board with food,
Such as the forest hoar
To our first fathers bore,
By us disdain'd, yet praised in hall and bower,
But, let who will the cup of joyance pour,
I never knew, I will not say of mirth,
But of repose, an hour,
When Phœbus leaves, and stars salute the earth.

Yon shepherd, when the mighty star of day
He sees descending to its western bed,
And the wide Orient all with shade embrown'd,

Takes his old crook, and from the fountain head,
Green mead, and beechen bower, pursues his way,
Calling, with welcome voice, his flocks around;
Then far from human sound,
Some desert cave he strows
With leaves and verdant boughs,
And lays him down, without a thought, to sleep.
Ah, cruel Love! – then dost thou bid me keep
My idle chase, the airy steps pursuing
Of her I ever weep,
Who flies me still, my endless toil renewing.

E'en the rude seaman, in some cave confined,
Pillows his head, as daylight quits the scene,
On the hard deck, with vilest mat o'erspread;
And when the Sun in orient wave serene
Bathes his resplendent front, and leaves behind
Those antique pillars of his boundless bed;
Forgetfulness has shed
O'er man, and beast, and flower,
Her mild restoring power:
But my determined grief finds no repose;
And every day but aggravates the woes
Of that remorseless flood, that, ten long years,
Flowing, yet ever flows,
Nor know I what can check its ceaseless tears.

J.H. Merivale.

What time towards the western skies
The sun with parting radiance flies,
And other climes gilds with expected light,
Some aged pilgrim dame who strays
Alone, fatigued, through pathless ways,
Hastens her step, and dreads the approach of night
Then, the day's journey o'er, she'll steep
Her sense awhile in grateful sleep;
Forgetting all the pain, and peril past;
But I, alas! find no repose,
Each sun to me brings added woes,
While light's eternal orb rolls from us fast.

When the sun's wheels no longer glow,
And hills their lengthen'd shadows throw,
The hind collects his tools, and carols gay;
Then spreads his board with frugal fare,
Such as those homely acorns were,
Which all revere, yet casting them away,
Let those, who pleasure can enjoy,
In cheerfulness their hours employ;
While I, of all earth's wretches most unblest,
Whether the sun fierce darts his beams,
Whether the moon more mildly gleams,
Taste no delight, no momentary rest!

When the swain views the star of day
Quench in the pillowing waves its ray,
And scatter darkness o'er the eastern skies
Rising, his custom'd crook he takes,
The beech-wood, fountain, plain forsakes,
As calmly homeward with his flock he hies
Remote from man, then on his bed
In cot, or cave, with fresh leaves spread,
He courts soft slumber, and suspense from care,
While thou, fell Love, bidst me pursue
That voice, those footsteps which subdue
My soul; yet movest not th' obdurate fair!

Lock'd in some bay, to taste repose
On the hard deck, the sailor throws

His coarse garb o'er him, when the car of light
Granada, with Marocco leaves,
The Pillars famed, Iberia's waves,
And the world's hush'd, and all its race, in night.
But never will my sorrows cease,
Successive days their sum increase,
Though just ten annual suns have mark'd my pain;
Say, to this bosom's poignant grief
Who shall administer relief?
Say, who at length shall free me from my chain?

And, since there's comfort in the strain,
I see at eve along each plain.
And furrow'd hill, the unyoked team return:
Why at that hour will no one stay
My sighs, or bear my yoke away?
Why bathed in tears must I unceasing mourn?
Wretch that I was, to fix my sight
First on that face with such delight,
Till on my thought its charms were strong imprest,
Which force shall not efface, nor art,
Ere from this frame my soul dispart!
Nor know I then if passion's votaries rest.

O hasty strain, devoid of worth,
Sad as the bard who brought thee forth,
Show not thyself, be with the world at strife,
From nook to nook indulge thy grief;
While thy lorn parent seeks relief,
Nursing that amorous flame which feeds his life!

Dr Nott

SONNET XLII.

Poco era ad appressarsi agli occhi miei.

SUCH ARE HIS SUFFERINGS THAT HE ENVIES THE INSENSIBILITY OF MARBLE.

Had but the light which dazzled them afar
Drawn but a little nearer to mine eyes,
Methinks I would have wholly changed my form,
Even as in Thessaly her form she changed:
But if I cannot lose myself in her
More than I have – small mercy though it won –
I would to-day in aspect thoughtful be,
Of harder stone than chisel ever wrought,
Of adamant, or marble cold and white,
Perchance through terror, or of jasper rare
And therefore prized by the blind greedy crowd.
Then were I free from this hard heavy yoke
Which makes me envy Atlas, old and worn,
Who with his shoulders brings Morocco night.

Anonymous

MADRIGALE I.

Non al suo amante più Diana piacque.

ANYTHING THAT REMINDS HIM OF LAURA RENEWS HIS TORMENTS.

Not Dian to her lover was more dear,
When fortune 'mid the waters cold and clear,
Gave him her naked beauties all to see,
Than seem'd the rustic ruddy nymph to me,
Who, in yon flashing stream, the light veil laved,
Whence Laura's lovely tresses lately waved;
I saw, and through me felt an amorous chill,
Though summer burn, to tremble and to thrill.

Robert Macgregor.

CANZONE VI.

Spirto gentil che quelle membra reggi.

TO RIENZI, BESEECHING HIM TO RESTORE TO ROME HER ANCIENT LIBERTY.

Spirit heroic! who with fire divine
Kindlest those limbs, awhile which pilgrim hold
On earth a Chieftain, gracious, wise, and bold;
Since, rightly, now the rod of state is thine
Rome and her wandering children to confine,
And yet reclaim her to the old good way:
To thee I speak, for elsewhere not a ray
Of virtue can I find, extinct below,
Nor one who feels of evil deeds the shame.
Why Italy still waits, and what her aim
I know not, callous to her proper woe,
Indolent, aged, slow,
Still will she sleep? Is none to rouse her found?
Oh! that my wakening hands were through her tresses wound.

So grievous is the spell, the trance so deep,
Loud though we call, my hope is faint that e'er
She yet will waken from her heavy sleep:
But not, methinks, without some better end
Was this our Rome entrusted to thy care,
Who surest may revive and best defend.
Fearlessly then upon that reverend head,
'Mid her dishevell'd locks, thy fingers spread,
And lift at length the sluggard from the dust;
I, day and night, who her prostration mourn,
For this, in thee, have fix'd my certain trust,
That, if her sons yet turn.
And their eyes ever to true honour raise.
The glory is reserved for thy illustrious days!

Her ancient walls, which still with fear and love
The world admires, whene'er it calls to mind
The days of Eld, and turns to look behind;
Her hoar and cavern'd monuments above
The dust of men, whose fame, until the world
In dissolution sink, can never fail;
Her all, that in one ruin now lies hurl'd,
Hopes to have heal'd by thee its every ail.
O faithful Brutus! noble Scipios dead!
To you what triumph, where ye now are blest,
If of our worthy choice the fame have spread:
And how his laurell'd crest,
Will old Fabricius rear, with joy elate,
That his own Rome again shall beauteous be and great!

And, if for things of earth its care Heaven show,
The souls who dwell above in joy and peace,
And their mere mortal frames have left below,
Implore thee this long civil strife may cease,
Which kills all confidence, nips every good,
Which bars the way to many a roof, where men
Once holy, hospitable lived, the den
Of fearless rapine now and frequent blood,
Whose doors to virtue only are denied.
While beneath plunder'd Saints, in outraged fanes
Plots Faction, and Revenge the altar stains;
And, contrast sad and wide,
The very bells which sweetly wont to fling
Summons to prayer and praise now Battle's tocsin ring!

Pale weeping women, and a friendless crowd
Of tender years, infirm and desolate Age,
Which hates itself and its superfluous days,
With each blest order to religion vow'd,
Whom works of love through lives of want engage,
To thee for help their hands and voices raise;
While our poor panic-stricken land displays
The thousand wounds which now so mar her frame,
That e'en from foes compassion they command;
Or more if Christendom thy care may claim.
Lo! God's own house on fire, while not a hand

Moves to subdue the flame:
– Heal thou these wounds, this feverish tumult end,
And on the holy work Heaven's blessing shall descend!

Often against our marble Column high
Wolf, Lion, Bear, proud Eagle, and base Snake
Even to their own injury insult shower;
Lifts against thee and theirs her mournful cry,
The noble Dame who calls thee here to break
Away the evil weeds which will not flower.
A thousand years and more! and gallant men
There fix'd her seat in beauty and in power;
The breed of patriot hearts has fail'd since then!
And, in their stead, upstart and haughty now,
A race, which ne'er to her in reverence bends,
Her husband, father thou!
Like care from thee and counsel she attends,
As o'er his other works the Sire of all extends.

'Tis seldom e'en that with our fairest scheme
Some adverse fortune will not mix, and mar
With instant ill ambition's noblest dreams;
But thou, once ta'en thy path, so walk that I
May pardon her past faults, great as they are,
If now at least she give herself the lie.
For never, in all memory, as to thee,
To mortal man so sure and straight the way
Of everlasting honour open lay,
For thine the power and will, if right I see,
To lift our empire to its old proud state.
Let this thy glory be!
They succour'd her when young, and strong, and great,
He, in her weak old age, warded the stroke of Fate.
Forth on thy way! my Song, and, where the bold
Tarpeian lifts his brow, shouldst thou behold,
Of others' weal more thoughtful than his own,
The chief, by general Italy revered,
Tell him from me, to whom he is but known
As one to Virtue and by Fame endear'd,
Till stamp'd upon his heart the sad truth be,
That, day by day to thee,

With suppliant attitude and streaming eyes,
For justice and relief our seven-hill'd city cries.

Robert Macgregor.

MADRIGALE II.

Perchè al viso d' Amor portava insegna.

A LOVE JOURNEY – DANGER IN THE PATH – HE TURNS BACK.

Bright in whose face Love's conquering ensign stream'd,
A foreign fair so won me, young and vain,
That of her sex all others worthless seem'd:
Her as I follow'd o'er the verdant plain,
I heard a loud voice speaking from afar,
"How lost in these lone woods his footsteps are!"
Then paused I, and, beneath the tall beech shade,
All wrapt in thought, around me well survey'd,
Till, seeing how much danger block'd my way,
Homeward I turn'd me though at noon of day.

Robert Macgregor.

BALLATA III.

Quel foco, ch' io pensai che fosse spento.

HE THOUGHT HIMSELF FREE, BUT FINDS THAT HE IS MORE THAN EVER ENTHRALLED BY LOVE.

That fire for ever which I thought at rest,
Quench'd in the chill blood of my ripen'd years,
Awakes new flames and torment in my breast.
Its sparks were never all, from what I see,
Extinct, but merely slumbering, smoulder'd o'er;
Haply this second error worse may be,
For, by the tears, which I, in torrents, pour,
Grief, through these eyes, distill'd from my heart's core,
Which holds within itself the spark and bait,
Remains not as it was, but grows more great.
What fire, save mine, had not been quench'd and kill'd
Beneath the flood these sad eyes ceaseless shed?
Struggling 'mid opposites – so Love has will'd –
Now here, now there, my vain life must be led,
For in so many ways his snares are spread,
When most I hope him from my heart expell'd
Then most of her fair face its slave I'm held.

Robert Macgregor.

SONNET XLIII.

Se col cieco desir che 'l cor distrugge.

BLIGHTED HOPE.

Either that blind desire, which life destroys
Counting the hours, deceives my misery,
Or, even while yet I speak, the moment flies,
Promised at once to pity and to me.
Alas! what baneful shade o'erhangs and dries
The seed so near its full maturity?
'Twixt me and hope what brazen walls arise?
From murderous wolves not even my fold is free.
Ah, woe is me! Too clearly now I find
That felon Love, to aggravate my pain,
Mine easy heart hath thus to hope inclined;
And now the maxim sage I call to mind,
That mortal bliss must doubtful still remain
Till death from earthly bonds the soul unbind.

Lord Charlemont.

Counting the hours, lest I myself mislead
By blind desire wherewith my heart is torn,
E'en while I speak away the moments speed,
To me and pity which alike were sworn.
What shade so cruel as to blight the seed
Whence the wish'd fruitage should so soon be born?
What beast within my fold has leap'd to feed?
What wall is built between the hand and corn?
Alas! I know not, but, if right I guess,
Love to such joyful hope has only led
To plunge my weary life in worse distress;
And I remember now what once I read,
Until the moment of his full release
Man's bliss begins not, nor his troubles cease.

Robert Macgregor.

SONNET XLIV.

Mie venture al venir son tarde e pigre.

FEW ARE THE SWEETS, BUT MANY THE BITTERS OF LOVE.

Ever my hap is slack and slow in coming,
Desire increasing, ay my hope uncertain
With doubtful love, that but increaseth pain;
For, tiger-like, so swift it is in parting.
Alas! the snow black shall it be and scalding,
The sea waterless, and fish upon the mountain,
The Thames shall back return into his fountain,
And where he rose the sun shall take [his] lodging,
Ere I in this find peace or quietness;
Or that Love, or my Lady, right wisely,
Leave to conspire against me wrongfully.
And if I have, after such bitterness,
One drop of sweet, my mouth is out of taste,
That all my trust and travail is but waste.

Sir Thomas Wyatt.

Late to arrive my fortunes are and slow –
Hopes are unsure, desires ascend and swell,
Suspense, expectancy in me rebel –
But swifter to depart than tigers go.
Tepid and dark shall be the cold pure snow,
The ocean dry, its fish on mountains dwell,
The sun set in the East, by that old well
Alike whence Tigris and Euphrates flow,
Ere in this strife I peace or truce shall find,
Ere Love or Laura practise kinder ways,
Sworn friends, against me wrongfully combined.
After such bitters, if some sweet allays,
Balk'd by long fasts my palate spurns the fare,
Sole grace from them that falleth to my share.

Robert Macgregor.

SONNET XLV.

La guancia che fu già piangendo stanca.

TO HIS FRIEND AGAPITO, WITH A PRESENT.

Thy weary cheek that channell'd sorrow shows,
My much loved lord, upon the one repose;
More careful of thyself against Love be,
Tyrant who smiles his votaries wan to see;
And with the other close the left-hand path
Too easy entrance where his message hath;
In sun and storm thyself the same display,
Bccausc timc faileth for the lengthen'd way.
And, with the third, drink of the precious herb
Which purges every thought that would disturb,
Sweet in the end though sour at first in taste:
But me enshrine where your best joys are placed,
So that I fear not the grim bark of Styx,
If with such prayer of mine pride do not mix.

Robert Macgregor.

BALLATA IV.

Perchè quel che mi trasse ad amar prima.

HE WILL ALWAYS LOVE HER, THOUGH DENIED THE SIGHT OF HER.

Though cruelty denies my view
Those charms which led me first to love;
To passion yet will I be true,
Nor shall my will rebellious prove.
Amid the curls of golden hair
That wave those beauteous temples round,
Cupid spread craftily the snare
With which my captive heart he bound:
And from those eyes he caught the ray
Which thaw'd the ice that fenced my breast,
Chasing all other thoughts away,
With brightness suddenly imprest.
But now that hair of sunny gleam,
Ah me! is ravish'd from my sight;
Those beauteous eyes withdraw their beam,
And change to sadness past delight.
A glorious death by all is prized;
Tis death alone shall break my chain:
Oh! be Love's timid wail despised.
Lovers should nobly suffer pain.

Dr Nott

Though barr'd from all which led me first to love
By coldness or caprice,
Not yet from its firm bent can passion cease!
The snare was set amid those threads of gold,
To which Love bound me fast;
And from those bright eyes melted the long cold
Within my heart that pass'd;
So sweet the spell their sudden splendour cast,
Its single memory still
Deprives my soul of every other will.
But now, alas! from me of that fine hair
Is ravish'd the dear sight;
The lost light of those twin stars, chaste as fair,
Saddens me in her flight;
But, since a glorious death wins honour bright,
By death, and not through grief,
Love from such chain shall give at last relief.

Robert Macgregor.

SONNET XLVI.

L' arbor gentil che forte amai molt' anni.

IMPRECATION AGAINST THE LAUREL.

The graceful tree I loved so long and well,
Ere its fair boughs in scorn my flame declined,
Beneath its shade encouraged my poor mind
To bud and bloom, and 'mid its sorrow swell.
But now, my heart secure from such a spell,
Alas, from friendly it has grown unkind!
My thoughts entirely to one end confined,
Their painful sufferings how I still may tell.
What should he say, the sighing slave of love,
To whom my later rhymes gave hope of bliss,
Who for that laurel has lost all – but this?
May poet never pluck thee more, nor Jove
Exempt; but may the sun still hold in hate
On each green leaf till blight and blackness wait.

Robert Macgregor.

SONNET XLVII.

Benedetto sia 'l giorno e 'l mese e l' anno.

HE BLESSES ALL THE CIRCUMSTANCES OF HIS PASSION.

Blest be the day, and blest the month, the year,
The spring, the hour, the very moment blest,
The lovely scene, the spot, where first oppress'd
I sunk, of two bright eyes the prisoner:
And blest the first soft pang, to me most dear,
Which thrill'd my heart, when Love became its guest;
And blest the bow, the shafts which pierced my breast,
And even the wounds, which bosom'd thence I bear.
Blest too the strains which, pour'd through glade and grove,
Have made the woodlands echo with her name;
The sighs, the tears, the languishment, the love:
And blest those sonnets, sources of my fame;
And blest that thought – Oh! never to remove!
Which turns to her alone, from her alone which came.

Francis Wrangham.

Blest be the year, the month, the hour, the day,
The season and the time, and point of space,
And blest the beauteous country and the place
Where first of two bright eyes I felt the sway:
Blest the sweet pain of which I was the prey,
When newly doom'd Love's sovereign law to embrace,
And blest the bow and shaft to which I trace,
The wound that to my inmost heart found way:
Blest be the ceaseless accents of my tongue,
Unwearied breathing my loved lady's name:
Blest my fond wishes, sighs, and tears, and pains:
Blest be the lays in which her praise I sung,
That on all sides acquired to her fair fame,
And blest my thoughts! for o'er them all she reigns.

Lady Dacre.

SONNET XLVIII.

Padre del ciel, dopo i perduti giorni.

CONSCIOUS OF HIS FOLLY, HE PRAYS GOD TO TURN HIM TO A BETTER LIFE.

Father of heaven! after the days misspent,
After the nights of wild tumultuous thought,
In that fierce passion's strong entanglement,
One, for my peace too lovely fair, had wrought;
Vouchsafe that, by thy grace, my spirit bent
On nobler aims, to holier ways be brought;
That so my foe, spreading with dark intent
His mortal snares, be foil'd, and held at nought.
E'en now th' eleventh year its course fulfils,
That I have bow'd me to the tyranny
Relentless most to fealty most tried.
Have mercy, Lord! on my unworthy ills:
Fix all my thoughts in contemplation high;
How on the cross this day a Saviour died.

Lady Dacre.

Father of heaven! despite my days all lost,
Despite my nights in doting folly spent
With that fierce passion which my bosom rent
At sight of her, too lovely for my cost;
Vouchsafe at length that, by thy grace, I turn
To wiser life, and enterprise more fair,
So that my cruel foe, in vain his snare
Set for my soul, may his defeat discern.
Already, Lord, the eleventh year circling wanes
Since first beneath his tyrant yoke I fell
Who still is fiercest where we least rebel:
Pity my undeserved and lingering pains,
To holier thoughts my wandering sense restore,
How on this day his cross thy Son our Saviour bore.

Robert Macgregor.

BALLATA V.

Volgendo gli occhi al mio novo colore.

HER KIND SALUTE SAVED HIM FROM DEATH.

Late as those eyes on my sunk cheek inclined,
Whose paleness to the world seems of the grave,
Compassion moved you to that greeting kind,
Whose soft smile to my worn heart spirit gave.
The poor frail life which yet to me is left
Was of your beauteous eyes the liberal gift,
And of that voice angelical and mild;
My present state derived from them I see;
As the rod quickens the slow sullen child,
So waken'd they the sleeping soul in me.
Thus, Lady, of my true heart both the keys
You hold in hand, and yet your captive please:
Ready to sail wherever winds may blow,
By me most prized whate'er to you I owe.

Robert Macgregor.

SONNET XLIX.

Se voi poteste per turbati segni.

HE ENTREATS LAURA NOT TO HATE THE HEART FROM WHICH SHE CAN NEVER BE ABSENT.

If, but by angry and disdainful sign,
By the averted head and downcast sight,
By readiness beyond thy sex for flight,
Deaf to all pure and worthy prayers of mine,
Thou canst, by these or other arts of thine,
'Scape from my breast – where Love on slip so slight
Grafts every day new boughs – of such despite
A fitting cause I then might well divine:
For gentle plant in arid soil to be
Seems little suited: so it better were,
And this e'en nature dictates, thence to stir.
But since thy destiny prohibits thee
Elsewhere to dwell, be this at least thy care
Not always to sojourn in hatred there.

Robert Macgregor.

SONNET L.

Lasso, che mal accorto fui da prima.

HE PRAYS LOVE TO KINDLE ALSO IN HER THE FLAME BY WHICH HE IS UNCEASINGLY TORMENTED.

Alas! this heart by me was little known
In those first days when Love its depths explored,
Where by degrees he made himself the lord
Of my whole life, and claim'd it as his own:
I did not think that, through his power alone,
A heart time-steel'd, and so with valour stored,
Such proof of failing firmness could afford,
And fell by wrong self-confidence o'erthrown.
Henceforward all defence too late will come,
Save this, to prove, enough or little, here
If to these mortal prayers Love lend his ear.
Not now my prayer – nor can such e'er have room –
That with more mercy he consume my heart,
But in the fire that she may bear her part.

Robert Macgregor.

SESTINA III.

L' aere gravato, e l' importuna nebbia.

HE COMPARES LAURA TO WINTER, AND FORESEES THAT SHE WILL ALWAYS BE THE SAME.

The overcharged air, the impending cloud,
Compress'd together by impetuous winds,
Must presently discharge themselves in rain;
Already as of crystal are the streams,
And, for the fine grass late that clothed the vales,
Is nothing now but the hoar frost and ice.

And I, within my heart, more cold than ice,
Of heavy thoughts have such a hovering cloud,
As sometimes rears itself in these our vales,
Lowly, and landlock'd against amorous winds,
Environ'd everywhere with stagnant streams,
When falls from soft'ning heaven the smaller rain.

Lasts but a brief while every heavy rain;
And summer melts away the snows and ice,
When proudly roll th' accumulated streams:
Nor ever hid the heavens so thick a cloud,
Which, overtaken by the furious winds,
Fled not from the first hills and quiet vales.

But ah! what profit me the flowering vales?
Alike I mourn in sunshine and in rain,
Suffering the same in warm and wintry winds;
For only then my lady shall want ice
At heart, and on her brow th' accustom'd cloud,
When dry shall be the seas, the lakes, and streams.

While to the sea descend the mountain streams,
As long as wild beasts love umbrageous vales,
O'er those bright eyes shall hang th' unfriendly cloud
My own that moistens with continual rain;

And in that lovely breast be harden'd ice
Which forces still from mine so dolorous winds.

Yet well ought I to pardon all the winds
But for the love of one, that 'mid two streams
Shut me among bright verdure and pure ice;
So that I pictured then in thousand vales
The shade wherein I was, which heat or rain
Esteemeth not, nor sound of broken cloud.

But fled not ever cloud before the winds,
As I that day: nor ever streams with rain
Nor ice, when April's sun opens the vales.

Robert Macgregor.

SONNET LI.

Del mar Tirreno alla sinistra riva.

THE FALL.

Upon the left shore of the Tyrrhene sea,
Where, broken by the winds, the waves complain,
Sudden I saw that honour'd green again,
Written for whom so many a page must be:
Love, ever in my soul his flame who fed,
Drew me with memories of those tresses fair;
Whence, in a rivulet, which silent there
Through long grass stole, I fell, as one struck dead.
Lone as I was, 'mid hills of oak and fir,
I felt ashamed; to heart of gentle mould
Blushes suffice: nor needs it other spur.
'Tis well at least, breaking bad customs old,
To change from eyes to feet: from these so wet
By those if milder April should be met.

Robert Macgregor.

SONNET LII.

L' aspetto sacro della terra vostra.

THE VIEW OF ROME PROMPTS HIM TO TEAR HIMSELF FROM LAURA, BUT LOVE WILL NOT ALLOW HIM.

The solemn aspect of this sacred shore
Wakes for the misspent past my bitter sighs;
'Pause, wretched man! and turn,' as conscience cries,
Pointing the heavenward way where I should soar.
But soon another thought gets mastery o'er
The first, that so to palter were unwise;
E'en now the time, if memory err not, flies,
When we should wait our lady-love before.
I, for his aim then well I apprehend,
Within me freeze, as one who, sudden, hears
News unexpected which his soul offend.
Returns my first thought then, that disappears;
Nor know I which shall conquer, but till now
Within me they contend, nor hope of rest allow!

Robert Macgregor.

SONNET LIII.

Ben sapev' io che natural consiglio.

FLEEING FROM LOVE, HE FALLS INTO THE HANDS OF HIS MINISTERS.

Full well I know that natural wisdom nought,
Love, 'gainst thy power, in any age prevail'd,
For snares oft set, fond oaths that ever fail'd,
Sore proofs of thy sharp talons long had taught;
But lately, and in me it wonder wrought –
With care this new experience be detail'd –
'Tween Tuscany and Elba as I sail'd
On the salt sea, it first my notice caught.
I fled from thy broad hands, and, by the way,
An unknown wanderer, 'neath the violence
Of winds, and waves, and skies, I helpless lay,
When, lo! thy ministers, I knew not whence,
Who quickly made me by fresh stings to feel
Ill who resists his fate, or would conceal.

Robert Macgregor.

CANZONE VII.

Lasso me, ch i' non so in qual parte pieghi.

HE WOULD CONSOLE HIMSELF WITH SONG, BUT IS CONSTRAINED TO WEEP.

Me wretched! for I know not whither tend
The hopes which have so long my heart betray'd:
If none there be who will compassion lend,
Wherefore to Heaven these often prayers for aid?
But if, belike, not yet denied to me
That, ere my own life end,
These sad notes mute shall bc,
Let not my Lord conceive the wish too free,
Yet once, amid sweet flowers, to touch the string,
"Reason and right it is that love I sing."

Reason indeed there were at last that I
Should sing, since I have sigh'd so long and late,
But that for me 'tis vain such art to try,
Brief pleasures balancing with sorrows great;
Could I, by some sweet verse, but cause to shine
Glad wonder and new joy
Within those eyes divine,
Bliss o'er all other lovers then were mine!
But more, if frankly fondly I could say,
"My lady asks, I therefore wake the lay."

Delicious, dangerous thoughts! that, to begin
A theme so high, have gently led me thus,
You know I ne'er can hope to pass within
Our lady's heart, so strongly steel'd from us;
She will not deign to look on thing so low,
Nor may our language win
Aught of her care: since Heaven ordains it so,
And vainly to oppose must irksome grow,
Even as I my heart to stone would turn,
"So in my verse would I be rude and stern."

What do I say? where am I? – My own heart
And its misplaced desires alone deceive!
Though my view travel utmost heaven athwart
No planet there condemns me thus to grieve:
Why, if the body's veil obscure my sight,
Blame to the stars impart.
Or other things as bright?
Within me reigns my tyrant, day and night,
Since, for his triumph, me a captive took
"Her lovely face, and lustrous eyes' dear look."

While all things else in Nature's boundless reign
Came good from the Eternal Master's mould,
I look for such desert in me in vain:
Me the light wounds that I around behold;
To the true splendour if I turn at last,
My eye would shrink in pain,
Whose own fault o'er it cast
Such film, and not the fatal day long past,
When first her angel beauty met my view,
"In the sweet season when my life was new."

Robert Macgregor.

CANZONE VIII.

Perchè la vita è breve.

IN PRAISE OF LAURA'S EYES: THE DIFFICULTY OF HIS THEME.

Since human life is frail,
And genius trembles at the lofty theme,
I little confidence in either place;
But let my tender wail
There, where it ought, deserved attention claim,
That wail which e'en in silence we may trace.
O beauteous eyes, where Love doth nestling stay!
To you I turn my insufficient lay,
Unapt to flow; but passion's goad I feel:
And he of you who sings
Such courteous habit by the strain is taught,
That, borne on amorous wings,
He soars above the reach of vulgar thought:
Exalted thus, I venture to reveal
What long my cautious heart has labour'd to conceal.

Yes, well do I perceive
To you how wrongful is my scanty praise;
Yet the strong impulse cannot be withstood,
That urges, since I view'd
What fancy to the sight before ne'er gave,
What ne'er before graced mine, or higher lays.
Bright authors of my sadly-pleasing state,
That you alone conceive me well I know,
When to your fierce beams I become as snow!
Your elegant disdain
Haply then kindles at my worthless strain.
Did not this dread create
Some mitigation of my bosom's heat,
Death would be bliss: for greater joy 'twould give
With them to suffer death, without them than to live.

If not consumèd quite,
I the weak object of a flame so strong:
'Tis not that safety springs from native might,
But that some fear restrains,
Which chills the current circling through my veins;
Strengthening this heart, that it may suffer long.
O hills, O vales, O forests, floods, and fields,
Ye who have witness'd how my sad life flows,
Oft have ye heard me call on death for aid.
Ah, state surcharged with woes!
To stay destroys, and flight no succour yields.
But had not higher dread
Withheld, some sudden effort I had made
To end my sorrows and protracted pains,
Of which the beauteous cause insensible remains.

Why lead me, grief, astray
From my first theme to chant a different lay?
Let me proceed where pleasure may invite.
'Tis not of you I 'plain,
O eyes, beyond compare serenely bright;
Nor yet of him who binds me in his chain.
Ye clearly can behold the hues that Love
Scatters ofttime on my dejected face;
And fancy may his inward workings trace
There where, whole nights and days,
He rules with power derived from your bright rays:
What rapture would ye prove,
If you, dear lights, upon yourselves could gaze!
But, frequent as you bend your beams on me,
What influence you possess you in another see.

Oh! if to you were known
That beauty which I sing, immense, divine.
As unto him on whom its glories shine!
The heart had then o'erflown
With joy unbounded, such as is denied
Unto that nature which its acts doth guide.
How happy is the soul for you that sighs,
Celestial lights! which lend a charm to life,

And make me bless what else I should not prize!
Ah! why, so seldom why
Afford what ne'er can cause satiety?
More often to your sight
Why not bring Love, who holds me constant strife?
And why so soon of joys despoil me quite,
Which ever and anon my tranced soul delight?

Yes, 'debted to your grace,
Frequent I feel throughout my inmost soul
Unwonted floods of sweetest rapture roll;
Relieving so the mind,
That all oppressive thoughts are left behind,
And of a thousand only one has place;
For which alone this life is dear to me.
Oh! might the blessing of duration prove,
Not equall'd then could my condition be!
But this would, haply, move
In others envy, in myself vain pride.
That pain should be allied
To pleasure is, alas! decreed above;
Then, stifling all the ardour of desire,
Homeward I turn my thoughts, and in myself retire.

So sweetly shines reveal'd
The amorous thought within your soul which dwells,
That other joys it from my heart expels:
Hence I aspire to frame
Lays whereon Hope may build a deathless name,
When in the tomb my dust shall lie conceal'd.
At your approach anguish and sorrow fly;
These, as your beams retire, again draw nigh;
Yet outward acts their influence ne'er betray,
For doting memory
Dwells on the past, and chases them away.
Whatever, then, of worth
My genius ripens owes to you its birth.
To you all honour and all praise is due –
Myself a barren soil, and cultured but by you.
Thy strains, O song! appease me not, but fire,
Chanting a theme that wings my wild desire:

Trust me, thou shalt ere long a sister-song acquire.

Dr Nott

Since mortal life is frail,
And my mind shrinks from lofty themes deterr'd,
But small the trust which I in either feel:
Yet hope I that my wail,
Which vainly I in silence would conceal,
Shall, where I wish, where most it ought, be heard.
Beautiful eyes! wherein Love makes his nest,
To you my song its feeble descant turns,
Slow of itself, but now by passion spurr'd;
Who sings of you is blest,
And from his theme such courteous habit learns
That, borne on wings of love,
Proudly he soars each viler thought above;
Encouraged thus, what long my harass'd heart
Has kept conceal'd, I venture to impart.

Yet do I know full well
How much my praise must wrongful prove to you,
But how the great desire can I oppose,
Which ever in me grows,
Since what surpasses thought 'twas mine to view,
Though that nor others' wit nor mine can tell?
Eyes! guilty authors of my cherish'd pain,
That you alone can judge me, well I know,
When from your burning beams I melt like snow,
Haply your sweet disdain
Offence in my unworthiness may see;
Ah! were there not such fear,
To calm the heat with which I kindle near,
'Twere bliss to die: for better far to me
Were death with them than life without could be.

If yet not wasted quite –
So frail a thing before so fierce a flame –
'Tis not from my own strength that safety came,
But that some fear gives might,
Freezing the warm blood coursing through its veins,
To my poor heart better to bear the strife.
O valleys, hills, O forests, floods, and plains,
Witnesses of my melancholy life!
For death how often have ye heard me pray!

Ah, miserable fate!
Where flight avails not, though 'tis death to stay;
But, if a dread more great
Restrain'd me not, despair would find a way,
Speedy and short, my lingering pains to close,
– Hers then the crime who still no mercy shows.

Why thus astray, O grief,
Lead me to speak what I would leave unsaid?
Leave me, where pleasure me impels, to tread:
Not now my song complains
Of you, sweet eyes, serene beyond belief,
Nor yet of him who binds me in such chains:
Right well may you observe the varying hues
Which o'er my visage oft the tyrant strews,
And thence may guess what war within he makes,
Where night and day he reigns,
Strong in the power which from your light he takes:
Blessèd ye were as bright,
Save that from you is barr'd your own dear sight:
Yet often as to me those orbs you turn,
What they to others are you well may learn.

If, as to us who gaze
Were known to you the charms incredible
And heavenly, of which I sing the praise,
No measured joy would swell
Your heart, and haply, therefore, 'tis denied
Unto the power which doth their motions guide.
Happy the soul for you which breathes the sigh,
Best lights of heaven! for whom I grateful bless
This life, which has for me no other joy.
Alas! so seldom why
Give me what I can ne'er too much possess?
Why not more often see
The ceaseless havoc which love makes of me?
And why that bliss so quickly from me steal,
From time to time which my rapt senses feel?

Yes, thanks, great thanks to you!
From time to time I feel through all my soul

A sweetness so unusual and new,
That every marring care
And gloomy vision thence begins to roll,
So that, from all, one only thought is there.
That – that alone consoles me life to bear:
And could but this my joy endure awhile,
Nought earthly could, methinks, then match my state.
Yet such great honour might
Envy in others, pride in me excite:
Thus still it seems the fate
Of man, that tears should chase his transient smile:
And, checking thus my burning wishes, I
Back to myself return, to muse and sigh.

The amorous anxious thought,
Which reigns within you, flashes so on me,
That from my heart it draws all other joy;
Whence works and words so wrought
Find scope and issue, that I hope to be
Immortal made, although all flesh must die.
At your approach ennui and anguish fly;
With your departure they return again:
But memory, on the past which doting dwells,
Denies them entrance then,
So that no outward act their influence tells;
Thus, if in me is nurst
Any good fruit, from you the seed came first:
To you, if such appear, the praise is due,
Barren myself till fertilized by you.
Thy strains appease me not, O song!
But rather fire me still that theme to sing
Where centre all my thoughts – therefore, ere long,
A sister ode to join thee will I bring.

Robert Macgregor.

CANZONE IX.

Gentil mia donna, i' veggio.

IN PRAISE OF LAURA'S EYES: THEY LEAD HIM TO CONTEMPLATE THE PATH OF LIFE.

Lady, in your bright eyes
Soft glancing round, I mark a holy light,
Pointing the arduous way that heavenward lies;
And to my practised sight,
From thence, where Love enthroned, asserts his might,
Visibly, palpably, the soul beams forth.
This is the beacon guides to deeds of worth,
And urges me to seek the glorious goal;
This bids me leave behind the vulgar throng,
Nor can the human tongue
Tell how those orbs divine o'er all my soul
Exert their sweet control,
Both when hoar winter's frosts around are flung,
And when the year puts on his youth again,
Jocund, as when this bosom first knew pain.

Oh! if in that high sphere,
From whence the Eternal Ruler of the stars
In this excelling work declared his might,
All be as fair and bright,
Loose me from forth my darksome prison here,
That to so glorious life the passage bars;
Then, in the wonted tumult of my breast,
I hail boon Nature, and the genial day
That gave me being, and a fate so blest,
And her who bade hope beam
Upon my soul; for till then burthensome
Was life itself become:
But now, elate with touch of self-esteem,
High thoughts and sweet within that heart arise,
Of which the warders are those beauteous eyes.

No joy so exquisite
Did Love or fickle Fortune ere devise,
In partial mood, for favour'd votaries,
But I would barter it
For one dear glance of those angelic eyes,
Whence springs my peace as from its living root.
O vivid lustre! of power absolute
O'er all my being – source of that delight,
By which consumed I sink, a willing prey.
As fades each lesser ray
Before your splendour more intense and bright,
So to my raptured heart,
When your surpassing sweetness you impart,
No other thought of feeling may remain
Where you, with Love himself, despotic reign.

All sweet emotions e'er
By happy lovers felt in every clime,
Together all, may not with mine compare,
When, as from time to time,
I catch from that dark radiance rich and deep
A ray in which, disporting, Love is seen;
And I believe that from my cradled sleep,
By Heaven provided this resource hath been,
'Gainst adverse fortune, and my nature frail.
Wrong'd am I by that veil,
And the fair hand which oft the light eclipse,
That all my bliss hath wrought;
And whence the passion struggling on my lips,
Both day and night, to vent the breast o'erfraught,
Still varying as I read her varying thought.

For that (with pain I find)
Not Nature's poor endowments may alone
Render me worthy of a look so kind,
I strive to raise my mind
To match with the exalted hopes I own,
And fires, though all engrossing, pure as mine.
If prone to good, averse to all things base,
Contemner of what worldlings covet most,
I may become by long self-discipline.

Haply this humble boast
May win me in her fair esteem a place;
For sure the end and aim
Of all my tears, my sorrowing heart's sole claim,
Were the soft trembling of relenting eyes,
The generous lover's last, best, dearest prize.

My lay, thy sister-song is gone before.
And now another in my teeming brain
Prepares itself: whence I resume the strain.

Lady Dacre.

CANZONE X.

Poichè per mio destino.

IN PRAISE OF LAURA'S EYES: IN THEM HE FINDS EVERY GOOD, AND HE CAN NEVER CEASE TO PRAISE THEM.

Since then by destiny
I am compell'd to sing the strong desire,
Which here condemns me ceaselessly to sigh,
May Love, whose quenchless fire
Excites me, be my guide and point the way,
And in the sweet task modulate my lay:
But gently be it, lest th' o'erpowering theme
Inflame and sting me, lest my fond heart may
Dissolve in too much softness, which I deem,
From its sad state, may be:
For in me – hence my terror and distress!
Not now as erst I see
Judgment to keep my mind's great passion less:
Nay, rather from mine own thoughts melt I so,
As melts before the summer sun the snow.

At first I fondly thought
Communing with mine ardent flame to win
Some brief repose, some time of truce within:
This was the hope which brought
Me courage what I suffer'd to explain,
Now, now it leaves me martyr to my pain:
But still, continuing mine amorous song,
Must I the lofty enterprise maintain;
So powerful is the wish that in me glows,
That Reason, which so long
Restrain'd it, now no longer can oppose.
Then teach me, Love, to sing
In such frank guise, that ever if the ear
Of my sweet foe should chance the notes to hear,
Pity, I ask no more, may in her spring.

If, as in other times,
When kindled to true virtue was mankind,
The genius, energy of man could find
Entrance in divers climes,
Mountains and seas o'erpassing, seeking there
Honour, and culling oft its garland fair,
Mine were such wish, not mine such need would be.
From shore to shore my weary course to trace,
Since God, and Love, and Nature deign for me
Each virtue and each grace
In those dear eyes where I rejoice to place.
In life to them must I
Turn as to founts whence peace and safety swell:
And e'en were death, which else I fear not, nigh,
Their sight alone would teach me to be well.

As, vex'd by the fierce wind,
The weary sailor lifts at night his gaze
To the twin lights which still our pole displays,
So, in the storms unkind
Of Love which I sustain, in those bright eyes
My guiding light and only solace lies:
But e'en in this far more is due to theft,
Which, taught by Love, from time to time, I make
Of secret glances than their gracious gift:
Yet that, though rare and slight,
Makes me from them perpetual model take;
Since first they blest my sight
Nothing of good without them have I tried,
Placing them over me to guard and guide,
Because mine own worth held itself but light.

Never the full effect
Can I imagine, and describe it less
Which o'er my heart those soft eyes still possess!
As worthless I reject
And mean all other joys that life confers,
E'en as all other beauties yield to hers.
A tranquil peace, alloy'd by no distress,
Such as in heaven eternally abides,
Moves from their lovely and bewitching smile.

So could I gaze, the while
Love, at his sweet will, governs them and guides,
– E'en though the sun were nigh,
Resting above us on his onward wheel –
On her, intensely with undazzled eye,
Nor of myself nor others think or feel.

Ah! that I should desire
Things that can never in this world be won,
Living on wishes hopeless to acquire.
Yet, were the knot undone,
Wherewith my weak tongue Love is wont to bind,
Checking its speech, when her sweet face puts on
All its great charms, then would I courage find,
Words on that point so apt and new to use,
As should make weep whoe'er might hear the tale.
But the old wounds I bear,
Stamp'd on my tortured heart, such power refuse;
Then grow I weak and pale,
And my blood hides itself I know not where;
Nor as I was remain I: hence I know
Love dooms my death and this the fatal blow.

Farewell, my song! already do I see
Heavily in my hand the tired pen move
From its long dear discourse with her I love;
Not so my thoughts from communing with me.

Robert Macgregor.

SONNET LIV.

Io son già stanco di pensar siccome.

HE WONDERS AT HIS LONG ENDURANCE OF SUCH TOIL AND SUFFERING.

I weary me alway with questions keen
How, why my thoughts ne'er turn from you away,
Wherefore in life they still prefer to stay,
When they might flee this sad and painful scene,
And how of the fine hair, the lovely mien,
Of the bright eyes which all my feelings sway,
Calling on your dear name by night and day,
My tongue ne'er silent in their praise has been,
And how my feet not tender are, nor tired,
Pursuing still with many a useless pace
Of your fair footsteps the elastic trace;
And whence the ink, the paper whence acquired,
Fill'd with your memories: if in this I err,
Not art's defect but Love's own fault it were.

Robert Macgregor.

SONNET LV.

I begli occhi, ond' i' fui percosso in guisa.

HE IS NEVER WEARY OF PRAISING THE EYES OF LAURA.

The bright eyes which so struck my fenceless side
That they alone which harm'd can heal the smart
Beyond or power of herbs or magic art,
Or stone which oceans from our shores divide,
The chance of other love have so denied
That one sweet thought alone contents my heart,
From following which if ne'er my tongue depart,
Pity the guided though you blame the guide.
These are the bright eyes which, in every land
But most in its own shrine, my heart, adored,
Have spread the triumphs of my conquering lord;
These are the same bright eyes which ever stand
Burning within me, e'en as vestal fires,
In singing which my fancy never tires.

Robert Macgregor.
Not all the spells of the magician's art,
Not potent herbs, nor travel o'er the main,
But those sweet eyes alone can soothe my pain,
And they which struck the blow must heal the smart;
Those eyes from meaner love have kept my heart,
Content one single image to retain,
And censure but the medium wild and vain,
If ill my words their honey'd sense impart;
These are those beauteous eyes which never fail
To prove Love's conquest, wheresoe'er they shine,
Although my breast hath oftenest felt their fire;
These are those beauteous eyes which still assail
And penetrate my soul with sparks divine,
So that of singing them I cannot tire.

Mrs Wrottesley.

SONNET LVI.

Amor con sue promesse lusingando.

LOVE CHAINS ARE STILL DEAR TO HIM.

By promise fair and artful flattery
Me Love contrived in prison old to snare,
And gave the keys to her my foe in care,
Who in self-exile dooms me still to lie.
Alas! his wiles I knew not until I
Was in their power, so sharp yet sweet to bear,
(Man scarce will credit it although I swear)
That I regain my freedom with a sigh,
And, as true suffering captives ever do,
Carry of my sore chains the greater part,
And on my brow and eyes so writ my heart
That when she witnesseth my cheek's wan hue
A sigh shall own: if right I read his face,
Between him and his tomb but small the space!

Robert Macgregor.

SONNET LVII.

Per mirar Policleto a prova fiso.

ON THE PORTRAIT OF LAURA PAINTED BY SIMON MEMMI.

Had Policletus seen her, or the rest
Who, in past time, won honour in this art,
A thousand years had but the meaner part
Shown of the beauty which o'ercame my breast.
But Simon sure, in Paradise the blest,
Whence came this noble lady of my heart,
Saw her, and took this wond'rous counterpart
Which should on earth her lovely face attest.
The work, indeed, was one, in heaven alone
To be conceived, not wrought by fellow-men,
Over whose souls the body's veil is thrown:
'Twas done of grace: and fail'd his pencil when
To earth he turn'd our cold and heat to bear,
And felt that his own eyes but mortal were.

Robert Macgregor.

Had Polycletus in proud rivalry
On her his model gazed a thousand years,
Not half the beauty to my soul appears,
In fatal conquest, e'er could he descry.
But, Simon, thou wast then in heaven's blest sky,
Ere she, my fair one, left her native spheres,
To trace a loveliness this world reveres
Was thus thy task, from heaven's reality.
Yes – thine the portrait heaven alone could wake,
This clime, nor earth, such beauty could conceive,
Where droops the spirit 'neath its earthly shrine:
The soul's reflected grace was thine to take,
Which not on earth thy painting could achieve,
Where mortal limits all the powers confine.
Miss Wollaston.

SONNET LVIII.

Quando giunse a Simon l' alto concetto.

HE DESIRES ONLY THAT MEMMI HAD BEEN ABLE TO IMPART SPEECH TO HIS PORTRAIT OF LAURA.

When, at my word, the high thought fired his mind,
Within that master-hand which placed the pen,
Had but the painter, in his fair work, then
Language and intellect to beauty join'd,
Less 'neath its care my spirit since had pined,
Which worthless held what still pleased other men;
And yet so mild she seems that my fond ken
Of peace sees promise in that aspect kind.
When further communing I hold with her
Benignantly she smiles, as if she heard
And well could answer to mine every word:
But far o'er mine thy pride and pleasure were,
Bright, warm and young, Pygmalion, to have press'd
Thine image long and oft, while mine not once has blest.

Robert Macgregor.

When Simon at my wish the proud design
Conceived, which in his hand the pencil placed,
Had he, while loveliness his picture graced,
But added speech and mind to charms divine;
What sighs he then had spared this breast of mine:
That bliss had given to higher bliss distaste:
For, when such meekness in her look was traced,
'Twould seem she soon to kindness might incline.
But, urging converse with the portray'd fair,
Methinks she deigns attention to my prayer,
Though wanting to reply the power of voice.
What praise thyself, Pygmalion, hast thou gain'd;
Forming that image, whence thou hast obtain'd
A thousand times what, once obtain'd, would me rejoice.

Dr Nott

SONNET LIX.

Se al principio risponde il fine e 'l mezzo.

IF HIS PASSION STILL INCREASE, HE MUST SOON DIE.

If, of this fourteenth year wherein I sigh,
The end and middle with its opening vie,
Nor air nor shade can give me now release,
I feel mine ardent passion so increase:
For Love, with whom my thought no medium knows,
Beneath whose yoke I never find repose,
So rules me through these eyes, on mine own ill
Too often turn'd, but half remains to kill.
Thus, day by day, I feel me sink apace,
And yet so secretly none else may trace,
Save she whose glances my fond bosom tear.
Scarcely till now this load of life I bear
Nor know how long with me will be her stay,
For death draws near, and hastens life away.

Robert Macgregor.

SESTINA IV.

Chi è fermato di menar sua vita.

HE PRAYS GOD TO GUIDE HIS FRAIL BARK TO A SAFE PORT.

Who is resolved to venture his vain life
On the deceitful wave and 'mid the rocks,
Alone, unfearing death, in little bark,
Can never be far distant from his end:
Therefore betimes he should return to port
While to the helm yet answers his true sail.

The gentle breezes to which helm and sail
I trusted, entering on this amorous life,
And hoping soon to make some better port,
Have led me since amid a thousand rocks,
And the sure causes of my mournful end
Are not alone without, but in my bark.

Long cabin'd and confined in this blind bark,
I wander'd, looking never at the sail,
Which, prematurely, bore me to my end;
Till He was pleased who brought me into life
So far to call me back from those sharp rocks,
That, distantly, at last was seen my port.

As lights at midnight seen in any port,
Sometimes from the main sea by passing bark,
Save when their ray is lost 'mid storms or rocks;
So I too from above the swollen sail
Saw the sure colours of that other life,
And could not help but sigh to reach my end.

Not that I yet am certain of that end,
For wishing with the dawn to be in port,
Is a long voyage for so short a life:
And then I fear to find me in frail bark,
Beyond my wishes full its every sail

With the strong wind which drove me on those rocks.

Escape I living from these doubtful rocks,
Or if my exile have but a fair end,
How happy shall I be to furl my sail,
And my last anchor cast in some sure port;
But, ah! I burn, and, as some blazing bark,
So hard to me to leave my wonted life.

Lord of my end and master of my life,
Before I lose my bark amid the rocks,
Direct to a good port its harass'd sail!

Robert Macgregor.

SONNET LX.

Io son sì stanco sotto 'l fascio antico.

HE CONFESSES HIS ERRORS, AND THROWS HIMSELF ON THE MERCY OF GOD.

I am so weary with the burden old
Of foregone faults, and power of custom base,
That much I fear to perish from the ways,
And fall into my enemy's grim fold.
True, a high friend, to free me, not with gold,
Came, of ineffable and utmost grace –
Then straightway vanished from before my face,
So that in vain I strive him to behold.
But his voice yet comes echoing below:
O ye that labour, the way open lies!
Come unto me lest some one shut the gate!
– What heavenly grace – what love will – or what fate –
The pinions of a dove on me bestow
That I may rest, and from the earth arise?

George Macdonald

Evil by custom, as by nature frail,
I am so wearied with the long disgrace,
That much I dread my fainting in the race
Should let th' original enemy prevail.
Once an Eternal Friend, that heard my cries,
Came to my rescue, glorious in his might,
Arm'd with all-conquering love, then took his flight,
That I in vain pursued Him with my eyes.
But his dear words, yet sounding, sweetly say,
"O ye that faint with travel, see the way!
Hopeless of other refuge, come to me."
What grace, what kindness, or what destiny
Will give me wings, as the fair-feather'd dove,
To raise me hence and seek my rest above?

Basil Kennet.

So weary am I 'neath the constant thrall
Of mine own vile heart, and the false world's taint,
That much I fear while on the way to faint,
And in the hands of my worst foe to fall.
Well came, ineffably, supremely kind,
A friend to free me from the guilty bond,
But too soon upward flew my sight beyond,
So that in vain I strive his track to find;
But still his words stamp'd on my heart remain,
All ye who labour, lo! the way in me;
Come unto me, nor let the world detain!
Oh! that to me, by grace divine, were given
Wings like a dove, then I away would flee,
And be at rest, up, up from earth to heaven!

Robert Macgregor.

SONNET LXI.

Io non fu' d' amar voi lassato unquanco.

UNLESS LAURA RELENT, HE IS RESOLVED TO ABANDON HER.

Yet was I never of your love aggrieved,
Nor never shall while that my life doth last:
But of hating myself, that date is past;
And tears continual sore have me wearied:
I will not yet in my grave be buried;
Nor on my tomb your name have fixèd fast,
As cruel cause, that did the spirit soon haste
From thc unhappy bones, by great sighs stirr'd.
Then if a heart of amorous faith and will
Content your mind withouten doing grief;
Please it you so to this to do relief:
If otherwise you seek for to fulfil
Your wrath, you err, and shall not as you ween;
And you yourself the cause thereof have been.

Sir Thomas Wyatt.

Weary I never was, nor can be e'er,
Lady, while life shall last, of loving you,
But brought, alas! myself in hate to view,
Perpetual tears have bred a blank despair:
I wish a tomb, whose marble fine and fair,
When this tired spirit and frail flesh are two,
May show your name, to which my death is due,
If e'en our names at last one stone may share;
Wherefore, if full of faith and love, a heart
Can, of worst torture short, suffice your hate,
Mercy at length may visit e'en my smart.
If otherwise your wrath itself would sate,
It is deceived: and none will credit show;
To Love and to myself my thanks for this I owe.

Robert Macgregor.

SONNET LXII.

Se bianche non son prima ambe le tempie.

THOUGH NOT SECURE AGAINST THE WILES OF LOVE, HE FEELS STRENGTH ENOUGH TO RESIST THEM.

Till silver'd o'er by age my temples grow,
Where Time by slow degrees now plants his grey,
Safe shall I never be, in danger's way
While Love still points and plies his fatal bow
I fear no more his tortures and his tricks,
That he will keep me further to ensnare
Nor opc my heart, that, from without, he there
His poisonous and ruthless shafts may fix.
No tears can now find issue from mine eyes,
But the way there so well they know to win,
That nothing now the pass to them denies.
Though the fierce ray rekindle me within,
It burns not all: her cruel and severe
Form may disturb, not break my slumbers here.

Robert Macgregor.

SONNET LXIII.

Occhi, piangete; accompagnate il core.

DIALOGUE BETWEEN THE POET AND HIS EYES.

Playne ye, myne eyes, accompanye my harte,
For, by your fault, lo, here is death at hand!
Ye brought hym first into this bitter band,
And of his harme as yett ye felt no part;
But now ye shall: Lo! here beginnes your smart.
Wett shall you be, ye shall it not withstand
With weepinge teares that shall make dymm your sight,
And mystic clowdes shall hang still in your light.
Blame but yourselves that kyndlyd have this brand,
With suche desyre to strayne that past your might;
But, since by you the hart hath caught his harme,
His flamèd heat shall sometyme make you warme.

Harrington.

P. Weep, wretched eyes, accompany the heart
Which only from your weakness death sustains.
E. Weep? evermore we weep; with keener pains
For others' error than our own we smart.
P. Love, entering first through you an easy part,
Took up his seat, where now supreme he reigns.
E. We oped to him the way, but Hope the veins
First fired of him now stricken by death's dart.
P. The lots, as seems to you, scarce equal fall
'Tween heart and eyes, for you, at first sight, were
Enamour'd of your common ill and shame.
E. This is the thought which grieves us most of all;
For perfect judgments are on earth so rare
That one man's fault is oft another's blame.

Robert Macgregor.

SONNET LXIV.

Io amai sempre, ed amo forte ancora.

HE LOVES, AND WILL ALWAYS LOVE, THE SPOT AND THE HOUR IN WHICH HE FIRST BECAME ENAMOURED OF LAURA.

I always loved, I love sincerely yet,
And to love more from day to day shall learn,
The charming spot where oft in grief I turn
When Love's severities my bosom fret:
My mind to love the time and hour is set
Which taught it each low care aside to spurn;
She too, of loveliest face, for whom I burn
Bids me her fair life love and sin forget.
Who ever thought to see in friendship join'd,
On all sides with my suffering heart to cope,
The gentle enemies I love so well?
Love now is paramount my heart to bind,
And, save that with desire increases hope,
Dead should I lie alive where I would dwell.

Robert Macgregor.

SONNET LXV.

Io avrò sempre in odio la fenestra.

BETTER IS IT TO DIE HAPPY THAN TO LIVE IN PAIN.

Always in hate the window shall I bear,
Whence Love has shot on me his shafts at will,
Because not one of them sufficed to kill:
For death is good when life is bright and fair,
But in this earthly jail its term to outwear
Is cause to me, alas! of infinite ill;
And mine is worse because immortal still,
Since from the heart the spirit may not tear.
Wretched! ere this who surely ought'st to know
By long experience, from his onward course
None can stay Time by flattery or by force.
Oft and again have I address'd it so:
Mourner, away! he parteth not too soon
Who leaves behind him far his life's calm June.

Robert Macgregor.

SONNET LXVI.

Sì tosto come avvien che l' arco scocchi.

HE CALLS THE EYES OF LAURA FOES, BECAUSE THEY KEEP HIM IN LIFE ONLY TO TORMENT HIM.

Instantly a good archer draws his bow
Small skill it needs, e'en from afar, to see
Which shaft, less fortunate, despised may be,
Which to its destined sign will certain go:
Lady, e'en thus of your bright eyes the blow,
You surely felt pass straight and deep in me,
Searching my life, whence – such is fate's decree –
Eternal tears my stricken heart overflow;
And well I know e'en then your pity said:
Fond wretch! to misery whom passion leads,
Be this the point at once to strike him dead.
But seeing now how sorrow sorrow breeds,
All that my cruel foes against me plot,
For my worse pain, and for my death is not.

Robert Macgregor.

SONNET LXVII.

Poi che mia speme è lunga a venir troppo.

HE COUNSELS LOVERS TO FLEE, RATHER THAN BE CONSUMED BY THE FLAMES OF LOVE.

Since my hope's fruit yet faileth to arrive,
And short the space vouchsafed me to survive,
Betimes of this aware I fain would be,
Swifter than light or wind from Love to flee:
And I do flee him, weak albeit and lame
O' my left side, where passion racked my frame.
Though now secure yet bear I on my face
Of the amorous encounter signal trace.
Wherefore I counsel each this way who comes,
Turn hence your footsteps, and, if Love consumes,
Think not in present pain his worst is done;
For, though I live, of thousand scapes not one!
'Gainst Love my enemy was strong indeed –
Lo! from his wounds e'en she is doom'd to bleed.

Robert Macgregor.

SONNET LXVIII.

Fuggendo la prigione ov' Amor m' ebbe.

HE LONGS TO RETURN TO THE CAPTIVITY OF LOVE.

Fleeing the prison which had long detain'd,
Where Love dealt with me as to him seem'd well,
Ladies, the time were long indeed to tell,
How much my heart its new-found freedom pain'd.
I felt within I could not, so bereaved,
Live e'en a day: and, midway, on my eyes
That traitor rose in so complete disguise,
A wiser than myself had been deceived:
Whence oft I've said, deep sighing for the past,
Alas! the yoke and chains of old to me
Were sweeter far than thus released to be.
Me wretched! but to learn mine ill at last;
With what sore trial must I now forget
Errors that round my path myself have set.

Robert Macgregor.

SONNET LXIX.

Erano i capei d' oro all' aura sparsi.

HE PAINTS THE BEAUTIES OF LAURA, PROTESTING HIS UNALTERABLE LOVE.

Loose to the breeze her golden tresses flow'd
Wildly in thousand mazy ringlets blown,
And from her eyes unconquer'd glances shone,
Those glances now so sparingly bestow'd.
And true or false, meseem'd some signs she show'd
As o'er her cheek soft pity's hue was thrown;
I, whose whole breast with love's soft food was sown,
What wonder if at once my bosom glow'd?
Graceful she moved, with more than mortal mien,
In form an angel: and her accents won
Upon the ear with more than human sound.
A spirit heavenly pure, a living sun,
Was what I saw; and if no more 'twere seen,
T' unbend the bow will never heal the wound.

Anonymous, Ox., 1795.

Her golden tresses on the wind she threw,
Which twisted them in many a beauteous braid;
In her fine eyes the burning glances play'd,
With lovely light, which now they seldom show:
Ah! then it seem'd her face wore pity's hue,
Yet haply fancy my fond sense betray'd;
Nor strange that I, in whose warm heart was laid
Love's fuel, suddenly enkindled grew!
Not like a mortal's did her step appear,
Angelic was her form; her voice, methought,
Pour'd more than human accents on the ear.
A living sun was what my vision caught,
A spirit pure; and though not such still found,
Unbending of the bow ne'er heals the wound.

Dr Nott

Her golden tresses to the gale were streaming,
That in a thousand knots did them entwine,
And the sweet rays which now so rarely shine
From her enchanting eyes, were brightly beaming,
And – was it fancy? – o'er that dear face gleaming
Methought I saw Compassion's tint divine;
What marvel that this ardent heart of mine
Blazed swiftly forth, impatient of Love's dreaming?
There was nought mortal in her stately tread
But grace angelic, and her speech awoke
Than human voices a far loftier sound,
A spirit of heaven, – a living sun she broke
Upon my sight; – what if these charms be fled? –
The slackening of the bow heals not the wound.

Mrs Wrottesley.

SONNET LXX.

La bella donna che cotanto amavi.

TO HIS BROTHER GERARDO, ON THE DEATH OF A LADY TO WHOM HE WAS ATTACHED.

The beauteous lady thou didst love so well
Too soon hath from our regions wing'd her flight,
To find, I ween, a home 'mid realms of light;
So much in virtue did she here excel
Thy heart's twin key of joy and woe can dwell
No more with her – then re-assume thy might,
Pursue her by the path most swift and right,
Nor let aught earthly stay thee by its spell.
Thus from thy heaviest burthen being freed,
Each other thou canst easier dispel,
And an unfreighted pilgrim seek thy sky;
Too well, thou seest, how much the soul hath need,
(Ere yet it tempt the shadowy vale) to quell
Each earthly hope, since all that lives must die.

Miss Wollaston.

The lovely lady who was long so dear
To thee, now suddenly is from us gone,
And, for this hope is sure, to heaven is flown,
So mild and angel-like her life was here!
Now from her thraldom since thy heart is clear,
Whose either key she, living, held alone,
Follow where she the safe short way has shown,
Nor let aught earthly longer interfere.
Thus disencumber'd from the heavier weight,
The lesser may aside be easier laid,
And the freed pilgrim win the crystal gate;
So teaching us, since all things that are made
Hasten to death, how light must be his soul
Who treads the perilous pass, unscathed and whole!

Robert Macgregor.

SONNET LXXI.

Piangete, donne, e con voi pianga Amore.

ON THE DEATH OF CINO DA PISTOIA.

Weep, beauteous damsels, and let Cupid weep,
Of every region weep, ye lover train;
He, who so skilfully attuned his strain
To your fond cause, is sunk in death's cold sleep!
Such limits let not my affliction keep,
As may the solace of soft tears restrain;
And, to relieve my bosom of its pain,
Be all my sighs tumultuous, utter'd deep!
Let song itself, and votaries of verse,
Breathe mournful accents o'er our Cino's bier,
Who late is gone to number with the blest!
Oh! weep, Pistoia, weep your sons perverse;
Its choicest habitant has fled our sphere,
And heaven may glory in its welcome guest!

Dr Nott

Ye damsels, pour your tears! weep with you. Love!
Weep, all ye lovers, through the peopled sphere!
Since he is dead who, while he linger'd here,
With all his might to do you honour strove.
For me, this tyrant grief my prayers shall move
Not to contest the comfort of a tear,
Nor check those sighs, that to my heart are dear,
Since ease from them alone it hopes to prove.
Ye verses, weep! – ye rhymes, your woes renew!
For Cino, master of the love-fraught lay,
E'en now is from our fond embraces torn!
Pistoia, weep, and all your thankless crew!
Your sweetest inmate now is reft away –
But, heaven, rejoice, and hail your son new-born!

Lord Charlemont.

SONNET LXXII.

Più volte Amor m' avea già detto: scrivi.

HE WRITES WHAT LOVE BIDS HIM.

White – to my heart Love oftentimes had said –
Write what thou seest in letters large of gold,
That livid are my votaries to behold,
And in a moment made alive and dead.
Once in thy heart my sovran influence spread
A public precedent to lovers told;
Though other duties drew thee from my fold,
I soon reclaim'd thee as thy footsteps fled.
And if the bright eyes which I show'd thee first,
If the fair face where most I loved to stay,
Thy young heart's icy hardness when I burst,
Restore to me the bow which all obey,
Then may thy cheek, which now so smooth appears,
Be channell'd with my daily drink of tears.

Robert Macgregor.

SONNET LXXIII.

Quando giugne per gli occhi al cor profondo.

HE DESCRIBES THE STATE OF TWO LOVERS, AND RETURNS IN THOUGHT TO HIS OWN SUFFERINGS.

When reaches through the eyes the conscious heart
Its imaged fate, all other thoughts depart;
The powers which from the soul their functions take
A dead weight on the frame its limbs then make.
From the first miracle a second springs,
At times the banish'd faculty that brings,
So fleeing from itself, to some new seat,
Which feeds revenge and makes e'en exile sweet.
Thus in both faces the pale tints were rife,
Because the strength which gave the glow of life
On neither side was where it wont to dwell –
I on that day these things remember'd well,
Of that fond couple when each varying mien
Told me in like estate what long myself had been.

Robert Macgregor.

SONNET LXXIV.

Così potess' io ben chiuder in versi.

HE COMPLAINS THAT TO HIM ALONE IS FAITH HURTFUL.

Could I, in melting verse, my thoughts but throw,
As in my heart their living load I bear,
No soul so cruel in the world was e'er
That would not at the tale with pity glow.
But ye, blest eyes, which dealt me the sore blow,
'Gainst which nor helm nor shield avail'd to spare
Within, without, behold me poor and bare,
Though never in laments is breathed my woe.
But since on me your bright glance ever shines,
E'en as a sunbeam through transparent glass,
Suffice then the desire without the lines.
Faith Peter bless'd and Mary, but, alas!
It proves an enemy to me alone,
Whose spirit save by you to none is known.

Robert Macgregor.

SONNET LXXV.

Io son dell' aspectar omai sì vinto.

HAVING ONCE SURRENDERED HIMSELF, HE IS COMPELLED EVER TO ENDURE THE PANGS OF LOVE.

Weary with expectation's endless round,
And overcome in this long war of sighs,
I hold desires in hate and hopes despise,
And every tie wherewith my breast is bound;
But the bright face which in my heart profound
Is stamp'd, and seen where'er I turn mine eyes,
Compels me where, against my will, arise
The same sharp pains that first my ruin crown'd.
Then was my error when the old way quite
Of liberty was bann'd and barr'd to me:
He follows ill who pleases but his sight:
To its own harm my soul ran wild and free,
Now doom'd at others' will to wait and wend;
Because that once it ventured to offend.

Robert Macgregor.

SONNET LXXVI.

Ahi bella libertà, come tu m' hai.

HE DEPLORES HIS LOST LIBERTY AND THE UNHAPPINESS OF HIS PRESENT STATE.

Alas! fair Liberty, thus left by thee,
Well hast thou taught my discontented heart
To mourn the peace it felt, ere yet Love's dart
Dealt me the wound which heal'd can never be;
Mine eyes so charm'd with their own weakness grow
That my dull mind of reason spurns the chain;
All worldly occupation they disdain,
Ah! that I should myself have train'd them so.
Naught, save of her who is my death, mine ear
Consents to learn; and from my tongue there flows
No accent save the name to me so dear;
Love to no other chase my spirit spurs,
No other path my feet pursue; nor knows
My hand to write in other praise but hers.

Robert Macgregor.

Alas, sweet Liberty! in speeding hence,
Too well didst thou reveal unto my heart
Its careless joy, ere Love ensheathed his dart,
Of whose dread wound I ne'er can lose the sense
My eyes, enamour'd of their grief intense,
Did in that hour from Reason's bridle start,
Thus used to woe, they have no wish to part;
Each other mortal work is an offence.
No other theme will now my soul content
Than she who plants my death, with whose blest name
I make the air resound in echoes sweet:
Love spurs me to her as his only bent,
My hand can trace nought other but her fame,
No other spot attracts my willing feet.

Miss Wollaston.

SONNET LXXVII.

Orso, al vostro destrier si può ben porre.

HE SYMPATHISES WITH HIS FRIEND ORSO AT HIS INABILITY TO ATTEND A TOURNAMENT.

Orso, a curb upon thy gallant horse
Well may we place to turn him from his course,
But who thy heart may bind against its will
Which honour courts and shuns dishonour still?
Sigh not! for nought its praise away can take,
Though Fate this journey hinder you to make.
For, as already voiced by general fame,
Now is it there, and none before it came.
Amid the camp, upon the day design'd,
Enough itself beneath those arms to find
Which youth, love, valour, and near blood concern,
Crying aloud: With noble fire I burn,
As my good lord unwillingly at home,
Who pines and languishes in vain to come.

Robert Macgregor.

SONNET LXXVIII.

Poi che voi ed io più volte abbiam provato.

TO A FRIEND, COUNSELLING HIM TO ABANDON EARTHLY PLEASURES.

Still has it been our bitter lot to prove
How hope, or e'er it reach fruition, flies!
Up then to that high good, which never dies,
Lift we the heart – to heaven's pure bliss above.
On earth, as in a tempting mead, we rove,
Where coil'd 'mid flowers the traitor serpent lies;
And, if some casual glimpse delight our eyes,
'Tis but to grieve the soul enthrall'd by Love.
Oh! then, as thou wouldst wish ere life's last day
To taste the sweets of calm unbroken rest,
Tread firm the narrow, shun the beaten way –
Ah! to thy friend too well may be address'd:
"Thou show'st a path, thyself most apt to stray,
Which late thy truant feet, fond youth, have never press'd."

Francis Wrangham.

Friend, as we both in confidence complain
To see our ill-placed hopes return in vain,
Let that chief good which must for ever please
Exalt our thought and fix our happiness.
This world as some gay flowery field is spread,
Which hides a serpent in its painted bed,
And most it wounds when most it charms our eyes,
At once the tempter and the paradise.
And would you, then, sweet peace of mind restore,
And in fair calm expect your parting hour,
Leave the mad train, and court the happy few.
Well may it be replied, "O friend, you show
Others the path, from which so often you
Have stray'd, and now stray farther than before."

Basil Kennet.

SONNET LXXIX.

Quella fenestra, ove l' un sol si vede.

RECOLLECTIONS OF LOVE.

That window where my sun is often seen
Refulgent, and the world's at morning's hours;
And that, where Boreas blows, when winter lowers,
And the short days reveal a clouded scene;
That bench of stone where, with a pensive mien,
My Laura sits, forgetting beauty's powers;
Haunts where her shadow strikes the walls or flowers,
And her feet press the paths or herbage green:
The place where Love assail'd me with success;
And spring, the fatal time that, first observed,
Revives the keen remembrance every year;
With looks and words, that o'er me have preserved
A power no length of time can render less,
Call to my eyes the sadly-soothing tear.

John Penn.

That window where my sun is ever seen,
Dazzling and bright, and Nature's at the none;
And that where still, when Boreas rude has blown
In the short days, the air thrills cold and keen:
The stone where, at high noon, her seat has been,
Pensive and parleying with herself alone:
Haunts where her bright form has its shadow thrown,
Or trod her fairy foot the carpet green:
The cruel spot where first Love spoil'd my rest,
And the new season which, from year to year,
Opes, on this day, the old wound in my breast:
The seraph face, the sweet words, chaste and dear,
Which in my suffering heart are deep impress'd,
All melt my fond eyes to the frequent tear.

Robert Macgregor.

SONNET LXXX.

Lasso! ben so che dolorose prede.

THOUGH FOR FOURTEEN YEARS HE HAS STRUGGLED UNSUCCESSFULLY, HE STILL HOPES TO CONQUER HIS PASSION.

Alas! well know I what sad havoc makes
Death of our kind, how Fate no mortal spares!
How soon the world whom once it loved forsakes,
How short the faith it to the friendless bears!
Much languishment, I see, small mercy wakes;
For the last day though now my heart prepares,
Love not a whit my cruel prison breaks,
And still my cheek grief's wonted tribute wears.
I mark the days, the moments, and the hours
Bear the full years along, nor find deceit,
Bow'd 'neath a greater force than magic spell.
For fourteen years have fought with varying powers
Desire and Reason: and the best shall beat;
If mortal spirits here can good foretell.

Robert Macgregor.

Alas! I know death makes us all his prey,
Nor aught of mercy shows to destined man;
How swift the world completes its circling span,
And faithless Time soon speeds him on his way.
My heart repeats the blast of earth's last day,
Yet for its grief no recompense can scan,
Love holds me still beneath its cruel ban,
And still my eyes their usual tribute pay.
My watchful senses mark how on their wing
The circling years transport their fleeter kin,
And still I bow enslaved as by a spell:
For fourteen years did reason proudly fling
Defiance at my tameless will, to win
A triumph blest, if Man can good foretell.

Miss Wollaston.

SONNET LXXXI.

Cesare, poi che 'l traditor d' Egitto.

THE COUNTENANCE DOES NOT ALWAYS TRULY INDICATE THE HEART.

When Egypt's traitor Pompey's honour'd head
To Cæsar sent; then, records so relate,
To shroud a gladness manifestly great,
Some feigned tears the specious monarch shed:
And, when misfortune her dark mantle spread
O'er Hannibal, and his afflicted state,
He laugh'd 'midst those who wept their adverse fate,
That rank despite to wreak defeat had bred.
Thus doth the mind oft variously conceal
Its several passions by a different veil;
Now with a countenance that's sad, now gay:
So mirth and song if sometimes I employ,
'Tis but to hide those sorrows that annoy,
'Tis but to chase my amorous cares away.

Dr Nott

Cæsar, when Egypt's cringing traitor brought
The gory gift of Pompey's honour'd head,
Check'd the full gladness of his instant thought,
And specious tears of well-feign'd pity shed:
And Hannibal, when adverse Fortune wrought
On his afflicted empire evils dread,
'Mid shamed and sorrowing friends, by laughter, sought
To ease the anger at his heart that fed.
Thus, as the mind its every feeling hides,
Beneath an aspect contrary, the mien,
Bright'ning with hope or charged with gloom, is seen.
Thus ever if I sing, or smile betides,
The outward joy serves only to conceal
The inner ail and anguish that I feel.

Robert Macgregor.

SONNET LXXXII.

Vinse Annibal, e non seppe usar poi.

TO STEFANO COLONNA, COUNSELLING HIM TO FOLLOW UP HIS VICTORY OVER THE ORSINI.

Hannibal conquer'd oft, but never knew
The fruits and gain of victory to get,
Wherefore, dear lord, be wise, take care that yet
A like misfortune happen not to you.
Still in their lair the cubs and she-bear,[3] who
Rough pasturage and sour in May have met,
With mad rage gnash their teeth and talons whet,
And vengeance of past loss on us pursue:
While this new grief disheartens and appalls,
Replace not in its sheath your honour'd sword,
But, boldly following where your fortune calls,
E'en to its goal be glory's path explored,
Which fame and honour to the world may give
That e'en for centuries after death will live.

Robert Macgregor.

3 *Orsa.* A play on the word *Orsim.*

SONNET LXXXIII.

L' aspettata virtù che 'n voi fioriva.

TO PAUDOLFO MALATESTA, LORD OF RIMINI.

Sweet virtue's blossom had its promise shed
Within thy breast (when Love became thy foe);
Fair as the flower, now its fruit doth glow,
And not by visions hath my hope been fed.
To hail thee thus, I by my heart am led,
That by my pen thy name renown should know;
No marble can the lasting fame bestow
Like that by poets' characters is spread.
Dost think Marcellus' or proud Cæsar's name,
Or Africanus, Paulus – still resound,
That sculptors proud have effigied their deed?
No, Pandolph, frail the statuary's fame,
For immortality alone is found
Within the records of a poet's meed.

Miss Wollaston.

The flower, in youth which virtue's promise bore,
When Love in your pure heart first sought to dwell,
Now beareth fruit that flower which matches well,
And my long hopes are richly come ashore,
Prompting my spirit some glad verse to pour
Where to due honour your high name may swell,
For what can finest marble truly tell
Of living mortal than the form he wore?
Think you great Cæsar's or Marcellus' name,
That Paulus, Africanus to our days,
By anvil or by hammer ever came?
No! frail the sculptor's power for lasting praise:
Our study, my Pandolfo, only can
Give immortality of fame to man.

Robert Macgregor.

CANZONE XI.[4]

Mai non vo' più cantar, com' io soleva.

ENIGMAS.

Never more shall I sing, as I have sung:
For still she heeded not; and I was scorn'd:
So e'en in loveliest spots is trouble found.
Unceasingly to sigh is no relief.
Already on the Alp snow gathers round:
Already day is near; and I awake.
An affable and modest air is sweet;
And in a lovely lady that she be
Noble and dignified, not proud and cold,
Well pleases it to find.
Love o'er his empire rules without a sword.
He who has miss'd his way let him turn back:
Who has no home the heath must be his bed:
Who lost or has not gold,
Will sate his thirst at the clear crystal spring.

I trusted in Saint Peter, not so now;
Let him who can my meaning understand.
A harsh rule is a heavy weight to bear.
I melt but where I must, and stand alone.
I think of him who falling died in Po;
Already thence the thrush has pass'd the brook
Come, see if I say sooth! No more for me.
A rock amid the waters is no joke,
Nor birdlime on the twig. Enough my grief
When a superfluous pride
In a fair lady many virtues hides.
There is who answereth without a call;
There is who, though entreated, fails and flies:
There is who melts 'neath ice:

4 This, the only known version, is included simply from a wish to represent the original completely, the poem being almost untranslateable into English verse. Italian critics are much divided as to its object. One of the most eminent (Bembo) considers it to be nothing more than an unconnected string of proverbs.

There is who day and night desires his death.

Love who loves you, is an old proverb now.
Well know I what I say. But let it pass;
'Tis meet, at their own cost, that men should learn.
A modest lady wearies her best friend.
Good figs are little known. To me it seems
Wise to eschew things hazardous and high;
In any country one may be at ease.
Infinite hope below kills hope above;
And I at times e'en thus have been the talk.
My brief life that remains
There is who'll spurn not if to Him devote.
I place my trust in Him who rules the world,
And who his followers shelters in the wood,
That with his pitying crook
Me will He guide with his own flock to feed.

Haply not every one who reads discerns;
Some set the snare at times who take no spoil;
Who strains too much may break the bow in twain.
Let not the law be lame when suitors watch.
To be at ease we many a mile descend.
To-day's great marvel is to-morrow's scorn.
A veil'd and virgin loveliness is best.
Blessed the key which pass'd within my heart,
And, quickening my dull spirit, set it free
From its old heavy chain,
And from my bosom banish'd many a sigh.
Where most I suffer'd once she suffers now;
Her equal sorrows mitigate my grief;
Thanks, then, to Love that I
Feel it no more, though he is still the same!

In silence words that wary are and wise;
The voice which drives from me all other care;
And the dark prison which that fair light hides:
As midnight on our hills the violets;
And the wild beasts within the walls who dwell;
The kind demeanour and the dear reserve;
And from two founts one stream which flow'd in peace

Where I desire, collected where I would.
Love and sore jealousy have seized my heart,
And the fair face whose guides
Conduct me by a plainer, shorter way
To my one hope, where all my torments end.
O treasured bliss, and all from thee which flows
Of peace, of war, or truce,
Never abandon me while life is left!

At my past loss I weep by turns and smile,
Because my faith is fix'd in what I hear.
The present I enjoy and better wait;
Silent, I count the years, yet crave their end,
And in a lovely bough I nestle so
That e'en her stern repulse I thank and praise,
Which has at length o'ercome my firm desire,
And inly shown me, I had been the talk,
And pointed at by hand: all this it quench'd.
So much am I urged on,
Needs must I own, thou wert not bold enough.
Who pierced me in my side she heals the wound,
For whom in heart more than in ink I write;
Who quickens me or kills,
And in one instant freezes me or fires.

Anonymous

MADRIGALE III.

Nova angeletta sovra l' ale accorta.

HE ALLEGORICALLY DESCRIBES THE ORIGIN OF HIS PASSION.

From heaven an angel upon radiant wings,
New lighted on that shore so fresh and fair,
To which, so doom'd, my faithful footstep clings:
Alone and friendless, when she found me there,
Of gold and silk a finely-woven net,
Where lay my path, 'mid seeming flowers she set:
Thus was I caught, and, for such sweet light shone
From out her eyes, I soon forgot to moan.

Robert Macgregor.

SONNET LXXXIV.

Non veggio ove scampar mi possa omai.

AFTER FIFTEEN YEARS HER EYES ARE MORE POWERFUL THAN AT FIRST.

No hope of respite, of escape no way,
Her bright eyes wage such constant havoc here;
Alas! excess of tyranny, I fear,
My doting heart, which ne'er has truce, will slay:
Fain would I flee, but ah! their amorous ray,
Which day and night on memory rises clear,
Shines with such power, in this the fifteenth year,
They dazzle more than in love's early day.
So wide and far their images are spread
That wheresoe'er I turn I alway see
Her, or some sister-light on hers that fed.
Springs such a wood from one fair laurel tree,
That my old foe, with admirable skill,
Amid its boughs misleads me at his will.

Robert Macgregor.

SONNET LXXXV.

Avventuroso più d' altro terreno.

HE APOSTROPHIZES THE SPOT WHERE LAURA FIRST SALUTED HIM.

Ah, happiest spot of earth! in this sweet place
Love first beheld my condescending fair
Retard her steps, to smile with courteous grace
On me, and smiling glad the ambient air.
The deep-cut image, wrought with skilful care,
Time shall from hardest adamant efface,
Ere from my mind that smile it shall erase,
Dear to my soul! which memory planted there.
Oft as I view thee, heart-enchanting soil!
With amorous awe I'll seek – delightful toil!
Where yet some traces of her footsteps lie.
And if fond Love still warms her generous breast,
Whene'er you see her, gentle friend! request
The tender tribute of a tear – a sigh.

Anonymous 1777.

Most fortunate and fair of spots terrene!
Where Love I saw her forward footstep stay,
And turn on me her bright eyes' heavenly ray,
Which round them make the atmosphere serene.
A solid form of adamant, I ween,
Would sooner shrink in lapse of time away,
Than from my mind that sweet salute decay,
Dear to my heart, in memory ever green.
And oft as I return to view this spot,
In its fair scenes I'll fondly stoop to seek
Where yet the traces of her light foot lie.
But if in valorous heart Love sleepeth not,
Whene'er you meet her, friend, for me bespeak
Some passing tears, perchance one pitying sigh.

Robert Macgregor.

SONNET LXXXVI.

Lasso! quante fiate Amor m' assale.

WHEN LOVE DISTURBS HIM, HE CALMS HIMSELF BY THINKING OF THE EYES AND WORDS OF LAURA.

Alas! how ceaselessly is urged Love's claim,
By day, by night, a thousand times I turn
Where best I may behold the dear lights burn
Which have immortalized my bosom's flame.
Thus grow I calm, and to such state am brought,
At noon, at break of day, at vesper-bell,
I find them in my mind so tranquil dwell,
I neither think nor care beside for aught.
The balmy air, which, from her angel mien,
Moves ever with her winning words and wise,
Makes wheresoe'er she breathes a sweet serene
As 'twere a gentle spirit from the skies,
Still in these scenes some comfort brings to me,
Nor elsewhere breathes my harass'd heart so free.

Robert Macgregor.

SONNET LXXXVII.

Perseguendomi Amor al luogo usato.

HE IS BEWILDERED AT THE UNEXPECTED ARRIVAL OF LAURA.

As Love his arts in haunts familiar tried,
Watchful as one expecting war is found,
Who all foresees and guards the passes round,
I in the armour of old thoughts relied:
Turning, I saw a shadow at my side
Cast by the sun, whose outline on the ground
I knew for hers, who – be my judgment sound –
Deserves in bliss immortal to abide.
I whisper'd to my heart, Nay, wherefore fear?
But scarcely did the thought arise within
Than the bright rays in which I burn were here.
As thunders with the lightning-flash begin,
So was I struck at once both blind and mute,
By her dear dazzling eyes and sweet salute.

Robert Macgregor.

SONNET LXXXVIII.

La donna che 'l mio cor nel viso porta.

HER KIND AND GENTLE SALUTATION THRILLS HIS HEART WITH PLEASURE.

She, in her face who doth my gone heart wear,
As lone I sate 'mid love-thoughts dear and true,
Appear'd before me: to show honour due,
I rose, with pallid brow and reverent air.
Soon as of such my state she was aware,
She turn'd on me with look so soft and new
As, in Jove's greatest fury, might subdue
His rage, and from his hand the thunders tear.
I started: on her further way she pass'd
Graceful, and speaking words I could not brook,
Nor of her lustrous eyes the loving look.
When on that dear salute my thoughts are cast,
So rich and varied do my pleasures flow,
No pain I feel, nor evil fear below.

Robert Macgregor.

SONNET LXXXIX.

Sennuccio, i' vo' che sappi in qual maniera.

HE RELATES TO HIS FRIEND SENNUCCIO HIS UNHAPPINESS, AND THE VARIED MOOD OF LAURA.

To thee, Sennuccio, fain would I declare,
To sadden life, what wrongs, what woes I find:
Still glow my wonted flames; and, though resign'd
To Laura's fickle will, no change I bear.
All humble now, then haughty is my fair;
Now meek, then proud; now pitying, then unkind:
Softness and tenderness now sway her mind;
Then do her looks disdain and anger wear.
Here would she sweetly sing, there sit awhile,
Here bend her step, and there her step retard;
Here her bright eyes my easy heart ensnared;
There would she speak fond words, here lovely smile;
There frown contempt; – such wayward cares I prove
By night, by day; so wills our tyrant Love!

Anonymous 1777.

Alas, Sennuccio! would thy mind could frame
What now I suffer! what my life's drear reign;
Consumed beneath my heart's continued pain,
At will she guides me – yet am I the same.
Now humble – then doth pride her soul inflame;
Now harsh – then gentle; cruel – kind again;
Now all reserve – then borne on frolic's vein;
Disdain alternates with a milder claim.
Here once she sat, and there so sweetly sang;
Here turn'd to look on me, and lingering stood;
There first her beauteous eyes my spirit stole:
And here she smiled, and there her accents rang,
Her speaking face here told another mood.
Thus Love, our sovereign, holds me in control.

Miss Wollaston.

SONNET XC.

Qui dove mezzo son, Sennuccio mio.

THE MERE SIGHT OF VAUCLUSE MAKES HIM FORGET ALL THE PERILS OF HIS JOURNEY.

Friend, on this spot, I life but half endure
(Would I were wholly here and you content),
Where from the storm and wind my course I bent,
Which suddenly had left the skies obscure.
Fain would I tell – for here I feel me sure –
Why lightnings now no fear to me present;
And why unmitigated, much less spent,
E'en as before my fierce desires allure.
Soon as I reach'd these realms of love, and saw
Where, sweet and pure, to life my Laura came,
Who calms the air, at rest the thunder lays;
Love in my soul, where she alone gives law,
Quench'd the cold fear and kindled the fast flame;
What were it then on her bright eyes to gaze!

Robert Macgregor.

SONNET XCI.

Dell' empia Babilonia, ond' è fuggita.

LEAVING ROME, HE DESIRES ONLY PEACE WITH LAURA AND PROSPERITY TO COLONNA.

Yes, out of impious Babylon I'm flown,
Whence flown all shame, whence banish'd is all good,
That nurse of error, and of guilt th' abode,
To lengthen out a life which else were gone:
There as Love prompts, while wandering alone,
I now a garland weave, and now an ode;
With him I commune, and in pensive mood
Hope better times; this only checks my moan.
Nor for the throng, nor fortune do I care,
Nor for myself, nor sublunary things,
No ardour outwardly, or inly springs:
I ask two persons only: let my fair
For me a kind and tender heart maintain;
And be my friend secure in his high post again.

Dr Nott

From impious Babylon, where all shame is dead,
And every good is banish'd to far climes,
Nurse of rank errors, centre of worst crimes,
Haply to lengthen life, I too am fled:
Alone, at last alone, and here, as led
At Love's sweet will, I posies weave or rhymes,
Self-parleying, and still on better times
Wrapt in fond thoughts whence only hope is fed.
Cares for the world or fortune I have none,
Nor much for self, nor any common theme:
Nor feel I in me, nor without, great heat.
Two friends alone I ask, and that the one
More merciful and meek to me may seem,
The other well as erst, and firm of feet.

Robert Macgregor.

SONNET XCII.

In mezzo di duo amanti onesta altera.

LAURA TURNING TO SALUTE HIM, THE SUN, THROUGH JEALOUSY, WITHDREW BEHIND A CLOUD.

'Tween two fond lovers I a lady spied,
Virtuous but haughty, and with her that lord,
By gods above and men below adored –
The sun on this, myself upon that side –
Soon as she found herself the sphere denied
Of her bright friend, on my fond eyes she pour'd
A flood of life and joy, which hope restored
Less cold to me will be her future pride.
Suddenly changed itself to cordial mirth
The jealous fear to which at his first sight
So high a rival in my heart gave birth;
As suddenly his sad and rueful plight
From further scrutiny a small cloud veil'd,
So much it ruffled him that then he fail'd.

Robert Macgregor.

SONNET XCIII.

Pien di quella ineffabile dolcezza.

WHEREVER HE IS, HE SEES ONLY LAURA.

O'erflowing with the sweets ineffable,
Which from that lovely face my fond eyes drew,
What time they seal'd, for very rapture, grew.
On meaner beauty never more to dwell,
Whom most I love I left: my mind so well
Its part, to muse on her, is train'd to do,
None else it sees; what is not hers to view,
As of old wont, with loathing I repel.
In a low valley shut from all around,
Sole consolation of my heart-deep sighs,
Pensive and slow, with Love I walk alone:
Not ladies here, but rocks and founts are found,
And of that day blest images arise,
Which my thought shapes where'er I turn mine eyes.

Robert Macgregor.

SONNET XCIV.

Se 'l sasso ond' è più chiusa questa valle.

COULD HE BUT SEE THE HOUSE OF LAURA, HIS SIGHS MIGHT REACH HER MORE QUICKLY.

If, which our valley bars, this wall of stone,
From which its present name we closely trace,
Were by disdainful nature rased, and thrown
Its back to Babel and to Rome its face;
Then had my sighs a better pathway known
To where their hope is yet in life and grace:
They now go singly, yet my voice all own;
And, where I send, not one but finds its place.
There too, as I perceive, such welcome sweet
They ever find, that none returns again,
But still delightedly with her remain.
My grief is from the eyes, each morn to meet –
Not the fair scenes my soul so long'd to see –
Toil for my weary limbs and tears for me.

Robert Macgregor.

SONNET XCV.

Rimansi addietro il sestodecim' anno.

THOUGH HE IS UNHAPPY, HIS LOVE REMAINS EVER UNCHANGED.

My sixteenth year of sighs its course has run,
I stand alone, already on the brow
Where Age descends: and yet it seems as now
My time of trial only were begun.
'Tis sweet to love, and good to be undone;
Though life be hard, more days may Heaven allow
Misfortune to outlive: else Death may bow
The bright head low my loving praise that won.
Here am I now who fain would be elsewhere;
More would I wish and yet no more I would;
I could no more and yet did all I could:
And new tears born of old desires declare
That still I am as I was wont to be,
And that a thousand changes change not me.

Robert Macgregor.

CANZONE XII.

Una donna più bella assai che 'l sole.

GLORY AND VIRTUE.

A lady, lovelier, brighter than the sun,
Like him superior o'er all time and space,
Of rare resistless grace,
Me to her train in early life had won:
She, from that hour, in act, and word and thought,
– For still the world thus covets what is rare –
In many ways though brought
Before my search, was still the same coy fair:
For her alone my plans, from what they were,
Grew changed, since nearer subject to her eyes;
Her love alone could spur
My young ambition to each hard emprize:
So, if in long-wish'd port I e'er arrive,
I hope, for aye through her,
When others deem me dead, in honour to survive.

Full of first hope, burning with youthful love,
She, at her will, as plainly now appears,
Has led me many years,
But for one end, my nature best to prove:
Oft showing me her shadow, veil, and dress,
But never her sweet face, till I, who right
Knew not her power to bless,
All my green youth for these, contented quite,
So spent, that still the memory is delight:
Since onward yet some glimpse of her is seen,
I now may own, of late,
Such as till then she ne'er for me had been,
She shows herself, shooting through all my heart
An icy cold so great
That save in her dear arms it ne'er can thence depart.

Not that in this cold fear I all did shrink,

For still my heart was to such boldness strung
That to her feet I clung,
As if more rapture from her eyes to drink:
And she – for now the veil was ta'en away
Which barr'd my sight – thus spoke me, "Friend, you see
How fair I am, and may
Ask, for your years, whatever fittest be."
"Lady," I said, "so long my love on thee
Has fix'd, that now I feel myself on fire,
What, in this state, to shun, and what desire."
She, thereon, with a voice so wond'rous sweet
And earnest look replied,
By turns with hope and fear it made my quick heart beat: –

"Rarely has man, in this full crowd below,
E'en partial knowledge of my worth possess'd
Who felt not in his breast
At least awhile some spark of spirit glow:
But soon my foe, each germ of good abhorr'd,
Quenches that light, and every virtue dies,
While reigns some other lord
Who promises a calmer life shall rise:
Love, of your mind, to him that naked lies,
So shows the great desire with which you burn,
That safely I divine
It yet shall win for you an honour'd urn;
Already one of my few friends you are,
And now shall see in sign
A lady who shall make your fond eyes happier far."

"It may not, cannot be," I thus began;
– When she, "Turn hither, and in yon calm nook
Upon the lady look
So seldom seen, so little sought of man!"
I turn'd, and o'er my brow the mantling shame,
Within me as I felt that new fire swell,
Of conscious treason came.
She softly smiled, "I understand you well;
E'en as the sun's more powerful rays dispel
And drive the meaner stars of heaven from sight,
So I less fair appear,

Dwindling and darken'd now in her more light;
But not for this I bar you from my train,
As one in jealous fear –
One birth, the elder she, produced us, sisters twain."

Meanwhile the cold and heavy chain was burst
Of silence, which a sense of shame had flung
Around my powerless tongue,
When I was conscious of her notice first:
And thus I spoke, "If what I hear be true,
Bless'd be the sire, and bless'd the natal day
Which graced our world with you!
Blest the long years pass'd in your search away!
From the right path if e'er I went astray,
It grieves me more than, haply, I can show:
But of your state, if I
Deserve more knowledge, more I long to know."
She paused, then, answering pensively, so bent
On me her eloquent eye,
That to my inmost heart her looks and language went: –

"As seem'd to our Eternal Father best,
We two were made immortal at our birth:
To man so small our worth
Better on us that death, like yours, should rest.
Though once beloved and lovely, young and bright,
So slighted are we now, my sister sweet
Already plumes for flight
Her wings to bear her to her own old seat;
Myself am but a shadow thin and fleet;
Thus have I told you, in brief words, whate'er
You sought of us to find:
And now farewell! before I mount in air
This favour take, nor fear that I forget."
Whereat she took and twined
A wreath of laurel green, and round my temples set.

My song! should any deem thy strain obscure,
Say, that I care not, and, ere long to hear,
In certain words and clear,
Truth's welcome message, that my hope is sure;

For this alone, unless I widely err
Of him who set me on the task, I came,
That others I might stir
To honourable acts of high and holy aim.

Robert Macgregor.

MADRIGALE IV.

Or vedi, Amor, che giovinetta donna.

A PRAYER TO LOVE THAT HE WILL TAKE VENGEANCE ON THE SCORNFUL PRIDE OF LAURA.

Now, Love, at length behold a youthful fair,
Who spurns thy rule, and, mocking all my care,
'Mid two such foes, is safe and fancy free.
Thou art well arm'd, 'mid flowers and verdure she,
In simplest robe and natural tresses found,
Against thee haughty still and harsh to me;
I am thy thrall: but, if thy bow be sound,
If yet one shaft be thine, in pity, take
Vengeance upon her for our common sake.

Robert Macgregor.

SONNET XCVI.

Quelle pietose rime, in ch' io m' accorsi.

TO ANTONIO OF FERRARA, WHO, IN A POEM, HAD LAMENTED PETRARCH'S SUPPOSED DEATH.

Those pious lines wherein are finely met
Proofs of high genius and a spirit kind,
Had so much influence on my grateful mind
That instantly in hand my pen I set
To tell you that death's final blow – which yet
Shall me and every mortal surely find –
I have not felt, though I, too, nearly join'd
The confines of his realm without regret;
But I turn'd back again because I read
Writ o'er the threshold that the time to me
Of life predestinate not all was fled,
Though its last day and hour I could not see.
Then once more let your sad heart comfort know,
And love the living worth which dead it honour'd so.

Robert Macgregor.

SONNET XCVII.

Dicesett' anni ha già rivolto il cielo.

E'EN IN OUR ASHES LIVE OUR WONTED FIRES.

The seventeenth summer now, alas! is gone,
And still with ardour unconsumed I glow;
Yet find, whene'er myself I seek to know,
Amidst the fire a frosty chill come on.
Truly 'tis said, 'Ere Habit quits her throne,
Years bleach the hair.' The senses feel life's snow,
But not less hot the tides of passion flow:
Such is our earthly nature's malison!
Oh! come the happy day, when doom'd to smart
No more, from flames and lingering sorrows free,
Calm I may note how fast youth's minutes flew!
Ah! will it e'er be mine the hour to see,
When with delight, nor duty nor my heart
Can blame, these eyes once more that angel face may view?

Francis Wrangham.

For seventeen summers heaven has o'er me roll'd
Since first I burn'd, nor e'er found respite thence,
But when to weigh our state my thoughts commence
I feel amidst the flames a frosty cold.
We change the form, not nature, is an old
And truthful proverb: thus, to dull the sense
Makes not the human feelings less intense;
The dark shades of our painful veil still hold.
Alas! alas! will e'er that day appear
When, my life's flight beholding, I may find
Issue from endless fire and lingering pain, –
The day which, crowning all my wishes here,
Of that fair face the angel air and kind
Shall to my longing eyes restore again?

Robert Macgregor.

SONNET XCVIII.

Quel vago impallidir che 'l dolce riso.

LEAVE-TAKING.

That witching paleness, which with cloud of love
Veil'd her sweet smile, majestically bright,
So thrill'd my heart, that from the bosom's night
Midway to meet it on her face it strove.
Then learnt I how, 'mid realms of joy above,
The blest behold the blest: in such pure light
I scann'd her tender thought, to others' sight
Viewless! – but my fond glances would not rove.
Each angel grace, each lowly courtesy,
E'er traced in dame by Love's soft power inspired,
Would seem but foils to those which prompt my lay:
Upon the ground was cast her gentle eye,
And still methought, though silent, she inquired,
"What bears my faithful friend so soon, so far away?"

Francis Wrangham.

There was a touching paleness on her face,
Which chased her smiles, but such sweet union made
Of pensive majesty and heavenly grace,
As if a passing cloud had veil'd her with its shade;
Then knew I how the blessed ones above
Gaze on each other in their perfect bliss,
For never yet was look of mortal love
So pure, so tender, so serene as this.
The softest glance fond woman ever sent
To him she loved, would cold and rayless be
Compared to this, which she divinely bent
Earthward, with angel sympathy, on me,
That seem'd with speechless tenderness to say,
"Who takes from me my faithful friend away?"

E. (*New Monthly Magazine.*)

SONNET XCIX.

Amor, Fortuna, e la mia mente schiva.

THE CAUSES OF HIS WOE.

Love, Fortune, and my melancholy mind,
Sick of the present, lingering on the past,
Afflict me so, that envious thoughts I cast
On those who life's dark shore have left behind.
Love racks my bosom: Fortune's wintry wind
Kills every comfort: my weak mind at last
Is chafed and pines, so many ills and vast
Expose its peace to constant strifes unkind.
Nor hope I better days shall turn again;
But what is left from bad to worse may pass:
For ah! already life is on the wane.
Not now of adamant, but frail as glass,
I see my best hopes fall from me or fade,
And low in dust my fond thoughts broken laid.

Robert Macgregor.

Love, Fortune, and my ever-faithful mind,
Which loathes the present in its memoried past,
So wound my spirit, that on all I cast
An envied thought who rest in darkness find.
My heart Love prostrates, Fortune more unkind
No comfort grants, until its sorrow vast
Impotent frets, then melts to tears at last:
Thus I to painful warfare am consign'd.
My halcyon days I hope not to return,
But paint my future by a darker tint;
My spring is gone – my summer well-nigh fled:
Ah! wretched me! too well do I discern
Each hope is now (unlike the diamond flint)
A fragile mirror, with its fragments shed.
Miss Wollaston.

CANZONE XIII.

Se 'l pensier che mi strugge.

HE SEEKS IN VAIN TO MITIGATE HIS WOE.

Oh! that my cheeks were taught
By the fond, wasting thought
To wear such hues as could its influence speak;
Then the dear, scornful fair
Might all my ardour share;
And where Love slumbers now he might awake!
Less oft the hill and mead
My wearied feet should tread;
Less oft, perhaps, these eyes with tears should stream;
If she, who cold as snow,
With equal fire would glow –
She who dissolves me, and converts to flame.

Since Love exerts his sway,
And bears my sense away,
I chant uncouth and inharmonious songs:
Nor leaves, nor blossoms show,
Nor rind, upon the bough,
What is the nature that thereto belongs.
Love, and those beauteous eyes,
Beneath whose shade he lies,
Discover all the heart can comprehend:
When vented are my cares
In loud complaints, and tears;
These harm myself, and others those offend.

Sweet lays of sportive vein,
Which help'd me to sustain
Love's first assault, the only arms I bore;
This flinty breast say who
Shall once again subdue,
That I with song may soothe me as before?
Some power appears to trace

Within me Laura's face,
Whispers her name; and straight in verse I strive
To picture her again,
But the fond effort's vain:
Me of my solace thus doth Fate deprive.

E'en as some babe unties
Its tongue in stammering guise,
Who cannot speak, yet will not silence keep:
So fond words I essay;
And listen'd be the lay
By my fair foe, ere in the tomb I sleep!
But if, of beauty vain,
She treats me with disdain;
Do thou, O verdant shore, attend my sighs:
Let them so freely flow,
That all the world may know,
My sorrow thou at least didst not despise!

And well art thou aware,
That never foot so fair
The soil e'er press'd as that which trod thee late;
My sunk soul and worn heart
Now seek thee, to impart
The secret griefs that on my passion wait.
If on thy margent green,
Or 'midst thy flowers, were seen
Some traces of her footsteps lingering there.
My wearied life 'twould cheer,
Bitter'd with many a tear:
Ah! now what means are left to soothe my care?

Where'er I bend mine eye,
What sweet serenity
I feel, to think here Laura shone of yore.
Each plant and scented bloom
I gather, seems to come
From where she wander'd on the custom'd shore:
Ofttimes in this retreat
A fresh and fragrant seat
She found; at least so fancy's vision shows:

And never let truth seek
Th' illusion dear to break –
O spirit blest, from whom such magic flows!

To thee, my simple song,
No polish doth belong;
Thyself art conscious of thy little worth!
Solicit not renown
Throughout the busy town,
But dwell within the shade that gave thee birth.

Dr Nott

CANZONE XIV.

Chiare, fresche e dolci acque.

TO THE FOUNTAIN OF VAUOLUSE – CONTEMPLATIONS OF DEATH.

Ye limpid brooks, by whose clear streams
My goddess laid her tender limbs!
Ye gentle boughs, whose friendly shade
Gave shelter to the lovely maid!
Ye herbs and flowers, so sweetly press'd
By her soft rising snowy breast!
Ye Zephyrs mild, that breathed around
The place where Love my heart did wound!
Now at my summons all appear,
And to my dying words give ear.

If then my destiny requires,
And Heaven with my fate conspires,
That Love these eyes should weeping close,
Here let me find a soft repose.
So Death will less my soul affright,
And, free from dread, my weary spright
Naked alone will dare t' essay
The still unknown, though beaten way;
Pleased that her mortal part will have
So safe a port, so sweet a grave.

The cruel fair, for whom I burn,
May one day to these shades return,
And smiling with superior grace,
Her lover seek around this place,
And when instead of me she finds
Some crumbling dust toss'd by the winds,
She may feel pity in her breast,
And, sighing, wish me happy rest,
Drying her eyes with her soft veil,
Such tears must sure with Heaven prevail.

Well I remember how the flowers
Descended from these boughs in showers,
Encircled in the fragrant cloud
She set, nor midst such glory proud.
These blossoms to her lap repair,
These fall upon her flowing hair,
(Like pearls enchased in gold they seem,)
These on the ground, these on the stream;
In giddy rounds these dancing say,
Here Love and Laura only sway.

In rapturous wonder oft I said,
Sure she in Paradise was made,
Thence sprang that bright angelic state,
Those looks, those words, that heavenly gait,
That beauteous smile, that voice divine,
Those graces that around her shine:
Transported I beheld the fair,
And sighing cried, How came I here?
In heaven, amongst th' immortal blest,
Here let me fix and ever rest.

R. Molesworth.

Ye waters clear and fresh, to whose blight wave
She all her beauties gave, –
Sole of her sex in my impassion'd mind!
Thou sacred branch so graced,
(With sighs e'en now retraced!)
On whose smooth shaft her heavenly form reclined!
Herbage and flowers that bent the robe beneath,
Whose graceful folds compress'd
Her pure angelic breast!
Ye airs serene, that breathe
Where Love first taught me in her eyes his lore!
Yet once more all attest,
The last sad plaintive lay my woe-worn heart may pour!

If so I must my destiny fulfil,
And Love to close these weeping eyes be doom'd
By Heaven's mysterious will,
Oh! grant that in this loved retreat, entomb'd,
My poor remains may lie,
And my freed soul regain its native sky!
Less rude shall Death appear,
If yet a hope so dear
Smooth the dread passage to eternity!
No shade so calm – serene,
My weary spirit finds on earth below;
No grave so still – so green,
In which my o'ertoil'd frame may rest from mortal woe!

Yet one day, haply, she – so heavenly fair!
So kind in cruelty! –
With careless steps may to these haunts repair,
And where her beaming eye
Met mine in days so blest,
A wistful glance may yet unconscious rest,
And seeking me around,
May mark among the stones a lowly mound,
That speaks of pity to the shuddering sense!
Then may she breathe a sigh,
Of power to win me mercy from above!
Doing Heaven violence,
All-beautiful in tears of late relenting love!

Still dear to memory! when, in odorous showers,
Scattering their balmy flowers,
To summer airs th' o'ershadowing branches bow'd,
The while, with humble state,
In all the pomp of tribute sweets she sate,
Wrapt in the roseate cloud!
Now clustering blossoms deck her vesture's hem,
Now her bright tresses gem, –
(In that all-blissful day,
Like burnish'd gold with orient pearls inwrought,)
Some strew the turf – some on the waters float!
Some, fluttering, seem to say
In wanton circlets toss'd, "Here Love holds sovereign sway!"

Oft I exclaim'd, in awful tremor rapt,
"Surely of heavenly birth
This gracious form that visits the low earth!"
So in oblivion lapp'd
Was reason's power, by the celestial mien,
The brow, – the accents mild –
The angelic smile serene!
That now all sense of sad reality
O'erborne by transport wild, –
"Alas! how came I here, and when?" I cry, –
Deeming my spirit pass'd into the sky!
E'en though the illusion cease,
In these dear haunts alone my tortured heart finds peace.

If thou wert graced with numbers sweet, my song!
To match thy wish to please;
Leaving these rocks and trees,
Thou boldly might'st go forth, and dare th' assembled throng.

Lady Dacre.

Clear, fresh, and dulcet streams,
Which the fair shape, who seems
To me sole woman, haunted at noon-tide;
Fair bough, so gently fit,
(I sigh to think of it,)
Which lent a pillar to her lovely side;
And turf, and flowers bright-eyed,
O'er which her folded gown
Flow'd like an angel's down;
And you, O holy air and hush'd,
Where first my heart at her sweet glances gush'd;
Give ear, give ear, with one consenting,
To my last words, my last and my lamenting.

If 'tis my fate below,
And Heaven will have it so,
That Love must close these dying eyes in tears,
May my poor dust be laid
In middle of your shade,
While my soul, naked, mounts to its own spheres.
The thought would calm my fears,
When taking, out of breath,
The doubtful step of death;
For never could my spirit find
A stiller port after the stormy wind;
Nor in more calm, abstracted bourne,
Slip from my travail'd flesh, and from my bones outworn.

Perhaps, some future hour,
To her accustom'd bower
Might come the untamed, and yet the gentle she;
And where she saw me first,
Might turn with eyes athirst
And kinder joy to look again for me;
Then, oh! the charity!
Seeing amidst the stones
The earth that held my bones,
A sigh for very love at last
Might ask of Heaven to pardon me the past:
And Heaven itself could not say nay,
As with her gentle veil she wiped the tears away.

How well I call to mind,
When from those boughs the wind
Shook down upon her bosom flower on flower;
And there she sat, meek-eyed,
In midst of all that pride,
Sprinkled and blushing through an amorous shower
Some to her hair paid dower,
And seem'd to dress the curls,
Queenlike, with gold and pearls;
Some, snowing, on her drapery stopp'd,
Some on the earth, some on the water dropp'd;
While others, fluttering from above,
Seem'd wheeling round in pomp, and saying, "Here reigns Love."

How often then I said,
Inward, and fill'd with dread,
"Doubtless this creature came from Paradise!"
For at her look the while,
Her voice, and her sweet smile,
And heavenly air, truth parted from mine eyes;
So that, with long-drawn sighs,
I said, as far from men,
"How came I here, and when?"
I had forgotten; and alas!
Fancied myself in heaven, not where I was;
And from that time till this, I bear
Such love for the green bower, I cannot rest elsewhere.

Leigh Hunt.

CANZONE XV.

In quella parte dov' Amor mi sprona.

HE FINDS HER IMAGE EVERYWHERE.

When Love, fond Love, commands the strain,
The coyest muse must sure obey;
Love bids my wounded breast complain,
And whispers the melodious lay:
Yet when such griefs restrain the muse's wing,
How shall she dare to soar, or how attempt to sing?

Oh! could my heart express its woe,
How poor, how wretched should I seem!
But as the plaintive accents flow,
Soft comfort spreads her golden gleam;
And each gay scene, that Nature holds to view,
Bids Laura's absent charms to memory bloom anew.

Though Fate's severe decrees remove
Her gladsome beauties from my sight,
Yet, urged by pity, friendly Love
Bids fond reflection yield delight;
If lavish spring with flowerets strews the mead,
Her lavish beauties all to fancy are displayed!

When to this globe the solar beams
Their full meridian blaze impart,
It pictures Laura, that inflames
With passion's fires each human heart:
And when the sun completes his daily race,
I see her riper age complete each growing grace.

When milder planets, warmer skies
O'er winter's frozen reign prevail;
When groves are tinged with vernal dyes,
And violets scent the wanton gale;
Those flowers, the verdure, then recall that day,

In which my Laura stole this heedless heart away.

The blush of health, that crimson'd o'er
Her youthful cheek; her modest mien;
The gay-green garment that she wore,
Have ever dear to memory been;
More dear they grow as time the more inflames
This tender breast o'ercome by passion's wild extremes!

The sun, whose cheering lustre warms
The bosom of yon snow-clad hill,
Seems a just emblem of the charms,
Whose power controls my vanquish'd will;
When near, they gild with joy this frozen heart,
Where ceaseless winter reigns, whene'er those charms depart.

Yon sun, too, paints the locks of gold,
That play around her face so fair –
Her face which, oft as I behold,
Prompts the soft sigh of amorous care!
While Laura smiles, all-conscious of that love
Which from this faithful breast no time can e'er remove.

If to the transient storm of night
Succeeds a star-bespangled sky,
And the clear rain-drops catch the light,
Glittering on all the foliage nigh;
Methinks her eyes I view, as on that day
When through the envious veil they shot their magic ray.

With brightness making heaven more bright,
As then they did, I see them now;
I see them, when the morning light
Purples the misty mountain's brow:
When day declines, and darkness spreads the pole;
Methinks 'tis Laura flies, and sadness wraps my soul.

In stately jars of burnish'd gold
Should lilies spread their silvery pride,
With fresh-blown roses that unfold
Their leaves, in heaven's own crimson dyed;

Then Laura's bloom I see, and sunny hair
Flowing adown her neck than ivory whiter far.

The flowerets brush'd by zephyr's wing,
Waving their heads in frolic play,
Oft to my fond remembrance bring
The happy spot, the happier day,
In which, disporting with the gale, I view'd
Those sweet unbraided locks, that all my heart subdued.

Oh! could I count those orbs that shine
Nightly o'er yon ethereal plain,
Or in some scanty vase confine
Each drop that ocean's bounds contain,
Then might I hope to fly from beauty's rays,
Laura o'er flaming worlds can spread bright beauty's blaze.

Should I all heaven, all earth explore,
I still should lovely Laura find;
Laura, whose beauties I adore,
Is ever present to my mind:
She's seen in all that strikes these partial eyes,
And her dear name still dwells in all my tender sighs.

But soft, my song, – not thine the power
To paint that never-dying flame,
Which gilds through life the gloomy hour,
Which nurtures this love-wasted frame;
For since with Laura dwells my wander'd heart,
Cheer'd by that fostering flame, I brave Death's ebon dart.

Anonymous, 1777.

CANZONE XVI.

Italia mia, benchè 'l parlar sia indarno.

TO THE PRINCES OF ITALY, EXHORTING THEM TO SET HER FREE.

O my own Italy! though words are vain
The mortal wounds to close,
Unnumber'd, that thy beauteous bosom stain,
Yet may it soothe my pain
To sigh forth Tyber's woes,
And Arno's wrongs, as on Po's sadden'd shore
Sorrowing I wander, and my numbers pour.
Ruler of heaven! By the all-pitying love
That could thy Godhead move
To dwell a lowly sojourner on earth,
Turn, Lord! on this thy chosen land thine eye:
See, God of Charity!
From what light cause this cruel war has birth;
And the hard hearts by savage discord steel'd,
Thou, Father! from on high,
Touch by my humble voice, that stubborn wrath may yield!

Ye, to whose sovereign hands the fates confide
Of this fair land the reins, –
(This land for which no pity wrings your breast) –
Why does the stranger's sword her plains invest?
That her green fields be dyed,
Hope ye, with blood from the Barbarians' veins?
Beguiled by error weak,
Ye see not, though to pierce so deep ye boast,
Who love, or faith, in venal bosoms seek:
When throng'd your standards most,
Ye are encompass'd most by hostile bands.
O hideous deluge gather'd in strange lands,
That rushing down amain
O'erwhelms our every native lovely plain!
Alas! if our own hands

Have thus our weal betray'd, who shall our cause sustain?

Well did kind Nature, guardian of our state,
Rear her rude Alpine heights,
A lofty rampart against German hate;
But blind ambition, seeking his own ill,
With ever restless will,
To the pure gales contagion foul invites:
Within the same strait fold
The gentle flocks and wolves relentless throng,
Where still meek innocence must suffer wrong:
And these, – oh, shame avow'd! –
Are of the lawless hordes no tie can hold:
Fame tells how Marius' sword
Erewhile their bosoms gored, –
Nor has Time's hand aught blurr'd the record proud!
When they who, thirsting, stoop'd to quaff the flood,
With the cool waters mix'd, drank of a comrade's blood!

Great Cæsar's name I pass, who o'er our plains
Pour'd forth the ensanguin'd tide,
Drawn by our own good swords from out their veins;
But now – nor know I what ill stars preside –
Heaven holds this land in hate!
To you the thanks! – whose hands control her helm! –
You, whose rash feuds despoil
Of all the beauteous earth the fairest realm!
Are ye impell'd by judgment, crime, or fate,
To oppress the desolate?
From broken fortunes, and from humble toil,
The hard-earn'd dole to wring,
While from afar ye bring
Dealers in blood, bartering their souls for hire?
In truth's great cause I sing.
Nor hatred nor disdain my earnest lay inspire.

Nor mark ye yet, confirm'd by proof on proof,
Bavaria's perfidy,
Who strikes in mockery, keeping death aloof?
(Shame, worse than aught of loss, in honour's eye!)
While ye, with honest rage, devoted pour

Your inmost bosom's gore! –
Yet give one hour to thought,
And ye shall own, how little he can hold
Another's glory dear, who sets his own at nought
O Latin blood of old!
Arise, and wrest from obloquy thy fame,
Nor bow before a name
Of hollow sound, whose power no laws enforce!
For if barbarians rude
Have higher minds subdued,
Ours! ours the crime! – not such wise Nature's course.

Ah! is not this the soil my foot first press'd?
And here, in cradled rest,
Was I not softly hush'd? – here fondly rear'd?
Ah! is not this my country? – so endear'd
By every filial tie!
In whose lap shrouded both my parents lie!
Oh! by this tender thought,
Your torpid bosoms to compassion wrought,
Look on the people's grief!
Who, after God, of you expect relief;
And if ye but relent,
Virtue shall rouse her in embattled might,
Against blind fury bent,
Nor long shall doubtful hang the unequal fight;
For no, – the ancient flame
Is not extinguish'd yet, that raised the Italian name!

Mark, sovereign Lords! how Time, with pinion strong,
Swift hurries life along!
E'en now, behold! Death presses on the rear.
We sojourn here a day – the next, are gone!
The soul disrobed – alone,
Must shuddering seek the doubtful pass we fear.
Oh! at the dreaded bourne,
Abase the lofty brow of wrath and scorn,
(Storms adverse to the eternal calm on high!)
And ye, whose cruelty
Has sought another's harm, by fairer deed
Of heart, or hand, or intellect, aspire

To win the honest meed
Of just renown – the noble mind's desire!
Thus sweet on earth the stay!
Thus to the spirit pure, unbarr'd is Heaven's way!

My song! with courtesy, and numbers sooth,
Thy daring reasons grace,
For thou the mighty, in their pride of place,
Must woo to gentle ruth,
Whose haughty will long evil customs nurse,
Ever to truth averse!
Thee better fortunes wait,
Among the virtuous few – the truly great!
Tell them – but who shall bid my terrors cease?
Peace! Peace! on thee I call! return, O heaven-born Peace!

Lady Dacre.
See Time, that flies, and spreads his hasty wing!
See Life, how swift it runs the race of years,
And on its weary shoulders death appears!
Now all is life and all is spring:
Think on the winter and the darker day
When the soul, naked and alone,
Must prove the dubious step, the still unknown,
Yet ever beaten way.
And through this fatal vale
Would you be wafted with some gentle gale?
Put off that eager strife and fierce disdain,
Clouds that involve our life's serene,
And storms that ruffle all the scene;
Your precious hours, misspent in others' pain,
On nobler deeds, worthy yourselves, bestow;
Whether with hand or wit you raise
Some monument of peaceful praise,
Some happy labour of fair love:
'Tis all of heaven that you can find below,
And opens into all above.

Basil Kennet.

CANZONE XVII.

Di pensier in pensier, di monte in monte.

DISTANCE AND SOLITUDE.

From hill to hill I roam, from thought to thought,
With Love my guide; the beaten path I fly,
For there in vain the tranquil life is sought:
If 'mid the waste well forth a lonely rill,
Or deep embosom'd a low valley lie,
In its calm shade my trembling heart's still;
And there, if Love so will,
I smile, or weep, or fondly hope, or fear.
While on my varying brow, that speaks the soul,
The wild emotions roll,
Now dark, now bright, as shifting skies appear;
That whosoe'er has proved the lover's state
Would say, He feels the flame, nor knows his future fate.

On mountains high, in forests drear and wide,
I find repose, and from the throng'd resort
Of man turn fearfully my eyes aside;
At each lone step thoughts ever new arise
Of her I love, who oft with cruel sport
Will mock the pangs I bear, the tears, the sighs;
Yet e'en these ills I prize,
Though bitter, sweet, nor would they were removed
For my heart whispers me, Love yet has power
To grant a happier hour:
Perchance, though self-despised, thou yet art loved:
E'en then my breast a passing sigh will heave,
Ah! when, or how, may I a hope so wild believe?

Where shadows of high rocking pines dark wave
I stay my footsteps, and on some rude stone
With thought intense her beauteous face engrave;
Roused from the trance, my bosom bathed I find
With tears, and cry, Ah! whither thus alone

Hast thou far wander'd, and whom left behind?
But as with fixed mind
On this fair image I impassion'd rest,
And, viewing her, forget awhile my ills,
Love my rapt fancy fills;
In its own error sweet the soul is blest,
While all around so bright the visions glide;
Oh! might the cheat endure, I ask not aught beside.

Her form portray'd within the lucid stream
Will oft appear, or on the verdant lawn,
Or glossy beech, or fleecy cloud, will gleam
So lovely fair, that Leda's self might say,
Her Helen sinks eclipsed, as at the dawn
A star when cover'd by the solar ray:
And, as o'er wilds I stray
Where the eye nought but savage nature meets,
There Fancy most her brightest tints employs;
But when rude truth destroys
The loved illusion of those dreamed sweets,
I sit me down on the cold rugged stone,
Less coid, less dead than I, and think, and weep alone.

Where the huge mountain rears his brow sublime,
On which no neighbouring height its shadow flings,
Led by desire intense the steep I climb;
And tracing in the boundless space each woe,
Whose sad remembrance my torn bosom wrings,
Tears, that bespeak the heart o'erfraught, will flow:
While, viewing all below,
From me, I cry, what worlds of air divide
The beauteous form, still absent and still near!
Then, chiding soft the tear,
I whisper low, haply she too has sigh'd
That thou art far away: a thought so sweet
Awhile my labouring soul will of its burthen cheat.

Go thou, my song, beyond that Alpine bound,
Where the pure smiling heavens are most serene,
There by a murmuring stream may I be found,
Whose gentle airs around

Waft grateful odours from the laurel green;
Nought but my empty form roams here unblest,
There dwells my heart with her who steals it from my breast.

Lady Dacre.

SONNET C.

Poi che 'l cammin m' è chiuso di mercede.

THOUGH FAR FROM LAURA, SOLITARY AND UNHAPPY, ENVY STILL PURSUES HIM.

Since mercy's door is closed, alas! to me,
And hopeless paths my poor life separate
From her in whom, I know not by what fate,
The guerdon lay of all my constancy,
My heart that lacks not other food, on sighs
I feed: to sorrow born, I live on tears:
Nor therefore mourn I: sweeter far appears
My present grief than others can surmise.
On thy dear portrait rests alone my view,
Which nor Praxiteles nor Xeuxis drew,
But a more bold and cunning pencil framed.
What shore can hide me, or what distance shield,
If by my cruel exile yet untamed
Insatiate Envy finds me here concealed?

Robert Macgregor.

SONNET CI.

Io canterei d' Amor sì novamente.

REPLY TO A SONNET OF JACOPO DA LENTINO.

Ways apt and new to sing of love I'd find,
Forcing from her hard heart full many a sigh,
And re-enkindle in her frozen mind
Desires a thousand, passionate and high;
O'er her fair face would see each swift change pass,
See her fond eyes at length where pity reigns,
As one who sorrows when too late, alas!
For his own error and another's pains;
See the fresh roses edging that fair snow
Move with her breath, that ivory descried,
Which turns to marble him who sees it near;
See all, for which in this brief life below
Myself I weary not but rather pride
That Heaven for later times has kept me here.

Robert Macgregor.

SONNET CII.

S' Amor non è, che dunque è quel ch' i' sento?

THE CONTRADICTIONS OF LOVE.

If no love is, O God, what fele I so?
And if love is, what thing and which is he?
If love be gode, from whence cometh my woe?
If it be wicke, a wonder thinketh me
When every torment and adversite
That cometh of him may to me savory thinke:
For aye more thurst I the more that I drinke.
And if that at my owne lust I brenne,
From whence cometh my wailing and my pleinte?
If harme agre me whereto pleine I thenne?
I not nere why unwery that I feinte.
O quickè deth, O surelè harme so quainte,
How may I see in me such quantite,
But if that I consent that so it be?

Geoffrey Chaucer.

If 'tis not love, what is it feel I then?
If 'tis, how strange a thing, sweet powers above!
If love be kind, why does it fatal prove?
If cruel, why so pleasing is the pain?
If 'tis my will to love, why weep, why plain?
If not my will, tears cannot love remove.
O living death! O rapturous pang! – why, love!
If I consent not, canst thou o'er me reign?
If I consent, 'tis wrongfully I mourn:
Thus on a stormy sea my bark is borne
By adverse winds, and with rough tempest tost;
Thus unenlightened, lost in error's maze,
My blind opinion ever dubious strays;
I'm froze by summer, scorched by winter's frost.

Anonymous, 1777.

SONNET CIII.

Amor m' ha posto come segno a strale.

LOVE'S ARMOURY.

Love makes me as the target for his dart,
As snow in sunshine, or as wax in flame,
Or gale-driven cloud; and, Laura, on thy name
I call, but thou no pity wilt impart.
Thy radiant eyes first caused my bosom's smart;
No time, no place can shield me from their beam;
From thee (but, ah, thou treat'st it as a dream!)
Proceed the torments of my suff'ring heart.
Each thought's an arrow, and thy face a sun,
My passion's flame: and these doth Love employ
To wound my breast, to dazzle, and destroy.
Thy heavenly song, thy speech with which I'm won,
All thy sweet breathings of such strong controul,
Form the dear gale that bears away my soul.

Dr Nott

Me Love has placed as mark before the dart,
As to the sun the snow, as wax to fire,
As clouds to wind: Lady, e'en now I tire,
Craving the mercy which never warms thy heart.
From those bright eyes was aim'd the mortal blow,
'Gainst which nor time nor place avail'd me aught;
From thee alone – nor let it strange be thought –
The sun, the fire, the wind whence I am so.
The darts are thoughts of thee, thy face the sun,
The fire my passion; such the weapons be
With which at will Love dazzles yet destroys.
Thy fragrant breath and angel voice – which won
My heart that from its thrall shall ne'er be free –
The wind which vapour-like my frail life flies.

Robert Macgregor.

SONNET CIV.

Pace non trovo, e non ho da far guerra.

LOVE'S INCONSISTENCY.

I fynde no peace and all my warre is done,
I feare and hope, I bourne and freese lyke yse;
I flye above the wynde, yet cannot ryse;
And nought I have, yet all the worlde I season,
That looseth, nor lacketh, holdes me in pryson,
And holdes me not, yet can I escape no wyse.
Nor lets me leeve, nor die at my devyce,
And yet of death it giveth none occasion.
Without eye I see, and without tongue I playne;
I desyre to perishe, yet aske I health;
I love another, and yet I hate my self;
I feede in sorrow and laughe in all my payne,
Lykewyse pleaseth me both death and lyf,
And my delight is cawser of my greif.

Sir Thomas Wyatt.[5]

5 Harrington's *Nugæ Antiquæ.*

Warfare I cannot wage, yet know not peace;
I fear, I hope, I burn, I freeze again;
Mount to the skies, then bow to earth my face;
Grasp the whole world, yet nothing can obtain.
His prisoner Love nor frees, nor will detain;
In toils he holds me not, nor will release;
He slays me not, nor yet will he unchain;
Nor joy allows, nor lets my sorrow cease.
Sightless I see my fair; though mute, I mourn;
I scorn existence, and yet court its stay;
Detest myself, and for another burn;
By grief I'm nurtured; and, though tearful, gay;
Death I despise, and life alike I hate:
Such, lady, dost thou make my wayward state!

Dr Nott

CANZONE XVIII.

Qual più diversa e nova.

HE COMPARES HIMSELF TO ALL THAT IS MOST STRANGE IN CREATION.

Whate'er most wild and new
Was ever found in any foreign land,
If viewed and valued true,
Most likens me 'neath Love's transforming hand.
Whence the bright day breaks through,
Alone and consortless, a bird there flies,
Who voluntary dies,
To live again regenerate and entire:
So ever my desire,
Alone, itself repairs, and on the crest
Of its own lofty thoughts turns to our sun,
There melts and is undone,
And sinking to its first state of unrest,
So burns and dies, yet still its strength resumes,
And, Phœnix-like, afresh in force and beauty blooms.

Where Indian billows sweep,
A wondrous stone there is, before whose strength
Stout navies, weak to keep
Their binding iron, sink engulf'd at length:
So prove I, in this deep
Of bitter grief, whom, with her own hard pride,
That fair rock knew to guide
Where now my life in wreck and ruin drives:
Thus too the soul deprives,
By theft, my heart, which once so stonelike was,
It kept my senses whole, now far dispersed:
For mine, O fate accurst!
A rock that lifeblood and not iron draws,
Whom still i' the flesh a magnet living, sweet,
Drags to the fatal shore a certain doom to meet.

Neath the far Ethiop skies
A beast is found, most mild and meek of air,
Which seems, yet in her eyes
Danger and dool and death she still does bear:
Much needs he to be wise
To look on hers whoever turns his mien:
Although her eyes unseen,
All else securely may be viewed at will
But I to mine own ill
Run ever in rash grief, though well I know
My sufferings past and future, still my mind
Its eager, deaf and blind
Desire o'ermasters and unhinges so,
That in her fine eyes and sweet sainted face,
Fatal, angelic, pure, my cause of death I trace.

In the rich South there flows
A fountain from the sun its name that wins,
This marvel still that shows,
Boiling at night, but chill when day begins;
Cold, yet more cold it grows
As the sun's mounting car we nearer see:
So happens it with me
(Who am, alas! of tears the source and seat),
When the bright light and sweet,
My only sun retires, and lone and drear
My eyes are left, in night's obscurest reign,
I burn, but if again
The gold rays of the living sun appear,
My slow blood stiffens, instantaneous, strange;
Within me and without I feel the frozen change!

Another fount of fame
Springs in Epirus, which, as bards have told,
Kindles the lurking flame,
And the live quenches, while itself is cold.
My soul, that, uncontroll'd,
And scathless from love's fire till now had pass'd,
Carelessly left at last
Near the cold fair for whom I ceaseless sigh,
Was kindled instantly:

Like martyrdom, ne'er known by day or night,
A heart of marble had to mercy shamed.
Which first her charms inflamed
Her fair and frozen virtue quenched the light;
That thus she crushed and kindled my heart's fire,
Well know I who have felt in long and useless ire.

Beyond our earth's known brinks,
In the famed Islands of the Blest, there be
Two founts: of this who drinks
Dies smiling: who of that to live is free.
A kindred fate Heaven links
To my sad life, who, smilingly, could die
For like o'erflowing joy,
But soon such bliss new cries of anguish stay.
Love! still who guidest my way,
Where, dim and dark, the shade of fame invites,
Not of that fount we speak, which, full each hour,
Ever with larger power
O'erflows, when Taurus with the Sun unites;
So are my eyes with constant sorrow wet,
But in that season most when I my Lady met.

Should any ask, my Song!
Or how or where I am, to such reply:
Where the tall mountain throws
Its shade, in the lone vale, whence Sorga flows,
He roams, where never eye
Save Love's, who leaves him not a step, is by,
And one dear image who his peace destroys,
Alone with whom to muse all else in life he flies.

Robert Macgregor.

SONNET CV.

Fiamma dal ciel su le tue treccie piova.

HE INVEIGHS AGAINST THE COURT OF ROME.

Vengeaunce must fall on thee, thow filthie whore
Of Babilon, thow breaker of Christ's fold,
That from achorns, and from the water colde,
Art riche become with making many poore.
Thow treason's neste that in thie harte dost holde
Of cankard malice, and of myschief more
Than pen can wryte, or may with tongue be tolde,
Slave to delights that chastitie hath solde;
For wyne and ease which settith all thie store
Uppon whoredome and none other lore,
In thye pallais of strompetts yonge and olde
Theare walks Plentie, and Belzebub thye Lorde:
Guydes thee and them, and doth thye raigne upholde:
It is but late, as wryting will recorde,
That poore thow weart withouten lande or goolde;
Yet now hathe golde and pryde, by one accorde,
In wickednesse so spreadd thie lyf abrode,
That it dothe stincke before the face of God.

Sir Thomas Wyatt?[1]

1 Harrington's *Nugæ Antiquæ.*

May fire from heaven rain down upon thy head,
Thou most accurst; who simple fare casts by,
Made rich and great by others' poverty;
How dost thou glory in thy vile misdeed!
Nest of all treachery, in which is bred
Whate'er of sin now through the world doth fly;
Of wine the slave, of sloth, of gluttony;
With sensuality's excesses fed!
Old men and harlots through thy chambers dance;
Then in the midst see Belzebub advance
With mirrors and provocatives obscene.
Erewhile thou wert not shelter'd, nursed on down;
But naked, barefoot on the straw wert thrown:
Now rank to heaven ascends thy life unclean.

Dr Nott

SONNET CVI.

L' avara Babilonia ha colmo 'l sacco.

HE PREDICTS TO ROME THE ARRIVAL OF SOME GREAT PERSONAGE WHO WILL BRING HER BACK TO HER OLD VIRTUE.

Covetous Babylon of wrath divine
By its worst crimes has drain'd the full cup now,
And for its future Gods to whom to bow
Not Pow'r nor Wisdom ta'en, but Love and Wine.
Though hoping reason, I consume and pine,
Yet shall her crown deck some new Soldan's brow,
Who shall again build up, and we avow
One faith in God, in Rome one head and shrine.
Her idols shall be shatter'd, in the dust
Her proud towers, enemies of Heaven, be hurl'd,
Her wardens into flames and exile thrust,
Fair souls and friends of virtue shall the world
Possess in peace; and we shall see it made
All gold, and fully its old works display'd.

Robert Macgregor.

SONNET CVII.

Fontana di dolore, albergo d' ira.

HE ATTRIBUTES THE WICKEDNESS OF THE COURT OF ROME TO ITS GREAT WEALTH.

Spring of all woe, O den of curssed ire,
Scoole of errour, temple of heresye;
Thow Pope, I meane, head of hypocrasye,
Thow and thie churche, unsaciat of desyre,
Have all the world filled full of myserye;
Well of disceate, thow dungeon full of fyre,
That hydes all truthe to breed idolatrie.
Thow wicked wretche, Chryste cannot be a lyer,
Behold, therefore, thie judgment hastelye;
Thye first founder was gentill povertie,
But there against is all thow dost requyre.
Thow shameless beaste wheare hast thow thie trust,
In thie whoredome, or in thie riche attyre?
Loe! Constantyne, that is turned into dust,
Shall not retourne for to mayntaine thie lust;
But now his heires, that might not sett thee higher,
For thie greate pryde shall teare thye seate asonder,
And scourdge thee so that all the world shall wonder.

Sir Thomas Wyatt?[2]

2 Harrington's *Nugæ Antiquæ*.

Fountain of sorrows, centre of mad ire,
Rank error's school and fane of heresy,
Once Rome, now Babylon, the false and free,
Whom fondly we lament and long desire.
O furnace of deceits, O prison dire,
Where good roots die and the ill-weed grows a tree
Hell upon earth, great marvel will it be
If Christ reject thee not in endless fire.
Founded in humble poverty and chaste,
Against thy founders lift'st thou now thy horn,
Impudent harlot! Is thy hope then placed
In thine adult'ries and thy wealth ill-born?
Since comes no Constantine his own to claim,
The vext world must endure, or end its shame.

Robert Macgregor.

SONNET CVIII.

Quanto più desiose l' ali spando.

FAR FROM HIS FRIENDS, HE FLIES TO THEM IN THOUGHT.

The more my own fond wishes would impel
My steps to you, sweet company of friends!
Fortune with their free course the more contends,
And elsewhere bids me roam, by snare and spell
The heart, sent forth by me though it rebel,
Is still with you where that fair vale extends,
In whose green windings most our sea ascends,
From which but yesterday I wept farewell.
It took the right-hand way, the left I tried,
I dragg'd by force in slavery to remain,
It left at liberty with Love its guide;
But patience is great comfort amid pain:
Long habits mutually form'd declare
That our communion must be brief and rare.

Robert Macgregor.

SONNET CIX.

Amor che nel pensier mio vive e regna.

THE COURAGE AND TIMIDITY OF LOVE.

The long Love that in my thought I harbour,
And in my heart doth keep his residence,
Into my face pressèth with bold pretence,
And there campèth displaying his bannèr.
She that me learns to love and to suffèr,
And wills that my trust, and lust's negligence
Be rein'd by reason, shame, and reverence,
With his hardiness takes displeasure.
Wherewith Love to the heart's forest he fleeth,
Leaving his enterprise with pain and cry,
And there him hideth, and not appearèth.
What may I do, when my master fearèth,
But in the field with him to live and die?
For good is the life, ending faithfully.

Sir Thomas Wyatt.

Love, that liveth and reigneth in my thought,
That built its seat within my captive breast;
Clad in the arms wherein with me he fought,
Oft in my face he doth his banner rest.
She, that me taught to love, and suffer pain;
My doubtful hope, and eke my hot desire
With shamefaced cloak to shadow and restrain,
Her smiling grace converteth straight to ire.
And coward love then to the heart apace
Taketh his flight; whereas he lurks, and plains
His purpose lost, and dare not show his face.
For my lord's guilt thus faultless bide I pains.
Yet from my lord shall not my foot remove:
Sweet is his death, that takes his end by love.

Surrey.

Love in my thought who ever lives and reigns,
And in my heart still holds the upper place,
At times come forward boldly in my face,
There plants his ensign and his post maintains:
She, who in love instructs us and its pains,
Would fain that reason, shame, respect should chase
Presumptuous hope and high desire abase,
And at our daring scarce herself restrains,
Love thereon to my heart retires dismay'd,
Abandons his attempt, and weeps and fears,
And hiding there, no more my friend appears.
What can the liege whose lord is thus afraid,
More than with him, till life's last gasp, to dwell?
For who well loving dies at least dies well.

Robert Macgregor.

SONNET CX.

Come talora al caldo tempo suole.

HE LIKENS HIMSELF TO THE INSECT WHICH, FLYING INTO ONE'S EYES, MEETS ITS DEATH.

As when at times in summer's scorching heats.
Lured by the light, the simple insect flies,
As a charm'd thing, into the passer's eyes,
Whence death the one and pain the other meets,
Thus ever I, my fatal sun to greet,
Rush to those eyes where so much sweetness lies
That reason's guiding hand fierce Love defies,
And by strong will is better judgment beat.
I clearly see they value me but ill,
And, for against their torture fails my strength.
That I am doom'd my life to lose at length:
But Love so dazzles and deludes me still,
My heart their pain and not my loss laments,
And blind, to its own death my soul consents.

Robert Macgregor.

SESTINA V.

Alia dolce ombra de le belle frondi.

HE TELLS THE STORY OF HIS LOVE, RESOLVING HENCEFORTH TO DEVOTE HIMSELF TO GOD.

Beneath the pleasant shade of beauteous leaves
I ran for shelter from a cruel light,
E'en here below that burnt me from high heaven,
When the last snow had ceased upon the hills,
And amorous airs renew'd the sweet spring time,

And on the upland flourish'd herbs and boughs.
Ne'er did the world behold such graceful boughs,
Nor ever wind rustled so verdant leaves,
As were by me beheld in that young time:
So that, though fearful of the ardent light,

I sought not refuge from the shadowing hills,
But of the plant accepted most in heaven.
A laurel then protected from that heaven:
Whence, oft enamour'd with its lovely boughs,
A roamer I have been through woods, o'er hills,

But never found I other trunk, nor leaves
Like these, so honour'd with supernal light,
Which changed not qualities with changing time.
Wherefore each hour more firm, from time to time
Following where I heard my call from heaven,
And guided ever by a soft clear light,

I turn'd, devoted still, to those first boughs,
Or when on earth are scatter'd the sere leaves,
Or when the sun restored makes green the hills.
The woods, the rocks, the fields, the floods, and hills,
All that is made, are conquer'd, changed by time:
And therefore ask I pardon of those leaves,

If after many years, revolving heaven
Sway'd me to flee from those entangling boughs,
When I begun to see its better light.
So dear to me at first was the sweet light,
That willingly I pass'd o'er difficult hills,

But to be nearer those beloved boughs;
Now shortening life, the apt place and full time
Show me another path to mount to heaven,
And to make fruit not merely flowers and leaves.
Other love, other leaves, and other light,
Other ascent to heaven by other hills
I seek – in sooth 'tis time – and other boughs.

Robert Macgregor.

SONNET CXI.

Quand' io v' odo parlar si dolcemente.

TO ONE WHO SPOKE TO HIM OF LAURA.

Whene'er you speak of her in that soft tone
Which Love himself his votaries surely taught,
My ardent passion to such fire is wrought,
That e'en the dead reviving warmth might own:
Where'er to me she, dear or kind, was known
There the bright lady is to mind now brought,
In the same bearing which, to waken thought,
Needed no sound but of my sighs alone.
Half-turn'd I see her looking, on the breeze
Her light hair flung; so true her memories roll
On my fond heart of which she keeps the keys;
But the surpassing bliss which floods my soul
So checks my tongue, to tell how, queen-like, there,
She sits as on her throne, I never dare.

Robert Macgregor.

SONNET CXII.

Nè così bello il sol giammai levarsi.

THE CHARMS OF LAURA WHEN SHE FIRST MET HIS SIGHT.

Ne'er can the sun such radiance soft display,
Piercing some cloud that would its light impair;
Ne'er tinged some showery arch the humid air,
With variegated lustre half so gay,
As when, sweet-smiling my fond heart away,
All-beauteous shone my captivating fair;
For charms what mortal can with her compare!
But truth, impartial truth! much more might say.
I saw young Cupid, saw his laughing eyes
With such bewitching, am'rous sweetness roll,
That every human glance I since despise.
Believe, dear friend! I saw the wanton boy;
Bent was his bow to wound my tender soul;
Yet, ah! once more I'd view the dang'rous joy.

Anonymous 1777.

Sun never rose so beautiful and bright
When skies above most clear and cloudless show'd,
Nor, after rain, the bow of heaven e'er glow'd
With tints so varied, delicate, and light,
As in rare beauty flash'd upon my sight,
The day I first took up this am'rous load,
That face whose fellow ne'er on earth abode –
Even my praise to paint it seems a slight!
Then saw I Love, who did her fine eyes bend
So sweetly, every other face obscure
Has from that hour till now appear'd to me.
The boy-god and his bow, I saw them, friend,
From whom life since has never been secure,
Whom still I madly yearn again to see.

Robert Macgregor.

SONNET CXIII.

Pommi ove 'l sol occide i fiori e l' erba.

HIS INVINCIBLE CONSTANCY.

Place me where herb and flower the sun has dried,
Or where numb winter's grasp holds sterner sway:
Place me where Phœbus sheds a temperate ray,
Where first he glows, where rests at eventide.
Place me in lowly state, in power and pride,
Where lour the skies, or where bland zephyrs play
Place me where blind night rules, or lengthened day,
In age mature, or in youth's boiling tide:
Place me in heaven, or in the abyss profound,
On lofty height, or in low vale obscure,
A spirit freed, or to the body bound;
Bank'd with the great, or all unknown to fame,
I still the same will be! the same endure!
And my trilustral sighs still breathe the same!

Lady Dacre.

Place me where Phœbus burns each herb, each flower;
Or where cold snows, and frost o'ercome his rays:
Place me where rolls his car with temp'rate blaze;
In climes that feel not, or that feel his power.
Place me where fortune may look bright, or lour;
Mid murky airs, or where soft zephyr plays:
Place me in night, in long or short-lived days,
Where age makes sad, or youth gilds ev'ry hour:
Place me on mountains high, in vallies drear,
In heaven, on earth, in depths unknown to-day;
Whether life fosters still, or flies this clay:
Place me where fame is distant, where she's near:
Still will I love; nor shall those sighs yet cease,
Which thrice five years have robb'd this breast of peace.

Anonymous 1777.

Place me where angry Titan burns the Moor,
And thirsty Afric fiery monsters brings,
Or where the new-born phœnix spreads her wings,
And troops of wond'ring birds her flight adore:
Place me by Gange, or Ind's empamper'd shore,
Where smiling heavens on earth cause double springs:
Place me where Neptune's quire of Syrens sings,
Or where, made hoarse through cold, he leaves to roar:
Me place where Fortune doth her darlings crown,
A wonder or a spark in Envy's eye,
Or late outrageous fates upon me frown,
And pity wailing, see disaster'd me.
Affection's print my mind so deep doth prove,
I may forget myself, but not my love.

Drummond.

SONNET CXIV.

O d' ardente virtute ornata e calda.

HE CELEBRATES LAURA'S BEAUTY AND VIRTUE.

O mind, by ardent virtue graced and warm'd.
To whom my pen so oft pours forth my heart;
Mansion of noble probity, who art
A tower of strength 'gainst all assault full arm'd.
O rose effulgent, in whose foldings, charm'd,
We view with fresh carnation snow take part!
O pleasure whence my wing'd ideas start
To that bless'd vision which no eye, unharm'd,
Created, may approach – thy name, if rhyme
Could bear to Bactra and to Thule's coast,
Nile, Tanaïs, and Calpe should resound,
And dread Olympus. – But a narrower bound
Confines my flight: and thee, our native clime
Between the Alps and Apennine must boast.

Capel Lofft.

With glowing virtue graced, of warm heart known,
Sweet Spirit! for whom so many a page I trace,
Tower in high worth which foundest well thy base!
Centre of honour, perfect, and alone!
O blushes! on fresh snow like roses thrown,
Wherein I read myself and mend apace;
O pleasures! lifting me to that fair face
Brightest of all on which the sun e'er shone.
Oh! if so far its sound may reach, your name
On my fond verse shall travel West and East,
From southern Nile to Thule's utmost bound.
But such full audience since I may not claim,
It shall be heard in that fair land at least
Which Apennine divides, which Alps and seas surround.

Robert Macgregor.

SONNET CXV.

Quando 'l voler, che con duo sproni ardenti.

HER LOOKS BOTH COMFORT AND CHECK HIM.

When, with two ardent spurs and a hard rein,
Passion, my daily life who rules and leads,
From time to time the usual law exceeds
That calm, at least in part, my spirits may gain,
It findeth her who, on my forehead plain,
The dread and daring of my deep heart reads,
And seeth Love, to punish its misdeeds,
Lighten her piercing eyes with worse disdain.
Wherefore – as one who fears the impending blow
Of angry Jove – it back in haste retires,
For great fears ever master great desires;
But the cold fire and shrinking hopes which so
Lodge in my heart, transparent as a glass,
O'er her sweet face at times make gleams of grace to pass.

Robert Macgregor.

SONNET CXVI.

Non Tesin, Po, Varo, Arno, Adige e Tebro.

HE EXTOLS THE LAUREL AND ITS FAVOURITE STREAM.

Not all the streams that water the bright earth,
Not all the trees to which its breast gives birth,
Can cooling drop or healing balm impart
To slack the fire which scorches my sad heart,
As one fair brook which ever weeps with me,
Or, which I praise and sing, as one dear tree.
This only help I find amid Love's strife;
Wherefore it me behoves to live my life
In arms, which else from me too rapid goes.
Thus on fresh shore the lovely laurel grows;
Who planted it, his high and graceful thought
'Neath its sweet shade, to Sorga's murmurs, wrote.

Robert Macgregor.

[IMITATION.]

Nor Arne, nor Mincius, nor stately Tiber,
Sebethus, nor the flood into whose streams
He fell who burnt the world with borrow'd beams;
Gold-rolling Tagus, Munda, famous Iber,
Sorgue, Rhone, Loire, Garron, nor proud-bank'd Seine,
Peneus, Phasis, Xanthus, humble Ladon,
Nor she whose nymphs excel her who loved Adon,
Fair Tamesis, nor Ister large, nor Rhine,
Euphrates, Tigris, Indus, Hermus, Gange,
Pearly Hydaspes, serpent-like Meander, –
The gulf bereft sweet Hero her Leander –
Nile, that far, far his hidden head doth range,
Have ever had so rare a cause of praise
As Ora, where this northern Phœnix stays.

Drummond.

BALLATA VI.

Di tempo in tempo mi si fa men dura.

THOUGH SHE BE LESS SEVERE, HE IS STILL NOT CONTENTED AND TRANQUIL AT HEART.

From time to time more clemency for me
In that sweet smile and angel form I trace;
Seem too her lovely face
And lustrous eyes at length more kind to be.
Yet, if thus honour'd, wherefore do my sighs
In doubt and sorrow flow,
Signs that too truly show
My anguish'd desperate life to common eyes?
Haply if, where she is, my glance I bend,
This harass'd heart to cheer,
Methinks that Love I hear
Pleading my cause, and see him succour lend.
Not therefore at an end the strife I deem,
Nor in sure rest my heart at last esteem;
For Love most burns within
When Hope most pricks us on the way to win.

Robert Macgregor.

From time to time less cruelty I trace
In her sweet smile and form divinely fair;
Less clouded doth appear
The heaven of her fine eyes and lovely face.
What then at last avail to me those sighs,
Which from my sorrows flow,
And in my semblance show
The life of anguish and despair I lead?
If towards her perchance I bend mine eyes,
Some solace to bestow
Upon my bosom's woe,
Methinks Love takes my part, and lends me aid:
Yet still I cannot find the conflict stay'd,
Nor tranquil is my heart in every state:
For, ah! my passion's heat
More strongly glows within as my fond hopes increase.

Dr Nott

SONNET CXVII.

Che fai, alma? che pensi? avrem mai pace?

DIALOGUE OF THE POET WITH HIS HEART.

P. What actions fire thee, and what musings fill?
Soul! is it peace, or truce, or war eterne?
H. Our lot I know not, but, as I discern,
Her bright eyes favour not our cherish'd ill.
P. What profit, with those eyes if she at will
Makes us in summer freeze, in winter burn?
H. From him, not her those orbs their movement learn.
P. What's he to us, she sees it and is still.
H. Sometimes, though mute the tongue, the heart laments
Fondly, and, though the face be calm and bright,
Bleeds inly, where no eye beholds its grief.
P. Nathless the mind not thus itself contents,
Breaking the stagnant woes which there unite,
For misery in fine hopes finds no relief.

Robert Macgregor.

P. What act, what dream, absorbs thee, O my soul?
Say, must we peace, a truce, or warfare hail?
H. Our fate I know not; but her eyes unveil
The grief our woe doth in her heart enrol.
P. But that is vain, since by her eyes' control
With nature I no sympathy inhale.
H. Yet guiltless she, for Love doth there prevail.
P. No balm to me, since she will not condole.
H. When man is mute, how oft the spirit grieves,
In clamorous woe! how oft the sparkling eye
Belies the inward tear, where none can gaze!
P. Yet restless still, the grief the mind conceives
Is not dispell'd, but stagnant seems to lie.
The wretched hope not, though hope aid might raise.

Miss Wollaston.

SONNET CXVIII.

Nom d' atra e tempestosa onda marina.

HE IS LED BY LOVE TO REASON.

No wearied mariner to port e'er fled
From the dark billow, when some tempest's nigh,
As from tumultuous gloomy thoughts I fly –
Thoughts by the force of goading passion bred:
Nor wrathful glance of heaven so surely sped
Destruction to man's sight, as does that eye
Within whose bright black orb Love's Deity
Sharpens each dart, and tips with gold its head.
Enthroned in radiance there he sits, not blind,
Quiver'd, and naked, or by shame just veil'd,
A live, not fabled boy, with changeful wing;
Thence unto me he lends instruction kind,
And arts of verse from meaner bards conceal'd,
Thus am I taught whate'er of love I write or sing.

Dr Nott

Ne'er from the black and tempest-troubled brine
The weary mariner fair haven sought,
As shelter I from the dark restless thought
Whereto hot wishes spur me and incline:
Nor mortal vision ever light divine
Dazzled, as mine, in their rare splendour caught
Those matchless orbs, with pride and passion fraught,
Where Love aye haunts his darts to gild and fine.
Him, blind no more, but quiver'd, there I view,
Naked, except so far as shame conceals,
A winged boy – no fable – quick and true.
What few perceive he thence to me reveals;
So read I clearly in her eyes' dear light
Whate'er of love I speak, whate'er I write.

Robert Macgregor.

SONNET CXIX.

Questa umil fera, un cor di tigre o d' orsa.

HE PRAYS HER EITHER TO WELCOME OR DISMISS HIM AT ONCE.

Fiercer than tiger, savager than bear,
In human guise an angel form appears,
Who between fear and hope, from smiles to tears
So tortures me that doubt becomes despair.
Ere long if she nor welcomes me, nor frees,
But, as her wont, between the two retains,
By the sweet poison circling through my veins,
My life, O Love! will soon be on its lees.
No longer can my virtue, worn and frail
With such severe vicissitudes, contend,
At once which burn and freeze, make red and pale:
By flight it hopes at length its grief to end,
As one who, hourly failing, feels death nigh:
Powerless he is indeed who cannot even die!

Robert Macgregor.

SONNET CXX.

Ite, caldi sospiri, al freddo core.

HE IMPLORES MERCY OR DEATH.

Go, my warm sighs, go to that frozen breast,
Burst the firm ice, that charity denies;
And, if a mortal prayer can reach the skies,
Let death or pity give my sorrows rest!
Go, softest thoughts! Be all you know express'd
Of that unnoticed by her lovely eyes,
Though fate and cruelty against me rise,
Error at least and hope shall be repress'd.
Tell her, though fully you can never tell,
That, while her days calm and serenely flow,
In darkness and anxiety I dwell;
Love guides your flight, my thoughts securely go,
Fortune may change, and all may yet be well;
If my sun's aspect not deceives my woe.

Lord Charlemont.

Go, burning sighs, to her cold bosom go,
Its circling ice which hinders pity rend,
And if to mortal prayer Heaven e'er attend,
Let death or mercy finish soon my woe.
Go forth, fond thoughts, and to our lady show
The love to which her bright looks never bend,
If still her harshness, or my star offend,
We shall at least our hopeless error know.
Go, in some chosen moment, gently say,
Our state disquieted and dark has been,
Even as hers pacific and serene.
Go, safe at last, for Love escorts your way:
From my sun's face if right the skies I guess
Well may my cruel fortune now be less.

Robert Macgregor.

SONNET CXXI.

Le stelle e 'l cielo e gli elementi a prova.

LAURA'S UNPARALLELED BEAUTY AND VIRTUE.

The stars, the elements, and Heaven have made
With blended powers a work beyond compare;
All their consenting influence, all their care,
To frame one perfect creature lent their aid.
Whence Nature views her loveliness display'd
With sun-like radiance sublimely fair:
Nor mortal eye can the pure splendour bear:
Love, sweetness, in unmeasured grace array'd.
The very air illumed by her sweet beams
Breathes purest excellence; and such delight
That all expression far beneath it gleams.
No base desire lives in that heavenly light,
Honour alone and virtue! – fancy's dreams
Never saw passion rise refined by rays so bright.

Capel Lofft.

The stars, the heaven, the elements, I ween,
Put forth their every art and utmost care
In that bright light, as fairest Nature fair,
Whose like on earth the sun has nowhere seen;
So noble, elegant, unique her mien,
Scarce mortal glance to rest on it may dare,
Love so much softness and such graces rare
Showers from those dazzling and resistless een.
The atmosphere, pervaded and made pure
By their sweet rays, kindles with goodness so,
Thought cannot equal it nor language show.
Here no ill wish, no base desires endure,
But honour, virtue. Here, if ever yet,
Has lust his death from supreme beauty met.

Robert Macgregor.

SONNET CXXII.

Non fur mai Giove e Cesare sì mossi.

LAURA IN TEARS.

High Jove to thunder ne'er was so intent,
So resolute great Cæsar ne'er to strike,
That pity had not quench'd the ire of both,
And from their hands the accustom'd weapons shook.
Madonna wept: my Lord decreed that I
Should see her then, and there her sorrows hear;
So joy, desire should fill me to the brim,
Thrilling my very marrow and my bones.
Love show'd to me, nay, sculptured on my heart,
That sweet and sparkling tear, and those soft words
Wrote with a diamond on its inmost core,
Where with his constant and ingenious keys
He still returneth often, to draw thence
True tears of mine and long and heavy sighs.

Robert Macgregor.

SONNET CXXIII.

I' vidi in terra angelici costumi.

THE EFFECTS OF HER GRIEF.

On earth reveal'd the beauties of the skies,
Angelic features, it was mine to hail;
Features, which wake my mingled joy and wail,
While all besides like dreams or shadows flies.
And fill'd with tears I saw those two bright eyes,
Which oft have turn'd the sun with envy pale;
And from those lips I heard – oh! such a tale,
As might awake brute Nature's sympathies!
Wit, pity, excellence, and grief, and love
With blended plaint so sweet a concert made,
As ne'er was given to mortal ear to prove:
And heaven itself such mute attention paid,
That not a breath disturb'd the listening grove –
Even æther's wildest gales the tuneful charm obey'd.

Francis Wrangham.

Yes, I beheld on earth angelic grace,
And charms divine which mortals rarely see,
Such as both glad and pain the memory;
Vain, light, unreal is all else I trace:
Tears I saw shower'd from those fine eyes apace,
Of which the sun ofttimes might envious be;
Accents I heard sigh'd forth so movingly,
As to stay floods, or mountains to displace.
Love and good sense, firmness, with pity join'd
And wailful grief, a sweeter concert made
Than ever yet was pour'd on human ear:
And heaven unto the music so inclined,
That not a leaf was seen to stir the shade;
Such melody had fraught the winds, the atmosphere.

Dr Nott

SONNET CXXIV.

Quel sempre acerbo ed onorato giorno.

HE RECALLS HER AS HE SAW HER WHEN IN TEARS.

That ever-painful, ever-honour'd day
So left her living image on my heart
Beyond or lover's wit or poet's art,
That oft to it will doting memory stray.
A gentle pity softening her bright mien,
Her sorrow there so sweet and sad was heard,
Doubt in the gazer's bosom almost stirr'd
Goddess or mortal, which made heaven serene.
Fine gold her hair, her face as sunlit snow,
Her brows and lashes jet, twin stars her eyne,
Whence the young archer oft took fatal aim;
Each loving lip – whence, utterance sweet and low
Her pent grief found – a rose which rare pearls line,
Her tears of crystal and her sighs of flame.

Robert Macgregor.

That ever-honour'd, yet too bitter day,
Her image hath so graven in my breast,
That only memory can return it dress'd
In living charms, no genius could portray:
Her air such graceful sadness did display,
Her plaintive, soft laments my ear so bless'd,
I ask'd if mortal, or a heavenly guest,
Did thus the threatening clouds in smiles array.
Her locks were gold, her cheeks were breathing snow,
Her brows with ebon arch'd – bright stars her eyes,
Wherein Love nestled, thence his dart to aim:
Her teeth were pearls – the rose's softest glow
Dwelt on that mouth, whence woke to speech grief's sighs
Her tears were crystal – and her breath was flame.

Miss Wollaston.

SONNET CXXV.

Ove ch' i' posi gli occhi lassi o giri.

HER IMAGE IS EVER IN HIS HEART.

Where'er I rest or turn my weary eyes,
To ease the longings which allure them still,
Love pictures my bright lady at his will,
That ever my desire may verdant rise.
Deep pity she with graceful grief applies –
Warm feelings ever gentle bosoms fill –
While captived equally my fond ears thrill
With her sweet accents and seraphic sighs.
Love and fair Truth were both allied to tell
The charms I saw were in the world alone,
That 'neath the stars their like was never known.
Nor ever words so dear and tender fell
On listening ear: nor tears so pure and bright
From such fine eyes e'er sparkled in the light.

Robert Macgregor.

SONNET CXXVI.

In qual parte del cielo, in quale idea.

HE EXTOLS THE BEAUTY AND VIRTUE OF LAURA.

Say from what part of heaven 'twas Nature drew,
From what idea, that so perfect mould
To form such features, bidding us behold,
In charms below, what she above could do?
What fountain-nymph, what dryad-maid e'er threw
Upon the wind such tresses of pure gold?
What heart such numerous virtues can unfold?
Although the chiefest all my fond hopes slew.
He for celestial charms may look in vain,
Who has not seen my fair one's radiant eyes,
And felt their glances pleasingly beguile.
How Love can heal his wounds, then wound again,
He only knows, who knows how sweet her sighs,
How sweet her converse, and how sweet her smile.

Dr Nott

In what celestial sphere – what realm of thought,
Dwelt the bright model from which Nature drew
That fair and beauteous face, in which we view
Her utmost power, on earth, divinely wrought?
What sylvan queen – what nymph by fountain sought,
Upon the breeze such golden tresses threw?
When did such virtues one sole breast imbue?
Though with my death her chief perfection's fraught.
For heavenly beauty he in vain inquires,
Who ne'er beheld her eyes' celestial stain,
Where'er she turns around their brilliant fires:
He knows not how Love wounds, and heals again,
Who knows not how she sweetly smiles, respires
The sweetest sighs, and speaks in sweetest strain!

Anonymous

SONNET CXXVII.

Amor ed io sì pien di maraviglia.

HER EVERY ACTION IS DIVINE.

As one who sees a thing incredible,
In mutual marvel Love and I combine,
Confessing, when she speaks or smiles divine,
None but herself can be her parallel.
Where the fine arches of that fair brow swell
So sparkle forth those twin true stars of mine,
Than whom no safer brighter beacons shine
His course to guide who'd wisely love and well.
What miracle is this, when, as a flower,
She sits on the rich grass, or to her breast,
Snow-white and soft, some fresh green shrub is press'd
And oh! how sweet, in some fair April hour,
To see her pass, alone, in pure thought there,
Weaving fresh garlands in her own bright hair.

Robert Macgregor.

SONNET CXXVIII.

O passi sparsi, o pensier vaghi e pronti.

EVERY CIRCUMSTANCE OF HIS PASSION IS A TORMENT TO HIM.

O scatter'd steps! O vague and busy thoughts!
O firm-set memory! O fierce desire!
O passion powerful! O failing heart!
O eyes of mine, not eyes, but fountains now!
O leaf, which honourest illustrious brows,
Sole sign of double valour, and best crown!
O painful life, O error oft and sweet!
That make me search the lone plains and hard hills.
O beauteous face! where Love together placed
The spurs and curb, to strive with which is vain,
They prick and turn me so at his sole will.
O gentle amorous souls, if such there be!
And you, O naked spirits of mere dust,
Tarry and see how great my suffering is!

Robert Macgregor.

SONNET CXXIX.

Lieti fiori e felici, e ben nate erbe.

HE ENVIES EVERY SPOT THAT SHE FREQUENTS.

Gay, joyous blooms, and herbage glad with showers,
O'er which my pensive fair is wont to stray!
Thou plain, that listest her melodious lay,
As her fair feet imprint thy waste of flowers!
Ye shrubs so trim; ye green, unfolding bowers;
Ye violets clad in amorous, pale array;
Thou shadowy grove, gilded by beauty's ray,
Whose top made proud majestically towers!
O pleasant country! O translucent stream,
Bathing her lovely face, her eyes so clear,
And catching of their living light the beam!
I envy ye her actions chaste and dear:
No rock shall stud thy waters, but shall learn
Henceforth with passion strong as mine to burn.

Dr Nott

O bright and happy flowers and herbage blest,
On which my lady treads! – O favour'd plain,
That hears her accents sweet, and can retain
The traces by her fairy steps impress'd! –
Pure shrubs, with tender verdure newly dress'd, –
Pale amorous violets, – leafy woods, whose reign
Thy sun's bright rays transpierce, and thus sustain
Your lofty stature, and umbrageous crest; –
O thou, fair country, and thou, crystal stream,
Which bathes her countenance and sparkling eyes,
Stealing fresh lustre from their living beam;
How do I envy thee these precious ties!
Thy rocky shores will soon be taught to gleam
With the same flame that burns in all my sighs.

Mrs Wrottesley.

SONNET CXXX.

Amor, che vedi ogni pensiero aperto.

HE CARES NOT FOR SUFFERINGS, SO THAT HE DISPLEASE NOT LAURA.

Love, thou who seest each secret thought display'd,
And the sad steps I take, with thee sole guide;
This throbbing breast, to thee thrown open wide,
To others' prying barr'd, thine eyes pervade.
Thou know'st what efforts, following thee, I made,
While still from height to height thy pinions glide;
Nor deign'st one pitying look to turn aside
On him who, fainting, treads a trackless glade.
I mark from far the mildly-beaming ray
To which thou goad'st me through the devious maze;
Alas! I want thy wings, to speed my way –
Henceforth, a distant homager, I'll gaze,
Content by silent longings to decay,
So that my sighs for her in her no anger raise.

Francis Wrangham.

O Love, that seest my heart without disguise,
And those hard toils from thee which I sustain,
Look to my inmost thought; behold the pain
To thee unveil'd, hid from all other eyes.
Thou know'st for thee this breast what suffering tries;
Me still from day to day o'er hill and plain
Thou chasest; heedless still, while I complain
As to my wearied steps new thorns arise.
True, I discern far off the cheering light
To which, through trackless wilds, thou urgest me:
But wings like thine to bear me to delight
I want: – Yet from these pangs I would not flee,
Finding this only favour in her sight,
That not displeased my love and death she see.

Capel Lofft.

SONNET CXXXI.

Or che 'l ciel e la terra e 'l vento tace.

NIGHT BRINGS PEACE TO ALL SAVE HIM.

O'er earth and sky her lone watch silence keeps,
And bird and beast in stirless slumber lie,
Her starry chariot Night conducts on high,
And in its bed the waveless ocean sleeps.
I wake, muse, burn, and weep; of all my pain
The one sweet cause appears before me still;
War is my lot, which grief and anger fill,
And thinking but of her some rest I gain.
Thus from one bright and living fountain flows
The bitter and the sweet on which I feed;
One hand alone can harm me or can heal:
And thus my martyrdom no limit knows,
A thousand deaths and lives each day I feel,
So distant are the paths to peace which lead.

Robert Macgregor.

’Tis now the hour when midnight silence reigns
O’er earth and sea, and whispering Zephyr dies
Within his rocky cell; and Morpheus chains
Each beast that roams the wood, and bird that wings the skies.
More blest those rangers of the earth and air,
Whom night awhile relieves from toil and pain;
Condemn’d to tears and sighs, and wasting care.
To me the circling sun descends in vain!
Ah me! that mingling miseries and joys,
Too near allied, from one sad fountain flow!
The magic hand that comforts and annoys
Can hope, and fell despair, and life, and death bestow!
Too great the bliss to find in death relief:
Fate has not yet fill’d up the measure of my grief.

Lord Woodhouselee.

SONNET CXXXII.

Come 'l candido piè per l' erba fresca.

HER WALK, LOOKS, WORDS, AND AIR.

As o'er the fresh grass her fair form its sweet
And graceful passage makes at evening hours,
Seems as around the newly-wakening flowers
Found virtue issue from her delicate feet.
Love, which in true hearts only has his seat,
Nor elsewhere deigns to prove his certain powers,
So warm a pleasure from her bright eyes showers,
No other bliss I ask, no better meat.
And with her soft look and light step agree
Her mild and modest, never eager air,
And sweetest words in constant union rare.
From these four sparks – nor only these we see –
Springs the great fire wherein I live and burn,
Which makes me from the sun as night-birds turn.

Robert Macgregor.

SONNET CXXXIII.

S' io fossi stato fermo alla spelunca.

TO ONE WHO DESIRED LATIN VERSE OF HIM.

Still had I sojourn'd in that Delphic cave
Where young Apollo prophet first became,
Verona, Mantua were not sole in fame,
But Florence, too, her poet now might have:
But since the waters of that spring no more
Enrich my land, needs must that I pursue
Some other planet, and, with sickle new,
Reap from my field of sticks and thorns its store.
Dried is the olive: elsewhere turn'd the stream
Whose source from famed Parnassus was derived.
Whereby of yore it throve in best esteem.
Me fortune thus, or fault perchance, deprived
Of all good fruit – unless eternal Jove
Shower on my head some favour from above.

Robert Macgregor.

SONNET CXXXIV.

Quando Amor i begli occhi a terra inchina.

LAURA SINGS.

If Love her beauteous eyes to earth incline,
And all her soul concentring in a sigh,
Then breathe it in her voice of melody,
Floating clear, soft, angelical, divine;
My heart, forth-stolen so gently, I resign,
And, all my hopes and wishes changed, I cry, –
"Oh, may my last breath pass thus blissfully,
If Heaven so sweet a death for me design!"
But the rapt sense, by such enchantment bound,
And the strong will, thus listening to possess
Heaven's joys on earth, my spirit's flight delay.
And thus I live; and thus drawn out and wound
Is my life's thread, in dreamy blessedness,
By this sole syren from the realms of day.

Lady Dacre.

Her bright and love-lit eyes on earth she bends –
Concentres her rich breath in one full sigh –
A brief pause – a fond hush – her voice on high,
Clear, soft, angelical, divine, ascends.
Such rapine sweet through all my heart extends,
New thoughts and wishes so within me vie,
Perforce I say, – "Thus be it mine to die,
If Heaven to me so fair a doom intends!"
But, ah! those sounds whose sweetness laps my sense,
The strong desire of more that in me yearns,
Restrain my spirit in its parting hence.
Thus at her will I live; thus winds and turns
The yarn of life which to my lot is given,
Earth's single siren, sent to us from heaven.

Robert Macgregor.

SONNET CXXXV.

Amor mi manda quel dolce pensero.

LIFE WILL FAIL HIM BEFORE HOPE.

Love to my mind recalling that sweet thought,
The ancient confidant our lives between,
Well comforts me, and says I ne'er have been
So near as now to what I hoped and sought.
I, who at times with dangerous falsehood fraught,
At times with partial truth, his words have seen,
Live in suspense, still missing the just mean,
'Twixt yea and nay a constant battle fought.
Meanwhile the years pass on: and I behold
In my true glass the adverse time draw near
Her promise and my hope which limits here.
So let it be: alone I grow not old;
Changes not e'en with age my loving troth;
My fear is this – the short life left us both.

Robert Macgregor.

SONNET CXXXVI.

Pien d' un vago pensier, che me desvia.

HIS TONGUE IS TIED BY EXCESS OF PASSION.

Such vain thought as wonted to mislead me
In desert hope, by well-assurèd moan,
Makes me from company to live alone,
In following her whom reason bids me flee.
She fleeth as fast by gentle cruelty;
And after her my heart would fain be gone,
But armèd sighs my way do stop anon,
'Twixt hope and dread locking my liberty;
Yet as I guess, under disdainful brow
One beam of ruth is in her cloudy look:
Which comforteth the mind, that erst for fear shook:
And therewithal bolded I seek the way how
To utter the smart I suffer within;
But such it is, I not how to begin.

Sir Thomas Wyatt

Full of a tender thought, which severs me
From all my kind, a lonely musing thing,
From my breast's solitude I sometimes spring,
Still seeking her whom most I ought to flee;
And see her pass though soft, so adverse she,
That my soul spreads for flight a trembling wing:
Of armèd sighs such legions does she bring,
The fair antagonist of Love and me.
Yet from beneath that dark disdainful brow,
Or much I err, one beam of pity flows,
Soothing with partial warmth my heart's distress:
Again my bosom feels its wonted glow!
But when my simple hope I would disclose,
My o'er-fraught faltering tongue the crowded thoughts oppress.

Francis Wrangham.

SONNET CXXXVII.

Più volte già dal bel sembiante umano.

LOVE UNMANS HIS RESOLUTION.

Oft as her angel face compassion wore,
With tears whose eloquence scarce fails to move,
With bland and courteous speech, I boldly strove
To soothe my foe, and in meek guise implore:
But soon her eyes inspire vain hopes no more;
For all my fortune, all my fate in love,
My life, my death, the good, the ills I prove,
To her are trusted by one sovereign power.
Hence 'tis, whene'er my lips would silence break,
Scarce can I hear the accents which I vent,
By passion render'd spiritless and weak.
Ah! now I find that fondness to excess
Fetters the tongue, and overpowers intent:
Faint is the flame that language can express!

Dr Nott

Oft have I meant my passion to declare,
When fancy read compliance in her eyes;
And oft with courteous speech, with love-lorn sighs,
Have wish'd to soften my obdurate fair:
But let that face one look of anger wear,
The intention fades; for all that fate supplies,
Or good, or ill, all, all that I can prize,
My life, my death, Love trusts to her dear care.
E'en I can scarcely hear my amorous moan,
So much my voice by passion is confined;
So faint, so timid are my accents grown!
Ah! now the force of love I plainly see;
What can the tongue, or what the impassion'd mind?
He that could speak his love, ne'er loved like me.

Anonymous 1777.

SONNET CXXXVIII.

Giunto m' ha Amor fra belle e crude braccia.

HE CANNOT END HER CRUELTY, NOR SHE HIS HOPE.

Me Love has left in fair cold arms to lie,
Which kill me wrongfully: if I complain,
My martyrdom is doubled, worse my pain:
Better in silence love, and loving die!
For she the frozen Rhine with burning eye
Can melt at will, the hard rock break in twain,
So equal to her beauty her disdain
That others' pleasure wakes her angry sigh.
A breathing moving marble all the rest,
Of very adamant is made her heart,
So hard, to move it baffles all my art.
Despite her lowering brow and haughty breast,
One thing she cannot, my fond heart deter
From tender hopes and passionate sighs for her.

Robert Macgregor.

SONNET CXXXIX.

O Invidia, nemica di virtute.

ENVY MAY DISTURB, BUT CANNOT DESTROY HIS HOPE.

O deadly Envy, virtue's constant foe,
With good and lovely eager to contest!
Stealthily, by what way, in that fair breast
Hast entrance found? by what arts changed it so?
Thence by the roots my weal hast thou uptorn,
Too blest in love hast shown me to that fair
Who welcomed once my chaste and humble prayer,
But seems to treat me now with hate and scorn.
But though you may by acts severe and ill
Sigh at my good and smile at my distress,
You cannot change for me a single thought.
Not though a thousand times each day she kill
Can I or hope in her or love her less.
For though she scare, Love confidence has taught.

Robert Macgregor.

SONNET CXL.

Mirando 'l sol de' begli occhi sereno.

THE SWEETS AND BITTERS OF LOVE.

Marking of those bright eyes the sun serene
Where reigneth Love, who mine obscures and grieves,
My hopeless heart the weary spirit leaves
Once more to gain its paradise terrene;
Then, finding full of bitter-sweet the scene,
And in the world how vast the web it weaves.
A secret sigh for baffled love it heaves,
Whose spurs so sharp, whose curb so hard have been.
By these two contrary and mix'd extremes,
With frozen or with fiery wishes fraught,
To stand 'tween misery and bliss she seems:
Seldom in glad and oft in gloomy thought,
But mostly contrite for its bold emprize,
For of like seed like fruit must ever rise!

Robert Macgregor.

SONNET CXLI.

Fera stella (se 'l cielo ha forza in noi).

TO PINE FOR HER IS BETTER THAN TO ENJOY HAPPINESS WITH ANY OTHER.

Ill-omen'd was that star's malignant gleam
That ruled my hapless birth; and dim the morn
That darted on my infant eyes the beam;
And harsh the wail, that told a man was born;
And hard the sterile earth, which first was worn
Beneath my infant feet; but harder far,
And harsher still, the tyrant maid, whose scorn,
In league with savage Love, inflamed the war
Of all my passions. – Love himself more tame,
With pity soothes my ills; while that cold heart,
Insensible to the devouring flame
Which wastes my vitals, triumphs in my smart.
One thought is comfort – that her scorn to bear,
Excels e'er prosperous love, with other earthly fair.

Lord Woodhouselee.

An evil star usher'd my natal morn
(If heaven have o'er us power, as some have said),
Hard was the cradle where I lay when born,
And hard the earth where first my young feet play'd;
Cruel the lady who, with eyes of scorn
And fatal bow, whose mark I still was made,
Dealt me the wound, O Love, which since I mourn
Whose cure thou only, with those arms, canst aid.
But, ah! to thee my torments pleasure bring:
She, too, severer would have wished the blow,
A spear-head thrust, and not an arrow-sting.
One comfort rests – better to suffer so
For her, than others to enjoy: and I,
Sworn on thy golden dart, on this for death rely.

Robert Macgregor.

SONNET CXLII.

Quando mi vene innanzi il tempo e 'l loco.

RECOLLECTIONS OF EARLY LOVE.

The time and scene where I a slave became
When I remember, and the knot so dear
Which Love's own hand so firmly fasten'd here,
Which made my bitter sweet, my grief a game;
My heart, with fuel stored, is, as a flame
Of those soft sighs familiar to mine ear,
So lit within, its very sufferings cheer;
On these I live, and other aid disclaim.
That sun, alone which beameth for my sight,
With his strong rays my ruin'd bosom burns
Now in the eve of life as in its prime,
And from afar so gives me warmth and light,
Fresh and entire, at every hour, returns
On memory the knot, the scene, the time.

Robert Macgregor.

SONNET CXLIII.

Per mezzo i boschi inospiti e selvaggi.

EVER THINKING ON HER, HE PASSES FEARLESS AND SAFE THROUGH THE FOREST OF ARDENNES.

Through woods inhospitable, wild, I rove,
Where armèd travellers bend their fearful way;
Nor danger dread, save from that sun of love,
Bright sun! which darts a soul-enflaming ray.
Of her I sing, all-thoughtless as I stray,
Whose sweet idea strong as heaven's shall prove:
And oft methinks these pines, these beeches, move
Like nymphs; 'mid which fond fancy sees her play
I seem to hear her, when the whispering gale
Steals through some thick-wove branch, when sings a bird,
When purls the stream along yon verdant vale.
How grateful might this darksome wood appear,
Where horror reigns, where scarce a sound is heard;
But, ah! 'tis far from all my heart holds dear.

Anonymous 1777.

Amid the wild wood's lone and difficult ways,
Where travel at great risk e'en men in arms,
I pass secure – for only me alarms
That sun, which darts of living love the rays –
Singing fond thoughts in simple lays to her
Whom time and space so little hide from me;
E'en here her form, nor hers alone, I see,
But maids and matrons in each beech and fir:
Methinks I hear her when the bird's soft moan,
The sighing leaves I hear, or through the dell
Where its bright lapse some murmuring rill pursues.
Rarely of shadowing wood the silence lone,
The solitary horror pleased so well,
Except that of my sun too much I lose.

Robert Macgregor.

SONNET CXLIV

Mille piagge in un giorno e mille rivi.

TO BE NEAR HER RECOMPENSES HIM FOR ALL THE PERILS OF THE WAY.

Love, who his votary wings in heart and feet,
To the third heaven that lightly he may soar,
In one short day has many a stream and shore
Given to me, in famed Ardennes, to meet.
Unarm'd and single to have pass'd is sweet
Where war in earnest strikes, nor tells before –
A helmless, sail-less ship 'mid ocean's roar –
My breast with dark and fearful thoughts replete;
But reach'd my dangerous journey's far extreme,
Remembering whence I came, and with whose wings,
From too great courage conscious terror springs.
But this fair country and belovèd stream
With smiling welcome reassures my heart,
Where dwells its sole light ready to depart.

Robert Macgregor.

SONNET CXLV.

Amor mi sprona in un tempo ed affrena.

HE HEARS THE VOICE OF REASON, BUT CANNOT OBEY.

Love in one instant spurs me and restrains,
Assures and frightens, freezes me and burns,
Smiles now and scowls, now summons me and spurns,
In hope now holds me, plunges now in pains:
Now high, now low, my weary heart he hurls,
Until fond passion loses quite the path,
And highest pleasure seems to stir but wrath –
My harass'd mind on such strange errors feeds!
A friendly thought there points the proper track,
Not of such grief as from the full eye breaks,
To go where soon it hopes to be at ease,
But, as if greater power thence turn'd it back,
Despite itself, another way it takes,
And to its own slow death and mine agrees.

Robert Macgregor.

SONNET CXLVI.

Geri, quando talor meco s' adira.

HE APPEASES HER BY HUMILITY, AND EXHORTS A FRIEND TO DO LIKEWISE.

When my sweet foe, so haughty oft and high,
Moved my brief ire no more my sight can thole,
One comfort is vouchsafed me lest I die,
Through whose sole strength survives my harass'd soul;
Where'er her eyes – all light which would deny
To my sad life – in scorn or anger roll,
Mine with such true humility reply,
Soon their meek glances all her rage control,
Were it not so, methinks I less could brook
To gaze on hers than on Medusa's mien,
Which turn'd to marble all who met her look.
My friend, act thus with thine, for closed I ween
All other aid, and nothing flight avails
Against the wings on which our master sails.

Robert Macgregor.

SONNET CXLVII.

Po, ben puo' tu portartene la scorza.

TO THE RIVER PO, ON QUITTING LAURA.

Thou Po to distant realms this frame mayst bear,
On thy all-powerful, thy impetuous tide;
But the free spirit that within doth bide
Nor for thy might, nor any might doth care:
Not varying here its course, nor shifting there,
Upon the favouring gale it joys to glide;
Plying its wings toward the laurel's pride,
In spite of sails or oars, of sea or air.
Monarch of floods, magnificent and strong,
That meet'st the sun as he leads on the day,
But in the west dost quit a fairer light;
Thy curvèd course this body wafts along;
My spirit on Love's pinions speeds its way,
And to its darling home directs its flight!

Dr Nott

Po, thou upon thy strong and rapid tide,
This frame corporeal mayst onward bear:
But a free spirit is concealèd there,
Which nor thy power nor any power can guide.
That spirit, light on breeze auspicious buoy'd,
With course unvarying backward cleaves the air –
Nor wave, nor wind, nor sail, nor oar its care –
And plies its wings, and seeks the laurel's pride.
'Tis thine, proud king of rivers, eastward borne
To meet the sun, as he leads on the day;
And from a brighter west 'tis thine to turn:
Thy hornèd flood these passive limbs obey –
But, uncontrollèd, to its sweet sojourn
On Love's untiring plumes my spirit speeds its way.

Francis Wrangham.

SONNET CXLVIII.

Amor fra l' orbe una leggiadra rete.

HE COMPARES HIMSELF TO A BIRD CAUGHT IN A NET.

Love 'mid the grass beneath a laurel green –
The plant divine which long my flame has fed,
Whose shade for me less bright than sad is seen –
A cunning net of gold and pearls had spread:
Its bait the seed he sows and reaps, I ween
Bitter and sweet, which I desire, yet dread:
Gentle and soft his call, as ne'er has been
Since first on Adam's eyes the day was shed:
And the bright light which disenthrones the sun
Was flashing round, and in her hand, more fair
Than snow or ivory, was the master rope.
So fell I in the snare; their slave so won
Her speech angelical and winning air,
Pleasure, and fond desire, and sanguine hope.

Robert Macgregor.

SONNET CXLIX.

Amor che 'ncende 'l cor d' ardente zelo.

LOVE AND JEALOUSY.

'Tis Love's caprice to freeze the bosom now
With bolts of ice, with shafts of flame now burn;
And which his lighter pang, I scarce discern –
Or hope or fear, or whelming fire or snow.
In heat I shiver, and in cold I glow,
Now thrill'd with love, with jealousy now torn:
As if her thin robe by a rival worn,
Or veil, had screen'd him from my vengeful blow
But more 'tis mine to burn by night, by day;
And how I love the death by which I die,
Nor thought can grasp, nor tongue of bard can sing:
Not so my freezing fire – impartially
She shines to all; and who would speed his way
To that high beam, in vain expands his fluttering wing.

Francis Wrangham.

Love with hot zeal now burns the heart within,
Now holds it fetter'd with a frozen fear,
Leaving it doubtful to our judgment here
If hope or dread, if flame or frost, shall win.
In June I shiver, burn December in,
Full of desires, from jealousy ne'er clear;
E'en as a lady who her loving fee
Hides 'neath a little veil of texture thin.
Of the two ills the first is all mine own,
By day, by night to burn; how sweet that pain
Dwells not in thought, nor ever poet sings:
Not so the other, my fair flame, is shown,
She levels all: who hopes the crest to gain
Of that proud light expands in vain his wings.

Robert Macgregor.

SONNET CL.

Se 'l dolce sguardo di costei m' ancide.

HE IS CONTINUALLY IN FEAR OF DISPLEASING HER.

If thus the dear glance of my lady slay,
On her sweet sprightly speech if dangers wait,
If o'er me Love usurp a power so great,
Oft as she speaks, or when her sun-smiles play;
Alas! what were it if she put away,
Or for my fault, or by my luckless fate,
Her eyes from pity, and to death's full hate,
Which now she keeps aloof, should then betray.
Thus if at heart with terror I am cold,
When o'er her fair face doubtful shadows spring,
The feeling has its source in sufferings old.
Woman by nature is a fickle thing,
And female hearts – time makes the proverb sure –
Can never long one state of love endure.

Robert Macgregor.

If the soft glance, the speech, both kind and wise,
Of that beloved one can wound me so,
And if, whene'er she lets her accents flow,
Or even smiles, Love gains such victories;
Alas! what should I do, were those dear eyes,
Which now secure my life through weal and woe,
From fault of mine, or evil fortune, slow
To shed on me their light in pity's guise?
And if my trembling spirit groweth cold
Whene'er I see change to her aspect spring,
This fear is only born of trials old;
(Woman by nature is a fickle thing,)
And hence I know her heart hath power to hold
But a brief space Love's sweet imagining!

Mrs Wrottesley.

SONNET CLI.

Amor, Natura, e la bell' alma umile.

DURING A SERIOUS ILLNESS OF LAURA.

Love, Nature, Laura's gentle self combines,
She where each lofty virtue dwells and reigns,
Against my peace: To pierce with mortal pains
Love toils – such ever are his stern designs.
Nature by bonds so slight to earth confines
Her slender form, a breath may break its chains;
And she, so much her heart the world disdains,
Longer to tread life's wearying round repines.
Hence still in her sweet frame we view decay
All that to earth can joy and radiance lend,
Or serve as mirror to this laggard age;
And Death's dread purpose should not Pity stay,
Too well I see where all those hopes must end,
With which I fondly soothed my lingering pilgrimage.

Francis Wrangham.

Love, Nature, and that gentle soul as bright,
Where every lofty virtue dwells and reigns,
Are sworn against my peace. As wont, Love strains
His every power that I may perish quite.
Nature her delicate form by bonds so slight
Holds in existence, that no help sustains;
She is so modest that she now disdains
Longer to brook this vile life's painful fight.
Thus fades and fails the spirit day by day,
Which on those dear and lovely limbs should wait,
Our mirror of true grace which wont to give:
And soon, if Mercy turn not Death away,
Alas! too well I see in what sad state
Are those vain hopes wherein I loved to live.

Robert Macgregor.

SONNET CLII.

Questa Fenice dell' aurata piuma.

HE COMPARES HER TO THE PHŒNIX.

This wondrous Phœnix with the golden plumes
Forms without art so rare a ring to deck
That beautiful and soft and snowy neck,
That every heart it melts, and mine consumes:
Forms, too, a natural diadem which lights
The air around, whence Love with silent steel
Draws liquid subtle fire, which still I feel
Fierce burning me though sharpest winter bites;
Border'd with azure, a rich purple vest,
Sprinkled with roses, veils her shoulders fair:
Rare garment hers, as grace unique, alone!
Fame, in the opulent and odorous breast
Of Arab mountains, buries her sole lair,
Who in our heaven so high a pitch has flown.

Robert Macgregor.

SONNET CLIII.

Se Virgilio ed Omero avessin visto.

THE MOST FAMOUS POETS OF ANTIQUITY WOULD HAVE SUNG HER ONLY, HAD THEY SEEN HER.

Had tuneful Maro seen, and Homer old,
The living sun which here mine eyes behold,
The best powers they had join'd of either lyre,
Sweetness and strength, that fame she might acquire;
Unsung had been, with vex'd Æneas, then
Achilles and Ulysses, godlike men,
And for nigh sixty years who ruled so well
The world; and who before Ægysthus fell;
Nay, that old flower of virtues and of arms,
As this new flower of chastity and charms,
A rival star, had scarce such radiance flung.
In rugged verse him honour'd Ennius sung,
I her in mine. Grant, Heaven! on my poor lays
She frown not, nor disdain my humble praise.

Anonymous

SONNET CLIV.

Giunto Alessandro alla famosa tomba.

HE FEARS THAT HE IS INCAPABLE OF WORTHILY CELEBRATING HER.

The son of Philip, when he saw the tomb
Of fierce Achilles, with a sigh, thus said:
"O happy, whose achievements erst found room
From that illustrious trumpet to be spread
O'er earth for ever!" – But, beyond the gloom
Of deep Oblivion shall that loveliest maid,
Whose like to view seems not of earthly doom,
By my imperfect accents be convey'd?
Her of the Homeric, the Orphèan Lyre,
Most worthy, or that shepherd, Mantua's pride,
To be the theme of their immortal lays;
Her stars and unpropitious fate denied
This palm: – and me bade to such height aspire,
Who, haply, dim her glories by my praise.

Capel Lofft.

When Alexander at the famous tomb
Of fierce Achilles stood, the ambitious sigh
Burst from his bosom – "Fortunate! on whom
Th' eternal bard shower'd honours bright and high."
But, ah! for so to each is fix'd his doom,
This pure fair dove, whose like by mortal eye
Was never seen, what poor and scanty room
For her great praise can my weak verse supply?
Whom, worthiest Homer's line and Orpheus' song,
Or his whom reverent Mantua still admires –
Sole and sufficient she to wake such lyres!
An adverse star, a fate here only wrong,
Entrusts to one who worships her dear name,
Yet haply injures by his praise her fame.

Robert Macgregor.

SONNET CLV.

Almo Sol, quella fronde ch' io sola amo.

TO THE SUN, WHOSE SETTING HID LAURA'S DWELLING FROM HIS VIEW.

O blessed Sun! that sole sweet leaf I love,
First loved by thee, in its fair seat, alone,
Bloometh without a peer, since from above
To Adam first our shining ill was shown.
Pause we to look on her! Although to stay
Thy course I pray thee, yet thy beams retire;
Their shades the mountains fling, and parting day
Parts me from all I most on earth desire.
The shadows from yon gentle heights that fall,
Where sparkles my sweet fire, where brightly grew
That stately laurel from a sucker small,
Increasing, as I speak, hide from my view
The beauteous landscape and the blessèd scene,
Where dwells my true heart with its only queen.

Robert Macgregor.

SONNET CLVI.

Passa la nave mia colma d' oblio.

UNDER THE FIGURE OF A TEMPEST-TOSSED VESSEL, HE DESCRIBES HIS OWN SAD STATE.

My bark, deep laden with oblivion, rides
O'er boisterous waves, through winter's midnight gloom,
'Twixt Scylla and Charybdis, while, in room
Of pilot, Love, mine enemy, presides;
At every oar a guilty fancy bides,
Holding at nought the tempest and the tomb;
A moist eternal wind the sails consume,
Of sighs, of hopes, and of desire besides.
A shower of tears, a fog of chill disdain
Bathes and relaxes the o'er-wearied cords,
With error and with ignorance entwined;
My two loved lights their wonted aid restrain;
Reason or Art, storm-quell'd, no help affords,
Nor hope remains the wish'd-for port to find.

Lord Charlemont.

My lethe-freighted bark with reckless prore
Cleaves the rough sea 'neath wintry midnight skies,
My old foe at the helm our compass eyes,
With Scylla and Charybdis on each shore,
A prompt and daring thought at every oar,
Which equally the storm and death defies,
While a perpetual humid wind of sighs,
Of hopes, and of desires, its light sail tore.
Bathe and relax its worn and weary shrouds
(Which ignorance with error intertwines),
Torrents of tears, of scorn and anger clouds;
Hidden the twin dear lights which were my signs;
Reason and Art amid the waves lie dead,
And hope of gaining port is almost fled.

Robert Macgregor.

SONNET CLVII.

Una candida cerva sopra l' erba.

THE VISION OF THE FAWN.

Beneath a laurel, two fair streams between,
At early sunrise of the opening year,
A milk-white fawn upon the meadow green,
Of gold its either horn, I saw appear;
So mild, yet so majestic, was its mien,
I left, to follow, all my labours here,
As miners after treasure, in the keen
Desire of new, forget the old to fear.
"Let none impede" – so, round its fair neck, run
The words in diamond and topaz writ –
"My lord to give me liberty sees fit."
And now the sun his noontide height had won
When I, with weary though unsated view,
Fell in the stream – and so my vision flew.

Robert Macgregor.

A form I saw with secret awe, nor ken I what it warns;
Pure as the snow, a gentle doe it seem'd, with silver horns:
Erect she stood, close by a wood, between two running streams;
And brightly shone the morning sun upon that land of dreams!
The pictured hind fancy design'd glowing with love and hope;
Graceful she stepp'd, but distant kept, like the timid antelope;
Playful, yet coy, with secret joy her image fill'd my soul;
And o'er the sense soft influence of sweet oblivion stole.
Gold I beheld and emerald on the collar that she wore;
Words, too – but theirs were characters of legendary lore.
"Cæsar's decree hath made me free; and through his solemn charge,
Untouch'd by men o'er hill and glen I wander here at large."
The sun had now, with radiant brow, climb'd his meridian throne,
Yet still mine eye untiringly gazed on that lovely one.
A voice was heard – quick disappear'd my dream – the spell was broken.
Then came distress: to the consciousness of life I had awoken.

Father Prout.

SONNET CLVIII.

Siccome eterna vita è veder Dio.

ALL HIS HAPPINESS IS IN GAZING UPON HER.

As life eternal is with God to be,
No void left craving, there of all possess'd,
So, lady mine, to be with you makes blest,
This brief frail span of mortal life to me.
So fair as now ne'er yet was mine to see –
If truth from eyes to heart be well express'd –
Lovely and blessèd spirit of my breast,
Which levels all high hopes and wishes free.
Nor would I more demand if less of haste
She show'd to part; for if, as legends tell
And credence find, are some who live by smell,
On water some, or fire who touch and taste,
All, things which neither strength nor sweetness give,
Why should not I upon your dear sight live?

Robert Macgregor.

SONNET CLIX.

Stiamo, Amor, a veder la gloria nostra.

TO LOVE, ON LAURA WALKING ABROAD.

Here stand we, Love, our glory to behold –
How, passing Nature, lovely, high, and rare!
Behold! what showers of sweetness falling there!
What floods of light by heaven to earth unroll'd!
How shine her robes, in purple, pearls, and gold,
So richly wrought, with skill beyond compare!
How glance her feet! – her beaming eyes how fair
Through the dark cloister which these hills enfold!
The verdant turf, and flowers of thousand hues
Beneath yon oak's old canopy of state,
Spring round her feet to pay their amorous duty.
The heavens, in joyful reverence, cannot choose
But light up all their fires, to celebrate
Her praise, whose presence charms their awful beauty.

J.H. Merivale.

Here tarry, Love, our glory to behold;
Nought in creation so sublime we trace;
Ah! see what sweetness showers upon that face,
Heaven's brightness to this earth those eyes unfold!
See, with what magic art, pearls, purple, gold,
That form transcendant, unexampled, grace:
Beneath the shadowing hills observe her pace,
Her glance replete with elegance untold!
The verdant turf, and flowers of every hue,
Clustering beneath yon aged holm-oak's gloom,
For the sweet pressure of her fair feet sue;
The orbs of fire that stud yon beauteous sky,
Cheer'd by her presence and her smiles, assume
Superior lustre and serenity.

Dr Nott

SONNET CLX.

Pasco la mente d' un sì nobil cibo.

TO SEE AND HEAR HER IS HIS GREATEST BLISS.

I feed my fancy on such noble food,
That Jove I envy not his godlike meal;
I see her – joy invades me like a flood,
And lethe of all other bliss I feel;
I hear her – instantly that music rare
Bids from my captive heart the fond sigh flow;
Borne by the hand of Love I know not where,
A double pleasure in one draught I know.
Even in heaven that dear voice pleaseth well,
So winning are its words, its sound so sweet,
None can conceive, save who had heard, their spell;
Thus, in the same small space, visibly, meet
All charms of eye and ear wherewith our race
Art, Genius, Nature, Heaven have join'd to grace.

Robert Macgregor.

Such noble aliment sustains my soul,
That Jove I envy not his godlike food;
I gaze on her – and feel each other good
Engulph'd in that blest draught at Lethe's bowl:
Her every word I in my heart enrol,
That on its grief it still may constant brood;
Prostrate by Love – my doom not understood
From that one form, I feel a twin control.
My spirit drinks the music of her voice,
Whose speaking harmony (to heaven so dear)
They only feel who in its tone partake:
Again within her face my eyes rejoice,
For in its gentle lineaments appear
What Genius, Nature, Art, and Heaven can wake.

Miss Wollaston.

SONNET CLXI.

L' aura gentil che rasserena i poggi.

JOURNEYING TO VISIT LAURA, HE FEELS RENEWED ARDOUR AS HE APPROACHES.

The gale, that o'er yon hills flings softer blue,
And wakes to life each bud that gems the glade,
I know; its breathings such impression made,
Wafting me fame, but wafting sorrow too:
My wearied soul to soothe, I bid adieu
To those dear Tuscan haunts I first survey'd;
And, to dispel the gloom around me spread,
I seek this day my cheering sun to view,
Whose sweet attraction is so strong, so great,
That Love again compels me to its light;
Then he so dazzles me, that vain were flight.
Not arms to brave, 'tis wings to 'scape, my fate
I ask; but by those beams I'm doom'd to die,
When distant which consume, and which enflame when nigh.

Dr Nott

The gentle air, which brightens each green hill,
Wakening the flowers that paint this bowery glade,
I recognise it by its soft breath still,
My sorrow and renown which long has made:
Again where erst my sick heart shelter sought,
From my dear native Tuscan air I flee:
That light may cheer my dark and troubled thought,
I seek my sun, and hope to-day to see.
That sun so great and genial sweetness brings,
That Love compels me to his beams again,
Which then so dazzle me that flight is vain:
I ask for my escape not arms, but wings:
Heaven by this light condemns me sure to die,
Which from afar consumes, and burns when nigh.

Robert Macgregor.

SONNET CLXII.

Di dì in dì vo cangiando il viso e 'l pelo.

HIS WOUNDS CAN BE HEALED ONLY BY PITY OR DEATH.

I alter day by day in hair and mien,
Yet shun not the old dangerous baits and dear,
Nor sever from the laurel, limed and green,
Which nor the scorching sun, nor fierce cold sear.
Dry shall the sea, the sky be starless seen,
Ere I shall cease to covet and to fear
Her lovely shadow, and – which ill I screen –
To like, yet loathe, the deep wound cherish'd here:
For never hope I respite from my pain,
From bones and nerves and flesh till I am free,
Unless mine enemy some pity deign,
Till things impossible accomplish'd be,
None but herself or death the blow can heal
Which Love from her bright eyes has left my heart to feel.

Robert Macgregor.

SONNET CLXIII.

L' aura serena che fra verdi fronde.

THE GENTLE BREEZE (L' AURA) RECALLS TO HIM THE TIME WHEN HE FIRST SAW HER.

The gentle gale, that plays my face around,
Murmuring sweet mischief through the verdant grove,
To fond remembrance brings the time, when Love
First gave his deep, although delightful wound;
Gave me to view that beauteous face, ne'er found
Veil'd, as disdain or jealousy might move;
To view her locks that shone bright gold above,
Then loose, but now with pearls and jewels bound:
Those locks she sweetly scatter'd to the wind,
And then coil'd up again so gracefully,
That but to think on it still thrills the sense.
These Time has in more sober braids confined;
And bound my heart with such a powerful tie,
That death alone can disengage it thence.

Dr Nott

The balmy airs that from yon leafy spray
My fever'd brow with playful murmurs greet,
Recall to my fond heart the fatal day
When Love his first wound dealt, so deep yet sweet,
And gave me the fair face – in scorn away
Since turn'd, or hid by jealousy – to meet;
The locks, which pearls and gems now oft array,
Whose shining tints with finest gold compete,
So sweetly on the wind were then display'd,
Or gather'd in with such a graceful art,
Their very thought with passion thrills my mind.
Time since has twined them in more sober braid,
And with a snare so powerful bound my heart,
Death from its fetters only can unbind.

Robert Macgregor.

SONNET CLXIV.

L' aura celeste che 'n quel verde Lauro.

HER HAIR AND EYES.

The heavenly airs from yon green laurel roll'd,
Where Love to Phœbus whilom dealt his stroke,
Where on my neck was placed so sweet a yoke,
That freedom thence I hope not to behold,
O'er me prevail, as o'er that Arab old
Medusa, when she changed him to an oak;
Nor ever can the fairy knot be broke
Whose light outshines the sun, not merely gold;
I mean of those bright locks the curlèd snare
Which folds and fastens with so sweet a grace
My soul, whose humbleness defends alone.
Her mere shade freezes with a cold despair
My heart, and tinges with pale fear my face;
And oh! her eyes have power to make me stone.

Robert Macgregor.

SONNET CLXV.

L' aura soave ch' al sol spiega e vibra.

HIS HEART LIES TANGLED IN HER HAIR.

The pleasant gale, that to the sun unplaits
And spreads the gold Love's fingers weave, and braid
O'er her fine eyes, and all around her head,
Fetters my heart, the wishful sigh creates:
No nerve but thrills, no artery but beats,
Approaching my fair arbiter with dread,
Who in her doubtful scale hath ofttimes weigh'd
Whether or death or life on me awaits;
Beholding, too, those eyes their fires display,
And on those shoulders shine such wreaths of hair,
Whose witching tangles my poor heart ensnare.
But how this magic's wrought I cannot say;
For twofold radiance doth my reason blind,
And sweetness to excess palls and o'erpowers my mind.

Dr Nott

The soft gale to the sun which shakes and spreads
The gold which Love's own hand has spun and wrought.
There, with her bright eyes and those fairy threads,
Binds my poor heart and sifts each idle thought.
My veins of blood, my bones of marrow fail,
Thrills all my frame when I, to hear or gaze,
Draw near to her, who oft, in balance frail,
My life and death together holds and weighs,
And see those love-fires shine wherein I burn,
And, as its snow each sweetest shoulder heaves,
Flash the fair tresses right and left by turn;
Verse fails to paint what fancy scarce conceives.
From two such lights is intellect distress'd,
And by such sweetness weary and oppress'd.

Robert Macgregor.

SONNET CLXVI.

O bella man, che mi distringi 'l core.

THE STOLEN GLOVE.

O beauteous hand! that dost my heart subdue,
And in a little space my life confine;
Hand where their skill and utmost efforts join
Nature and Heaven, their plastic powers to show!
Sweet fingers, seeming pearls of orient hue,
To my wounds only cruel, fingers fine!
Love, who towards me kindness doth design,
For once permits ye naked to our view.
Thou glove most dear, most elegant and white,
Encasing ivory tinted with the rose;
More precious covering ne'er met mortal sight.
Would I such portion of thy veil had gain'd!
O fleeting gifts which fortune's hand bestows!
'Tis justice to restore what theft alone obtain'd.

Dr Nott

O beauteous hand! which robb'st me of my heart,
And holdest all my life in little space;
Hand! which their utmost effort and best art
Nature and Heaven alike have join'd to grace;
O sister pearls of orient hue, ye fine
And fairy fingers! to my wounds alone
Cruel and cold, does Love awhile incline
In my behalf, that naked ye are shown?
O glove! most snowy, delicate, and dear,
Which spotless ivory and fresh roses set,
Where can on earth a sweeter spoil be met,
Unless her fair veil thus reward us here?
Inconstancy of human things! the theft
Late won and dearly prized too soon from me is reft!

Robert Macgregor.

SONNET CLXVII.

Non pur quell' una bella ignuda mano.

HE RETURNS THE GLOVE, BEWAILING THE EFFECT OF HER BEAUTY.

Not of one dear hand only I complain,
Which hides it, to my loss, again from view,
But its fair fellow and her soft arms too
Are prompt my meek and passive heart to pain.
Love spreads a thousand toils, nor one in vain,
Amid the many charms, bright, pure, and new,
That so her high and heavenly part endue,
No style can equal it, no mind attain.
That starry forehead and those tranquil eyes,
The fair angelic mouth, where pearl and rose
Contrast each other, whence rich music flows,
These fill the gazer with a fond surprise,
The fine head, the bright tresses which defied
The sun to match them in his noonday pride.

Robert Macgregor.

SONNET CLXVIII.

Mia ventura ed Amor m' avean sì adorno.

HE REGRETS HAVING RETURNED HER GLOVE.

Me Love and Fortune then supremely bless'd!
Her glove which gold and silken broidery bore!
I seem'd to reach of utmost bliss the crest,
Musing within myself on her who wore.
Ne'er on that day I think, of days the best,
Which made me rich, then beggar'd as before,
But rage and sorrow fill mine aching breast.
With slighted love and self-shame boiling o'er;
That on my precious prize in time of need
I kept not hold, nor made a firmer stand
'Gainst what at best was merely angel force,
That my feet were not wings their flight to speed,
And so at last take vengeance on the hand,
Make my poor eyes of tears the too oft source.

Robert Macgregor.

SONNET CLXIX.

D' un bel, chiaro, polito e vivo ghiaccio.

THOUGH RACKED BY AGONY, HE DOES NOT COMPLAIN OF HER.

The flames that ever on my bosom prey
From living ice or cold fair marble pour,
And so exhaust my veins and waste my core,
Almost insensibly I melt away.
Death, his stern arm already rear'd to slay,
As thunders angry heaven or lions roar,
Pursues my life that vainly flies before,
While I with terror shake, and mute obey.
And yet, were Love and Pity friends, they might
A double column for my succour throw
Between my worn soul and the mortal blow:
It may not be; such feelings in the sight
Of my loved foe and mistress never stir;
The fault is in my fortune, not in her.

Robert Macgregor.

SONNET CLXX.

Lasso, ch' i' ardo, ed altri non mel crede!

POSTERITY WILL ACCORD TO HIM THE PITY WHICH LAURA REFUSES.

Alas, with ardour past belief I glow!
None doubt this truth, except one only fair,
Who all excels, for whom alone I care;
She plainly sees, yet disbelieves my woe.
O rich in charms, but poor in faith! canst thou
Look in these eyes, nor read my whole heart there?
Were I not fated by my baleful star,
For me from pity's fount might favour flow.
My flame, of which thou tak'st so little heed,
And thy high praises pour'd through all my song,
O'er many a breast may future influence spread:
These, my sweet fair, so warns prophetic thought,
Closed thy bright eye, and mute thy poet's tongue,
E'en after death shall still with sparks be fraught.

Dr Nott

Alas! I burn, yet credence fail to gain
All others credit it save only she
All others who excels, alone for me;
She seems to doubt it still, yet sees it plain
Infinite beauty, little faith and slow,
Perceive ye not my whole heart in mine eyes?
Well might I hope, save for my hostile skies,
From mercy's fount some pitying balm to flow.
Yet this my flame which scarcely moves your care,
And your warm praises sung in these fond rhymes,
May thousands yet inflame in after times;
These I foresee in fancy, my sweet fair,
Though your bright eyes be closed and cold my breath,
Shall lighten other loves and live in death.

Robert Macgregor.

SONNET CLXXI.

Anima, che diverse cose tante.

HE REJOICES AT BEING ON EARTH WITH HER, AS HE IS THEREBY ENABLED BETTER TO IMITATE HER VIRTUES.

Soul! with such various faculties endued
To think, write, speak, to read, to see, to hear;
My doting eyes! and thou, my faithful ear!
Where drinks my heart her counsels wise and good;
Your fortune smiles; if after or before,
The path were won so badly follow'd yet,
Ye had not then her bright eyes' lustre met,
Nor traced her light feet earth's green carpet o'er.
Now with so clear a light, so sure a sign,
'Twere shame to err or halt on the brief way
Which makes thee worthy of a home divine.
That better course, my weary will, essay!
To pierce the cloud of her sweet scorn be thine,
Pursuing her pure steps and heavenly ray.

Robert Macgregor.

SONNET CLXXII.

Dolci ire, dolci sdegni e dolci paci.

HE CONSOLES HIMSELF WITH THE THOUGHT THAT HE WILL BE ENVIED BY POSTERITY.

Sweet scorn, sweet anger, and sweet misery,
Forgiveness sweet, sweet burden, and sweet ill;
Sweet accents that mine ear so sweetly thrill,
That sweetly bland, now sweetly fierce can be.
Mourn not, my soul, but suffer silently;
And those embitter'd sweets thy cup that fill
With the sweet honour blend of loving still
Her whom I told: "Thou only pleasest me."
Hereafter, moved with envy, some may say:
"For that high-boasted beauty of his day
Enough the bard has borne!" then heave a sigh.
Others: "Oh! why, most hostile Fortune, why
Could not these eyes that lovely form survey?
Why was she early born, or wherefore late was I?"

Dr Nott

Sweet anger, sweet disdain, and peace as sweet,
Sweet ill, sweet pain, sweet burthen that I bear,
Sweet speech as sweetly heard; sweet speech, my fair!
That now enflames my soul, now cools its heat.
Patient, my soul! endure the wrongs you meet;
And all th' embitter'd sweets you're doomed to share
Blend with that sweetest bliss, the maid to greet
In these soft words, "Thou only art my care!"
Haply some youth shall sighing envious say,
"Enough has borne the bard so fond, so true,
For that bright beauty, brightest of his day!"
While others cry, "Sad eyes! how hard your fate,
Why could I ne'er this matchless beauty view?
Why was she born so soon, or I so late?"

Anonymous 1777.

CANZONE XIX.

S' il dissi mai, ch' i' venga in odio a quella.

HE VEHEMENTLY REBUTS THE CHARGE OF LOVING ANOTHER.

Perdie! I said it not,
Nor never thought to do:
As well as I, ye wot
I have no power thereto.
And if I did, the lot
That first did me enchain
May never slake the knot,
But strait it to my pain.

And if I did, each thing
That may do harm or woe,
Continually may wring
My heart, where so I go!
Report may always ring
Of shame on me for aye,
If in my heart did spring
The words that you do say.

And if I did, each star
That is in heaven above,
May frown on me, to mar
The hope I have in love!
And if I did, such war
As they brought unto Troy,
Bring all my life afar
From all his lust and joy!

And if I did so say,
The beauty that me bound
Increase from day to day,
More cruel to my wound!
With all the moan that may

To plaint may turn my song;
My life may soon decay,
Without redress, by wrong!

If I be clear from thought,
Why do you then complain?
Then is this thing but sought
To turn my heart to pain.
Then this that you have wrought,
You must it now redress;
Of right, therefore, you ought
Such rigour to repress.

And as I have deserved,
So grant me now my hire;
You know I never swerved,
You never found me liar.
For Rachel have I served,
For Leah cared I never;
And her I have reserved
Within my heart for ever.

Sir Thomas Wyatt.

If I said so, may I be hated by
Her on whose love I live, without which I should die –
If I said so, my days be sad and short,
May my false soul some vile dominion court.
If I said so, may every star to me
Be hostile; round me grow
Pale fear and jealousy;
And she, my foe,
As cruel still and cold as fair she aye must be.

If I said so, may Love upon my heart
Expend his golden shafts, on her the leaden dart;
Be heaven and earth, and God and man my foe,
And she still more severe if I said so:
If I said so, may he whose blind lights lead
Me straightway to my grave,
Trample yet worse his slave,
Nor she behave
Gentle and kind to me in look, or word, or deed.

If I said so, then through my brief life may
All that is hateful block my worthless weary way:
If I said so, may the proud frost in thee
Grow prouder as more fierce the fire in me:
If I said so, no more then may the warm
Sun or bright moon be view'd,
Nor maid, nor matron's form,
But one dread storm
Such as proud Pharaoh saw when Israel he pursued.

If I said so, despite each contrite sigh,
Let courtesy for me and kindly feeling die:
If I said so, that voice to anger swell,
Which was so sweet when first her slave I fell:
If I said so, I should offend whom I,
E'en from my earliest breath
Until my day of death,
Would gladly take,
Alone in cloister'd cell my single saint to make.

But if I said not so, may she who first,

In life's green youth, my heart to hope so sweetly nursed,
Deign yet once more my weary bark to guide
With native kindness o'er the troublous tide;
And graceful, grateful, as her wont before,
When, for I could no more,
My all, myself I gave,
To be her slave,
Forget not the deep faith with which I still adore.

I did not, could not, never would say so,
For all that gold can give, cities or courts bestow:
Let truth, then, take her old proud seat on high,
And low on earth let baffled falsehood lie.
Thou know'st me, Love! if aught my state within
Belief or care may win,
Tell her that I would call
Him blest o'er all
Who, doom'd like me to pine, dies ere his strife begin.

Rachel I sought, not Leah, to secure,
Nor could I this vain life with other fair endure,
And, should from earth Heaven summon her again,
Myself would gladly die
For her, or with her, when
Elijah's fiery car her pure soul wafts on high.

Robert Macgregor.

CANZONE XX.

Ben mi credea passar mio tempo omai.

HE CANNOT LIVE WITHOUT SEEING HER, BUT WOULD NOT DIE THAT HE MAY STILL LOVE HER.

As pass'd the years which I have left behind,
To pass my future years I fondly thought,
Amid old studies, with desires the same;
But, from my lady since I fail to find
The accustom'd aid, the work himself has wrought
Let Love regard my tempter who became;
Yet scarce I feel the shame
That, at my age, he makes me thus a thief
Of that bewitching light
For which my life is steep'd in cureless grief;
In youth I better might
Have ta'en the part which now I needs must take,
For less dishonour boyish errors make.

Those sweet eyes whence alone my life had health
Were ever of their high and heavenly charms
So kind to me when first my thrall begun,
That, as a man whom not his proper wealth,
But some extern yet secret succour arms,
I lived, with them at ease, offending none:
Me now their glances shun
As one injurious and importunate,
Who, poor and hungry, did
Myself the very act, in better state
Which I, in others, chid.
From mercy thus if envy bar me, be
My amorous thirst and helplessness my plea.

In divers ways how often have I tried
If, reft of these, aught mortal could retain
E'en for a single day in life my frame:
But, ah! my soul, which has no rest beside,

Speeds back to those angelic lights again;
And I, though but of wax, turn to their flame,
Planting my mind's best aim
Where less the watch o'er what I love is sure:
As birds i' th' wild wood green,
Where less they fear, will sooner take the lure,
So on her lovely mien,
Now one and now another look I turn,
Wherewith at once I nourish me and burn.

Strange sustenance! upon my death I feed,
And live in flames, a salamander rare!
And yet no marvel, as from love it flows.
A blithe lamb 'mid the harass'd fleecy breed.
Whilom I lay, whom now to worst despair
Fortune and Love, as is their wont, expose.
Winter with cold and snows,
With violets and roses spring is rife,
And thus if I obtain
Some few poor aliments of else weak life,
Who can of theft complain?
So rich a fair should be content with this,
Though others live on hers, if nought she miss.

Who knows not what I am and still have been,
From the first day I saw those beauteous eyes,
Which alter'd of my life the natural mood?
Traverse all lands, explore each sea between,
Who can acquire all human qualities?
There some on odours live by Ind's vast flood;
Here light and fire are food
My frail and famish'd spirit to appease!
Love! more or nought bestow;
With lordly state low thrift but ill agrees;
Thou hast thy darts and bow,
Take with thy hands my not unwilling breath,
Life were well closed with honourable death.

Pent flames are strongest, and, if left to swell,
Not long by any means can rest unknown,
This own I, Love, and at your hands was taught.

When I thus silent burn'd, you knew it well;
Now e'en to me my cries are weary grown,
Annoy to far and near so long that wrought.
O false world! O vain thought!
O my hard fate! where now to follow thee?
Ah! from what meteor light
Sprung in my heart the constant hope which she,
Who, armour'd with your might,
Drags me to death, binds o'er it as a chain?
Yours is the fault, though mine the loss and pain.

Thus bear I of true love the pains along,
Asking forgiveness of another's debt,
And for mine own; whose eyes should rather shun
That too great light, and to the siren's song
My ears be closed: though scarce can I regret
That so sweet poison should my heart o'errun.
Yet would that all were done,
That who the first wound gave my last would deal;
For, if I right divine,
It were best mercy soon my fate to seal;
Since not a chance is mine
That he may treat me better than before,
'Tis well to die if death shut sorrow's door.

My song! with fearless feet
The field I keep, for death in flight were shame.
Myself I needs must blame
For these laments; tears, sighs, and death to meet,
Such fate for her is sweet.
Own, slave of Love, whose eyes these rhymes may catch,
Earth has no good that with my grief can match.

Robert Macgregor.

SONNET CLXXIII.

Rapido fiume che d' alpestra vena.

JOURNEYING ALONG THE RHONE TO AVIGNON, PETRARCH BIDS THE RIVER KISS LAURA'S HAND, AS IT WILL ARRIVE AT HER DWELLING BEFORE HIM.

Impetuous flood, that from the Alps' rude head,
Eating around thee, dost thy name obtain;[3]
Anxious like me both night and day to gain
Where thee pure nature, and me love doth lead;
Pour on: thy course nor sleep nor toils impede;
Yet, ere thou pay'st thy tribute to the main,
Oh, tarry where most verdant looks the plain,
Where most serenity the skies doth spread!
There beams my radiant sun of cheering ray,
Which deck thy left banks, and gems o'er with flowers;
E'en now, vain thought! perhaps she chides my stay:
Kiss then her feet, her hand so beauteous fair;
In place of language let thy kiss declare
Strong is my will, though feeble are my powers.

Dr Nott

3 Deriving it from *rodere*, to gnaw.

O rapid flood! which from thy mountain bed
Gnawest thy shores, whence (in my tongue) thy name;
Thou art my partner, night and day the same,
Where I by love, thou art by nature led:
Precede me now; no weariness doth shed
Its spell o'er thee, no sleep thy course can tame;
Yet ere the ocean waves thy tribute claim,
Pause, where the herb and air seem brighter fed.
There beams our sun of life, whose genial ray
With brighter verdure thy left shore adorns;
Perchance (vain hope!) e'en now my stay she mourns.
Kiss then her foot, her lovely hand, and may
Thy kiss to her in place of language speak,
The spirit is willing, but the flesh is weak.

Miss Wollaston.

SONNET CLXXIV.

I' dolci colli ov' io lasciai me stesso.

HE LEAVES VAUCLUSE, BUT HIS SPIRIT REMAINS THERE WITH LAURA.

The loved hills where I left myself behind,
Whence ever 'twas so hard my steps to tear,
Before me rise; at each remove I bear
The dear load to my lot by Love consign'd.
Often I wonder inly in my mind,
That still the fair yoke holds me, which despair
Would vainly break, that yet I breathe this air;
Though long the chain, its links but closer bind.
And as a stag, sore struck by hunter's dart,
Whose poison'd iron rankles in his breast,
Flies and more grieves the more the chase is press'd,
So I, with Love's keen arrow in my heart,
Endure at once my death and my delight,
Rack'd with long grief, and weary with vain flight.

Robert Macgregor.

Those gentle hills which hold my spirit still
(For though I fly, my heart there must remain),
Are e'er before me, whilst my burthen's pain,
By love bestow'd, I bear with patient will.
I marvel oft that I can yet fulfil
That yoke's sweet duties, which my soul enchain,
I seek release, but find the effort vain;
The more I fly, the nearer seems my ill.
So, like the stag, who, wounded by the dart,
Its poison'd iron rankling in his side,
Flies swifter at each quickening anguish'd throb, –
I feel the fatal arrow at my heart;
Yet with its poison, joy awakes its tide;
My flight exhausts me – grief my life doth rob!

Miss Wollaston.

SONNET CLXXV.

Non dall' Ispano Ibero all' Indo Idaspe.

HIS WOES ARE UNEXAMPLED.

From Spanish Ebro to Hydaspes old,
Exploring ocean in its every nook,
From the Red Sea to the cold Caspian shore,
In earth, in heaven one only Phœnix dwells.
What fortunate, or what disastrous bird
Omen'd my fate? which Parca winds my yarn,
That I alone find Pity deaf as asp,
And wretched live who happy hoped to be?
Let me not speak of her, but him her guide,
Who all her heart with love and sweetness fills –
Gifts which, from him o'erflowing, follow her,
Who, that my sweets may sour and cruel be,
Dissembleth, careth not, or will not see
That silver'd, ere my time, these temples are.

Robert Macgregor.

SONNET CLXXVI.

Voglia mi sprona; Amor mi guida e scorge.

HE DESCRIBES HIS STATE, SPECIFYING THE DATE OF HIS ATTACHMENT.

Passion impels me, Love escorts and leads,
Pleasure attracts me, habits old enchain,
Hope with its flatteries comforts me again,
And, at my harass'd heart, with fond touch pleads.
Poor wretch! it trusts her still, and little heeds
The blind and faithless leader of our train;
Reason is dead, the senses only reign:
One fond desire another still succeeds.
Virtue and honour, beauty, courtesy,
With winning words and many a graceful way,
My heart entangled in that laurel sweet.
In thirteen hundred seven and twenty, I
– 'Twas April, the first hour, on its sixth day –
Enter'd Love's labyrinth, whence is no retreat.

Robert Macgregor.

By will impell'd, Love o'er my path presides;
By Pleasure led, o'ercome by Habit's reign,
Sweet Hope deludes, and comforts me again;
At her bright touch, my heart's despair subsides.
It takes her proffer'd hand, and there confides.
To doubt its blind disloyal guide were vain;
Each sense usurps poor Reason's broken rein;
On each desire, another wilder rides!
Grace, virtue, honour, beauty, words so dear,
Have twined me with that laurell'd bough, whose power
My heart hath tangled in its lab'rinth sweet:
The thirteen hundred twenty-seventh year,
The sixth of April's suns – in that first hour,
My entrance mark'd, whence I see no retreat.

Miss Wollaston.

SONNET CLXXVII.

Beato in sogno, e di languir contento.

THOUGH SO LONG LOVE'S FAITHFUL SERVANT, HIS ONLY REWARD HAS BEEN TEARS.

Happy in visions, and content to pine,
Shadows to clasp, to chase the summer gale,
On shoreless and unfathom'd sea to sail,
To build on sand, and in the air design,
The sun to gaze on till these eyes of mine
Abash'd before his noonday splendour fail,
To chase adown some soft and sloping vale,
The wingèd stag with maim'd and heavy kine;
Weary and blind, save my own harm to all,
Which day and night I seek with throbbing heart,
On Love, on Laura, and on Death I call.
Thus twenty years of long and cruel smart,
In tears and sighs I've pass'd, because I took
Under ill stars, alas! both bait and hook.

Robert Macgregor.

SONNET CLXXVIII.

Grazie ch' a pochi 'l ciel largo destina.

THE ENCHANTMENTS THAT ENTHRALL HIM

Graces, that liberal Heaven on few bestows;
Rare excellence, scarce known to human kind;
With youth's bright locks age's ripe judgment join'd;
Celestial charms, which a meek mortal shows;
An elegance unmatch'd; and lips, whence flows
Music that can the sense in fetters bind;
A goddess step; a lovely ardent mind,
That breaks the stubborn, and the haughty bows;
Eyes, whose refulgence petrifies the heart,
To glooms, to shades that can a light impart,
Lift high the lover's soul, or plunge it low;
Speech link'd by tenderness and dignity;
With many a sweetly-interrupted sigh;
Such are the witcheries that transform me so.

Dr Nott

Graces which liberal Heaven grants few to share:
Rare virtue seldom witness'd by mankind;
Experienced judgment with fair hair combined;
High heavenly beauty in a humble fair;
A gracefulness most excellent and rare;
A voice whose music sinks into the mind;
An angel gait; wit glowing and refined,
The hard to break, the high and haughty tear,
And brilliant eyes which turn the heart to stone,
Strong to enlighten hell and night, and take
Souls from our bodies and their own to make;
A speech where genius high yet gentle shone,
Evermore broken by the balmiest sighs
– Such magic spells transform'd me in this wise.

Robert Macgregor.

SESTINA VI.

Anzi tre di creata era alma in parte.

THE HISTORY OF HIS LOVE; AND PRAYER FOR HELP.

Life's three first stages train'd my soul in part
To place its care on objects high and new,
And to disparage what men often prize,
But, left alone, and of her fatal course
As yet uncertain, frolicsome, and free,
She enter'd at spring-time a lovely wood.

A tender flower there was, born in that wood
The day before, whose root was in a part
High and impervious e'en to spirit free;
For many snares were there of forms so new,
And such desire impell'd my sanguine course,
That to lose freedom were to gain a prize.

Dear, sweet, yet perilous and painful prize!
Which quickly drew me to that verdant wood,
Doom'd to mislead me midway in life's course;
The world I since have ransack'd part by part,
For rhymes, or stones, or sap of simples new,
Which yet might give me back the spirit, free.

But ah! I feel my body must be free
From that hard knot which is its richest prize,
Ere medicine old or incantations new
Can heal the wounds which pierced me in that wood,
Thorny and troublous, where I play'd such part,
Leaving it halt who enter'd with hot course.

Yes! full of snares and sticks, a difficult course
Have I to run, where easy foot and sure
Were rather needed, healthy in each part;
Thou, Lord, who still of pity hast the prize,
Stretch to me thy right hand in this wild wood,

And let thy sun dispel my darkness new.

Look on my state, amid temptations new,
Which, interrupting my life's tranquil course,
Have made me denizen of darkling wood;
If good, restore me, fetterless and free,
My wand'ring consort, and be thine the prize
If yet with thee I find her in blest part.

Lo! thus in part I put my questions new,
If mine be any prize, or run its course,
Be my soul free, or captived in close wood.

Robert Macgregor.

SONNET CLXXIX.

In nobil sangue vita umile e queta.

SHE UNITES IN HERSELF THE HIGHEST EXCELLENCES OF VIRTUE AND BEAUTY.

High birth in humble life, reserved yet kind,
On youth's gay flower ripe fruits of age and rare,
A virtuous heart, therewith a lofty mind,
A happy spirit in a pensive air;
Her planet, nay, heaven's king, has fitly shrined
All gifts and graces in this lady fair,
True honour, purest praises, worth refined,
Above what rapt dreams of best poets are.
Virtue and Love so rich in her unite,
With natural beauty dignified address,
Gestures that still a silent grace express,
And in her eyes I know not what strange light,
That makes the noonday dark, the dusk night clear,
Bitter the sweet, and e'en sad absence dear.

Robert Macgregor.

Though nobly born, so humbly calm she dwells,
So bright her intellect – so pure her mind –
The blossom and its bloom in her we find;
With pensive look, her heart with mirth rebels:
Thus by her planets' union she excels,
(Nay – His, the stars' proud sov'reign, who enshrined
There honour, worth, and fortitude combined!)
Which to the bard inspired, his hope dispels.
Love blooms in her, but 'tis his home most pure;
Her daily virtues blend with native grace;
Her noiseless movements speak, though she is mute:
Such power her eyes, they can the day obscure,
Illume the night, – the honey's sweetness chase,
And wake its stream, where gall doth oft pollute.

Miss Wollaston.

SONNET CLXXX.

Tutto 'l di piango; e poi la notte, quando.

HER CRUELTY RENDERS LIFE WORSE THAN DEATH TO HIM.

Through the long lingering day, estranged from rest,
My sorrows flow unceasing; doubly flow,
Painful prerogative of lover's woe!
In that still hour, when slumber soothes th' unblest.
With such deep anguish is my heart opprest,
So stream mine eyes with tears! Of things below
Most miserable I; for Cupid's bow
Has banish'd quiet from this heaving breast.
Ah me! while thus in suffering, morn to morn
And eve to eve succeeds, of death I view
(So should this life be named) one-half gone by –
Yet this I weep not, but another's scorn;
That she, my friend, so tender and so true,
Should see me hopeless burn, and yet her aid deny.

Francis Wrangham.

SONNET CLXXXI.

Già desiai con sì giusta querela.

HE LIVES DESTITUTE OF ALL HOPE SAVE THAT OF RENDERING HER IMMORTAL.

Erewhile I labour'd with complaint so true,
And in such fervid rhymes to make me heard,
Seem'd as at last some spark of pity stirr'd
In the hard heart which frost in summer knew.
Th' unfriendly cloud, whose cold veil o'er it grew,
Broke at the first breath of mine ardent word
Or low'ring still she others' blame incurr'd
Her bright and killing eyes who thus withdrew
No ruth for self I crave, for her no hate;
I wish not this – *that* passes power of mine:
Such was mine evil star and cruel fate.
But I shall ever sing her charms divine,
That, when I have resign'd this mortal breath,
The world may know how sweet to me was death.

Robert Macgregor.

SONNET CLXXXII.

Tra quantunque leggiadre donne e belle.

ALL NATURE WOULD BE IN DARKNESS WERE SHE, ITS SUN, TO PERISH.

Where'er she moves, whatever dames among,
Beauteous or graceful, matchless she below.
With her fair face she makes all others show
Dim, as the day's bright orb night's starry throng.
And Love still whispers, with prophetic tongue, –
"Long as on earth is seen that glittering brow,
Shall life have charms: but she shall cease to glow
And with her all my power shall fleet along,
Should Nature from the skies their twin-lights wrest;
Hush every breeze, each herb and flower destroy;
Strip man of reason – speech; from Ocean's breast
His tides, his tenants chase – such, earth's annoy;
Yea, still more darken'd were it and unblest,
Had she, thy Laura, closed her eyes to love and joy."

Francis Wrangham.

Whene'er amidst the damsels, blooming bright,
She shows herself, whose like was never made,
At her approach all other beauties fade,
As at morn's orient glow the gems of night.
Love seems to whisper, – "While to mortal sight
Her graces shall on earth be yet display'd,
Life shall be blest; 'till soon with her decay'd,
The virtues, and my reign shall sink outright."
Of moon and sun, should nature rob the sky,
The air of winds, the earth of herbs and leaves,
Mankind of speech and intellectual eye,
The ocean's bed of fish, and dancing waves;
Even so shall all things dark and lonely lye,
When of her beauty Death the world bereaves!

Lord Charlemont.

SONNET CLXXXIII.

Il cantar novo e 'l pianger degli augelli.

MORNING.

The birds' sweet wail, their renovated song,
At break of morn, make all the vales resound;
With lapse of crystal waters pouring round,
In clear, swift runnels, the fresh shores among.
She, whose pure passion knows nor guile nor wrong,
With front of snow, with golden tresses crown'd,
Combing her aged husband's hoar locks found,
Wakes me when sportful wakes the warbling throng.
Thus, roused from sleep, I greet the dawning day,
And its succeeding sun, with one more bright,
Still dazzling, as in early youth, my sight:
Both suns I've seen at once uplift their ray;
This drives the radiance of the stars away,
But that which gilds my life eclipses e'en his light.

Dr Nott

Soon as gay morn ascends her purple car,
The plaintive warblings of the new-waked grove,
The murmuring streams, through flowery meads that rove,
Fill with sweet melody the valleys fair.
Aurora, famed for constancy in love,
Whose face with snow, whose locks with gold compare.
Smoothing her aged husband's silvery hair,
Bids me the joys of rural music prove.
Then, waking, I salute the sun of day;
But chief that beauteous sun, whose cheering ray
Once gilt, nay gilds e'en now, life's scene so bright.
Dear suns! which oft I've seen together rise;
This dims each meaner lustre of the skies,
And that sweet sun I love dims every light.

Anonymous 1777.

SONNET CLXXXIV.

Onde tolse Amor l' oro e di qual vena.

THE CHARMS OF HER COUNTENANCE AND VOICE.

Whence could Love take the gold, and from what vein,
To form those bright twin locks? What thorn could grow
Those roses? And what mead that white bestow
Of the fresh dews, which pulse and breath obtain?
Whence came those pearls that modestly restrain
Accents which courteous, sweet, and rare can flow?
And whence those charms that so divinely show,
Spread o'er a face serene as heaven's blue plain?
Taught by what angel, or what tuneful sphere,
Was that celestial song, which doth dispense
Such potent magic to the ravish'd ear?
What sun illumed those bright commanding eyes,
Which now look peaceful, now in hostile guise;
Now torture me with hope, and now with fear?

Dr Nott

Say, from what vein did Love procure the gold
To make those sunny tresses? From what thorn
Stole he the rose, and whence the dew of morn,
Bidding them breathe and live in Beauty's mould?
What depth of ocean gave the pearls that told
Those gentle accents sweet, though rarely born?
Whence came so many graces to adorn
That brow more fair than summer skies unfold?
Oh! say what angels lead, what spheres control
The song divine which wastes my life away?
(Who can with trifles now my senses move?)
What sun gave birth unto the lofty soul
Of those enchanting eyes, whose glances stray
To burn and freeze my heart – the sport of Love?

Mrs Wrottesley.

SONNET CLXXXV.

Qual mio destin, qual forza o qual inganno.

THOUGH HER EYES DESTROY HIM, HE CANNOT TEAR HIMSELF AWAY.

What destiny of mine, what fraud or force,
Unarm'd again conducts me to the field,
Where never came I but with shame to yield
'Scape I or fall, which better is or worse?
– Not worse, but better; from so sweet a source
Shine in my heart those lights, so bright reveal'd
The fatal fire, e'en now as then, which seal'd
My doom, though twenty years have roll'd their course
I feel death's messengers when those dear eyes,
Dazzling me from afar, I see appear,
And if on me they turn as she draw near,
Love with such sweetness tempts me then and tries,
Tell it I cannot, nor recall in sooth,
For wit and language fail to reach the truth!

Robert Macgregor.

SONNET CLXXXVI.

Liete e pensose, accompagnate e sole.

NOT FINDING HER WITH HER FRIENDS, HE ASKS THEM WHY SHE IS ABSENT.

P. Pensive and glad, accompanied, alone,
Ladies who cheat the time with converse gay,
Where does my life, where does my death delay?
Why not with you her form, as usual, shown?
L. Glad are we her rare lustre to have known,
And sad from her dear company to stay,
Which jealousy and envy keep away
O'er other's bliss, as their own ill who moan.
P. Who lovers can restrain, or give them law?
L. No one the soul, harshness and rage the frame;
As erst in us, this now in her appears.
As oft the face, betrays the heart, we saw
Clouds that, obscuring her high beauty, came,
And in her eyes the dewy trace of tears.

Robert Macgregor.

SONNET CLXXXVII.

Quando 'l sol bagna in mur l' aurato carro.

HIS NIGHTS ARE, LIKE HIS DAYS, PASSED IN TORMENT.

When in the sea sinks the sun's golden light,
And on my mind and nature darkness lies,
With the pale moon, faint stars and clouded skies
I pass a weary and a painful night:
To her who hears me not I then rehearse
My sad life's fruitless toils, early and late;
And with the world and with my gloomy fate,
With Love, with Laura and myself, converse.
Sleep is forbid me: I have no repose,
But sighs and groans instead, till morn returns,
And tears, with which mine eyes a sad heart feeds;
Then comes the dawn, the thick air clearer grows,
But not my soul; the sun which in it burns
Alone can cure the grief his fierce warmth breeds.

Dr Nott

When Phœbus lashes to the western main
His fiery steeds, and shades the lurid air;
Grief shades my soul, my night is spent in care;
Yon moon, yon stars, yon heaven begin my pain.
Wretch that I am! full oft I urge in vain
To heedless beings all those pangs I bear;
Of the false world, of an unpitying fair,
Of Love, and fickle fortune I complain!
From eve's last glance, till morning's earliest ray,
Sleep shuns my couch; rest quits my tearful eye;
And my rack'd breast heaves many a plaintive sigh.
Then bright Aurora cheers the rising day,
But cheers not me – for to my sorrowing heart
One sun alone can cheering light impart!

Anonymous 1777.

SONNET CLXXVIII.

S' una fede amorosa, un cor non finto.

THE MISERY OF HIS LOVE.

If faith most true, a heart that cannot feign,
If Love's sweet languishment and chasten'd thought,
And wishes pure by nobler feelings taught,
If in a labyrinth wanderings long and vain,
If on the brow each pang pourtray'd to bear,
Or from the heart low broken sounds to draw,
Withheld by shame, or check'd by pious awe,
If on the faded cheek Love's hue to wear,
If than myself to hold one far more dear,
If sighs that cease not, tears that ever flow,
Wrung from the heart by all Love's various woe,
In absence if consumed, and chill'd when near, –
If these be ills in which I waste my prime,
Though I the sufferer be, yours, lady, is the crime.

Lady Dacre.

If fondest faith, a heart to guile unknown,
By melting languors the soft wish betray'd;
If chaste desires, with temper'd warmth display'd;
If weary wanderings, comfortless and lone;
If every thought in every feature shown,
Or in faint tones and broken sounds convey'd,
As fear or shame my pallid cheek array'd
In violet hues, with Love's thick blushes strown;
If more than self another to hold dear;
If still to weep and heave incessant sighs,
To feed on passion, or in grief to pine,
To glow when distant, and to freeze when near, –
If hence my bosom's anguish takes its rise,
Thine, lady, is the crime, the punishment is mine.

Francis Wrangham.

SONNET CLXXXIX.

Dodici donne onestamente lasse.

HAPPY WHO STEERED THE BOAT, OR DROVE THE CAR, WHEREIN SHE SAT AND SANG.

Twelve ladies, their rare toil who lightly bore,
Rather twelve stars encircling a bright sun,
I saw, gay-seated a small bark upon,
Whose like the waters never cleaved before:
Not such took Jason to the fleece of yore,
Whose fatal gold has ev'ry heart now won,
Nor such the shepherd boy's, by whom undone
Troy mourns, whose fame has pass'd the wide world o'er.
I saw them next on a triumphal car,
Where, known by her chaste cherub ways, aside
My Laura sate and to them sweetly sung.
Things not of earth to man such visions are!
Blest Tiphys! blest Automedon! to guide
The bark, or car of band so bright and young.

Robert Macgregor.

SONNET CXC

Passer mai solitario in alcun tetto.

FAR FROM HIS BELOVED, LIFE IS MISERABLE BY NIGHT AS BY DAY.

Never was bird, spoil'd of its young, more sad,
Or wild beast in his lair more lone than me,
Now that no more that lovely face I see,
The only sun my fond eyes ever had.
In ceaseless sorrow is my chief delight:
My food to poison turns, to grief my joy;
The night is torture, dark the clearest sky,
And my lone pillow a hard field of fight.
Sleep is indeed, as has been well express'd.
Akin to death, for it the heart removes
From the dear thought in which alone I live.
Land above all with plenty, beauty bless'd!
Ye flowery plains, green banks and shady groves!
Ye hold the treasure for whose loss I grieve!

Robert Macgregor.

SONNET CXCI.

Aura, che quelle chiome bionde e crespe.

HE ENVIES THE BREEZE WHICH SPORTS WITH HER, THE STREAM THAT FLOWS TOWARDS HER.

Ye laughing gales, that sporting with my fair,
The silky tangles of her locks unbraid;
And down her breast their golden treasures spread;
Then in fresh mazes weave her curling hair,
You kiss those bright destructive eyes, that bear
The flaming darts by which my heart has bled;
My trembling heart! that oft has fondly stray'd
To seek the nymph, whose eyes such terrors wear.
Methinks she's found – but oh! 'tis fancy's cheat!
Methinks she's seen – but oh! 'tis love's deceit!
Methinks she's near – but truth cries "'tis not so!"
Go happy gale, and with my Laura dwell!
Go happy stream, and to my Laura tell
What envied joys in thy clear crystal flow!

Anonymous 1777.

Thou gale, that movest, and disportest round
Those bright crisp'd locks, by them moved sweetly too,
That all their fine gold scatter'st to the view,
Then coil'st them up in beauteous braids fresh wound;
About those eyes thou playest, where abound
The am'rous swarms, whose stings my tears renew!
And I my treasure tremblingly pursue,
Like some scared thing that stumbles o'er the ground.
Methinks I find her now, and now perceive
She's distant; now I soar, and now descend;
Now what I wish, now what is true believe.
Stay and enjoy, blest air, the living beam;
And thou, O rapid, and translucent stream,
Why can't I change my course, and thine attend?

Dr Nott

SONNET CXCII.

Amor con la man destra il lato manco.

UNDER THE FIGURE OF A LAUREL, HE RELATES THE GROWTH OF HIS LOVE.

My poor heart op'ning with his puissant hand,
Love planted there, as in its home, to dwell
A Laurel, green and bright, whose hues might well
In rivalry with proudest emeralds stand:
Plough'd by my pen and by my heart-sighs fann'd,
Cool'd by the soft rain from mine eyes that fell,
It grew in grace, upbreathing a sweet smell,
Unparallel'd in any age or land.
Fair fame, bright honour, virtue firm, rare grace,
The chastest beauty in celestial frame, –
These be the roots whence birth so noble came.
Such ever in my mind her form I trace,
A happy burden and a holy thing,
To which on rev'rent knee with loving prayer I cling.

Robert Macgregor.

SONNET CXCIII.

Cantai, or piango; e non men di dolcezza.

THOUGH IN THE MIDST OF PAIN, HE DEEMS HIMSELF THE HAPPIEST OF MEN.

I sang, who now lament; nor less delight
Than in my song I found, in tears I find;
For on the cause and not effect inclined,
My senses still desire to scale that height:
Whence, mildly if she smile or hardly smite,
Cruel and cold her acts, or meek and kind,
All I endure, nor care what weights they bind,
E'en though her rage would break my armour quite.
Let Love and Laura, world and fortune join,
And still pursue their usual course for me,
I care not, if unblest, in life to be.
Let me or burn to death or living pine,
No gentler state than mine beneath the sun,
Since from a source so sweet my bitters run.

Robert Macgregor.

SONNET CXCIV.

I' piansi, or canto; che 'l celeste lume.

AT HER RETURN, HIS SORROWS VANISH.

I wept, but now I sing; its heavenly light
That living sun conceals not from my view,
But virtuous love therein revealeth true
His holy purposes and precious might;
Whence, as his wont, such flood of sorrow springs
To shorten of my life the friendless course,
Nor bridge, nor ford, nor oar, nor sails have force
To forward mine escape, nor even wings.
But so profound and of so full a vein
My suff'ring is, so far its shore appears,
Scarcely to reach it can e'en thought contrive:
Nor palm, nor laurel pity prompts to gain,
But tranquil olive, and the dark sky clears,
And checks my grief and wills me to survive.

Robert Macgregor.

SONNET CXCV.

I' mi vivea di mia sorte contento.

HE FEARS THAT AN ILLNESS WHICH HAS ATTACKED THE EYES OF LAURA MAY DEPRIVE HIM OF THEIR SIGHT.

I lived so tranquil, with my lot content,
No sorrow visited, nor envy pined,
To other loves if fortune were more kind
One pang of mine their thousand joys outwent;
But those bright eyes, whence never I repent
The pains I feel, nor wish them less to find,
So dark a cloud and heavy now does blind,
Seems as my sun of life in them were spent.
O Nature! mother pitiful yet stern,
Whence is the power which prompts thy wayward deeds,
Such lovely things to make and mar in turn?
True, from one living fount all power proceeds:
But how couldst Thou consent, great God of Heaven,
That aught should rob the world of what thy love had given?

Robert Macgregor.

SONNET CXCVI.

Vincitore Alessandro l' ira vinse.

THE EVIL RESULTS OF UNRESTRAINED ANGER.

What though the ablest artists of old time
Left us the sculptured bust, the imaged form
Of conq'ring Alexander, wrath o'ercame
And made him for the while than Philip less?
Wrath to such fury valiant Tydeus drove
That dying he devour'd his slaughter'd foe;
Wrath made not Sylla merely blear of eye,
But blind to all, and kill'd him in the end.
Well Valentinian knew that to such pain
Wrath leads, and Ajax, he whose death it wrought.
Strong against many, 'gainst himself at last.
Wrath is brief madness, and, when unrestrain'd,
Long madness, which its master often leads
To shame and crime, and haply e'en to death.

Anonymous

SONNET CXCVII.

Qual ventura mi fu, quando dall' uno.

HE REJOICES AT PARTICIPATING IN HER SUFFERINGS.

Strange, passing strange adventure! when from one
Of the two brightest eyes which ever were,
Beholding it with pain dis urb'd and dim,
Moved influence which my own made dull and weak.
I had return'd, to break the weary fast
Of seeing her, my sole care in this world,
Kinder to me were Heaven and Love than e'en
If all their other gifts together join'd,
When from the right eye – rather the right sun –
Of my dear Lady to my right eye came
The ill which less my pain than pleasure makes;
As if it intellect possess'd and wings
It pass'd, as stars that shoot along the sky:
Nature and pity then pursued their course.

Anonymous

SONNET CXCVIII.

O cameretta che già fosti un porto.

HE NO LONGER FINDS RELIEF IN SOLITUDE.

Thou little chamber'd haven to the woes
Whose daily tempest overwhelms my soul!
From shame, I in Heaven's light my grief control;
Thou art its fountain, which each night o'erflows.
My couch! that oft hath woo'd me to repose,
'Mid sorrows vast – Love's iv'ried hand hath stole
Griefs turgid stream, which o'er thee it doth roll,
That hand which good on all but me bestows.
Not only quiet and sweet rest I fly,
But from myself and thought, whose vain pursuit
On pinion'd fancy doth my soul transport:
The multitude I did so long defy,
Now as my hope and refuge I salute,
So much I tremble solitude to court.

Miss Wollaston.

Room! which to me hast been a port and shield
From life's rude daily tempests for long years,
Now the full fountain of my nightly tears
Which in the day I bear for shame conceal'd:
Bed! which, in woes so great, wert wont to yield
Comfort and rest, an urn of doubts and fears
Love o'er thee now from those fair hands uprears,
Cruel and cold to me alone reveal'd.
But e'en than solitude and rest, I flee
More from myself and melancholy thought,
In whose vain quest my soul has heavenward flown.
The crowd long hateful, hostile e'en to me,
Strange though it sound, for refuge have I sought,
Such fear have I to find myself alone!

Robert Macgregor.

SONNET CXCIX.

Lasso! Amor mi trasporta ov' io non voglio.

HE EXCUSES HIMSELF FOR VISITING LAURA TOO OFTEN, AND LOVING HER TOO MUCH.

Alas! Love bears me where I would not go,
And well I see how duty is transgress'd,
And how to her who, queen-like, rules my breast,
More than my wont importunate I grow.
Never from rocks wise sailor guarded so
His ship of richest merchandise possess'd,
As evermore I shield my bark distress'd
From shocks of her hard pride that would o'erthrow
Torrents of tears, fierce winds of infinite sighs
– For, in my sea, nights horrible and dark
And pitiless winter reign – have driven my bark,
Sail-less and helm-less where it shatter'd lies,
Or, drifting at the mercy of the main,
Trouble to others bears, distress to me and pain.

Robert Macgregor.

SONNET CC.

Amor, io fallo e veggio il mio fallire.

HE PRAYS LOVE, WHO IS THE CAUSE OF HIS OFFENCES, TO OBTAIN PARDON FOR HIM.

O Love, I err, and I mine error own,
As one who burns, whose fire within him lies
And aggravates his grief, while reason dies,
With its own martyrdom almost o'erthrown.
I strove mine ardent longing to restrain,
Her fair calm face that I might ne'er disturb:
I can no more; falls from my hand the curb,
And my despairing soul is bold again;
Wherefore if higher than her wont she aim,
The act is thine, who firest and spur'st her so,
No way too rough or steep for her to go:
But the rare heavenly gifts are most to blame
Shrined in herself: let her at least feel this,
Lest of my faults her pardon I should miss.

Robert Macgregor.

SESTINA VII.

Non ha tanti animali il mar fra l' onde.

HE DESPAIRS OF ESCAPE FROM THE TORMENTS BY WHICH HE IS SURROUNDED.

Nor Ocean holds such swarms amid his waves,
Not overhead, where circles the pale moon,
Were stars so numerous ever seen by night,
Nor dwell so many birds among the woods,
Nor plants so many clothe the field or hill,
As holds my tost heart busy thoughts each eve.

Each day I hope that this my latest eve
Shall part from my quick clay the sad salt waves,
And leave me in last sleep on some cold hill;
So many torments man beneath the moon
Ne'er bore as I have borne; this know the woods
Through which I wander lonely day and night.

For never have I had a tranquil night,
But ceaseless sighs instead from morn till eve,
Since love first made me tenant of the woods:
The sea, ere I can rest, shall lose his waves,
The sun his light shall borrow from the moon,
And April flowers be blasted o'er each hill.

Thus, to myself a prey, from hill to hill,
Pensive by day I roam, and weep at night,
No one state mine, but changeful as the moon;
And when I see approaching the brown eve,
Sighs from my bosom, from my eyes fall waves,
The herbs to moisten and to move the woods.

Hostile the cities, friendly are the woods
To thoughts like mine, which, on this lofty hill,
Mingle their murmur with the moaning waves,
Through the sweet silence of the spangled night,

So that the livelong day I wait the eve,
When the sun sets and rises the fair moon.

Would, like Endymion, 'neath the enamour'd moon,
That slumbering I were laid in leafy woods,
And that ere vesper she who makes my eve,
With Love and Luna on that favour'd hill,
Alone, would come, and stay but one sweet night,
While stood the sun nor sought his western waves.

Upon the hard waves, 'neath the beaming moon,
Song, that art born of night amid the woods,
Thou shalt a rich hill see to-morrow eve!

Robert Macgregor.

Count the ocean's finny droves;
Count the twinkling host of stars.
Round the night's pale orb that moves;
Count the groves' wing'd choristers;
Count each verdant blade that grows;
Counted then will be my woes.

When shall these eyes cease to weep;
When shall this world-wearied frame,
Cover'd by the cold sod, sleep? –
Sure, beneath yon planet's beam,
None like me have made such moan;
This to every bower is known.

Sad my nights; from morn till eve,
Tenanting the woods, I sigh:
But, ere I shall cease to grieve,
Ocean's vast bed shall be dry,
Suns their light from moons shall gain.
And spring wither on each plain.

Pensive, weeping, night and day,
From this shore to that I fly,
Changeful as the lunar ray;
And, when evening veils the sky,
Then my tears might swell the floods,
Then my sighs might bow the woods!

Towns I hate, the shades I love;
For relief to yon green height,
Where the rill resounds, I rove
At the grateful calm of night;
There I wait the day's decline,
For the welcome moon to shine.

Oh, that in some lone retreat,
Like Endymion I were lain;
And that she, who rules my fate,
There one night to stay would deign;
Never from his billowy bed
More might Phœbus lift his head!

Song, that on the wood-hung stream
In the silent hour wert born,
Witness'd but by Cynthia's beam.
Soon as breaks to-morrow's morn,
Thou shalt seek a glorious plain,
There with Laura to remain!

Lady Dacre.

SESTINA VIII.

Là ver l' aurora, che sì dolce l' aura.

SHE IS MOVED NEITHER BY HIS VERSES NOR HIS TEARS.

When music warbles from each thorn,
And Zephyr's dewy wings
Sweep the young flowers; what time the morn
Her crimson radiance flings:
Then, as the smiling year renews,
I feel renew'd Love's tender pain;
Renew'd is Laura's cold disdain;
And I for comfort court the weeping muse.

Oh! could my sighs in accents flow
So musically lorn,
That thou might'st catch my am'rous woe,
And cease, proud Maid! thy scorn:
Yet, ere within thy icy breast
The smallest spark of passion's found,
Winter's cold temples shall be bound
With all the blooms that paint spring's glowing vest.

The drops that bathe the grief-dew'd eye,
The love-impassion'd strain
To move thy flinty bosom try
Full oft; – but, ah! in vain
Would tears, and melting song avail;
As vainly might the silken breeze,
That bends the flowers, that fans the trees,
Some rugged rock's tremendous brow assail.

Both gods and men alike are sway'd
By Love, as poets tell; –
And I, when flowers in every shade
Their bursting gems reveal,
First felt his all-subduing power:
While Laura knows not yet the smart;

Nor heeds the tortures of my heart,
My prayers, my plaints, and sorrow's pearly shower!

Thy wrongs, my soul! with patience bear,
While life shall warm this clay;
And soothing sounds to Laura's ear
My numbers shall convey;
Numbers with forceful magic charm
All nature o'er the frost-bound earth,
Wake summer's fragrant buds to birth,
And the fierce serpent of its rage disarm.

The blossom'd shrubs in smiles are drest,
Now laughs his purple plain;
And shall the nymph a foe profest
To tenderness remain?
But oh! what solace shall I find,
If fortune dooms me yet to bear
The frowns of my relentless Fair,
Save with soft moan to vex the pitying wind?
In baffling nets the light-wing'd gale
I'd fetter as it blows,
The vernal rose that scents the vale
I'd cull on wintery snows;
Still I'd ne'er hope that mind to move
Which dares defy the wiles of verse, and Love.

Anonymous 1777.

SONNET CCI.

Real natura, angelico intelletto.

ON THE KISS OF HONOUR GIVEN BY CHARLES OF LUXEMBURG TO LAURA AT A BANQUET.

A kingly nature, an angelic mind,
A spotless soul, prompt aspect and keen eye,
Quick penetration, contemplation high
And truly worthy of the breast which shrined:
In bright assembly lovely ladies join'd
To grace that festival with gratulant joy,
Amid so many and fair faces nigh
Soon his good judgment did the fairest find.
Of riper age and higher rank the rest
Gently he beckon'd with his hand aside,
And lovingly drew near the perfect one:
So courteously her eyes and brow he press'd,
All at his choice in fond approval vied –
Envy through my sole veins at that sweet freedom run.

Robert Macgregor.

A sovereign nature, – an exalted mind, –
A soul proud – sleepless – with a lynx's eye, –
An instant foresight, – thought as towering high,
E'en as the heart in which they are enshrined:
A bright assembly on that day combined
Each other in his honour to outvie,
When 'mid the fair his judgment did descry
That sweet perfection all to her resign'd.
Unmindful of her rival sisterhood,
He motion'd silently his preference,
And fondly welcomed her, that humblest one:
So pure a kiss he gave, that all who stood,
Though fair, rejoiced in beauty's recompense:
By that strange act nay heart was quite undone!

Miss Wollaston.

SONNET CCII.

I' ho pregato Amor, e nel riprego.

HE PLEADS THE EXCESS OF HIS PASSION IN PALLIATION OF HIS FAULT.

Oft have I pray'd to Love, and still I pray,
My charming agony, my bitter joy!
That he would crave your grace, if consciously
From the right path my guilty footsteps stray.
That Reason, which o'er happier minds holds sway,
Is quell'd of Appetite, I not deny;
And hence, through tracks my better thoughts would fly,
The victor hurries me perforce away,
You, in whose bosom Genius, Virtue reign
With mingled blaze lit by auspicious skies –
Ne'er shower'd kind star its beams on aught so rare!
You, you should say with pity, not disdain;
"How could he 'scape, lost wretch! these lightning eyes –
So passionate he, and I so direly fair?"

Francis Wrangham.

SONNET CCIII.

L' alto signor, dinanzi a cui non vale.

HIS SORROW FOR THE ILLNESS OF LAURA INCREASES, NOT LESSENS, HIS FLAME.

The sovereign Lord, 'gainst whom of no avail
Concealment, or resistance is, or flight,
My mind had kindled to a new delight
By his own amorous and ardent ail:
Though his first blow, transfixing my best mail
Were mortal sure, to push his triumph quite
He took a shaft of sorrow in his right,
So my soft heart on both sides to assail.
A burning wound the one shed fire and flame,
The other tears, which ever grief distils,
Through eyes for your weak health that are as rills.
But no relief from either fountain came
My bosom's conflagration to abate,
Nay, passion grew by very pity great.

Robert Macgregor.

SONNET CCIV.

Mira quel colle, o stanco mio cor vago.

HE BIDS HIS HEART RETURN TO LAURA, NOT PERCEIVING THAT IT HAD NEVER LEFT HER.

P. Look on that hill, my fond but harass'd heart!
Yestreen we left her there, who 'gan to take
Some care of us and friendlier looks to dart;
Now from our eyes she draws a very lake:
Return alone – I love to be apart –
Try, if perchance the day will ever break
To mitigate our still increasing smart,
Partner and prophet of my lifelong ache.
H. O wretch! in whom vain thoughts and idle swell,
Thou, who thyself hast tutor'd to forget,
Speak'st to thy heart as if 'twere with thee yet?
When to thy greatest bliss thou saidst farewell,
Thou didst depart alone: it stay'd with her,
Nor cares from those bright eyes, its home, to stir.

Robert Macgregor.

SONNET CCV.

Fresco ambroso fiorito e verde colle.

HE CONGRATULATES HIS HEART ON ITS REMAINING WITH HER.

O hill with green o'erspread, with groves o'erhung!
Where musing now, now trilling her sweet lay,
Most like what bards of heavenly spirits say,
Sits she by fame through every region sung:
My heart, which wisely unto her has clung –
More wise, if there, in absence blest, it stay!
Notes now the turf o'er which her soft steps stray,
Now where her angel-eyes' mild beam is flung;
Then throbs and murmurs, as they onward rove,
"Ah! were he here, that man of wretched lot,
Doom'd but to taste the bitterness of love!"
She, conscious, smiles: our feelings tally not:
Heartless am I, mere stone; heaven is thy grove –
O dear delightful shade, O consecrated spot!

Francis Wrangham.

Fresh, shaded hill! with flowers and verdure crown'd,
Where, in fond musings, or with music sweet,
To earth a heaven-sent spirit takes her seat!
She who from all the world has honour found.
Forsaking me, to her my fond heart bound
– Divorce for aye were welcome as discreet –
Notes where the turf is mark'd by her fair feet,
Or from these eyes for her in sorrow drown'd,
Then inly whispers as her steps advance,
"Would for awhile that wreteh were here alone
Who pines already o'er his bitter lot."
She conscious smiles. Not equal is the chance;
An Eden thou, while I a heartless stone.
O holy, happy, and beloved spot!

Robert Macgregor.

SONNET CCVI.

Il mal mi preme, e mi spaventa il peggio.

TO A FRIEND, IN LOVE LIKE HIMSELF, HE CAN GIVE NO ADVICE BUT TO RAISE HIS SOUL TO GOD.

Evil oppresses me and worse dismay,
To which a plain and ample way I find;
Driven like thee by frantic passion, blind,
Urged by harsh thoughts I bend like thee my way.
Nor know I if for war or peace to pray:
To war is ruin, shame to peace, assign'd.
But wherefore languish thus? – Rather, resign'd,
Whate'er the Will Supreme ordains, obey.
However ill that honour me beseem
By thee conferr'd, whom that affection cheats
Which many a perfect eye to error sways,
To raise thy spirit to that realm supreme
My counsel is, and win those blissful seats:
For short the time, and few the allotted days.

Capel Lofft.

The bad oppresses me, the worse dismays,
To which so broad and plain a path I see;
My spirit, to like frenzy led with thee,
Tried by the same hard thoughts, in dotage strays,
Nor knows if peace or war of God it prays,
Though great the loss and deep the shame to me.
But why pine longer? Best our lot will be,
What Heaven's high will ordains when man obeys.
Though I of that great honour worthless prove
Offer'd by thee – herein Love leads to err
Who often makes the sound eye to see wrong –
My counsel this, instant on Heaven above
Thy soul to elevate, thy heart to spur,
For though the time be short, the way is long.

Robert Macgregor.

SONNET CCVII.

Due rose fresche, e colte in paradiso.

THE TWO ROSES.

Two brilliant roses, fresh from Paradise,
Which there, on May-day morn, in beauty sprung
Fair gift, and by a lover old and wise
Equally offer'd to two lovers young:
At speech so tender and such winning guise,
As transports from a savage might have wrung,
A living lustre lit their mutual eyes,
And instant on their cheeks a soft blush hung.
The sun ne'er look'd upon a lovelier pair,
With a sweet smile and gentle sigh he said,
Pressing the hands of both and turn'd away.
Of words and roses each alike had share.
E'en now my worn heart thrill with joy and dread,
O happy eloquence! O blessed day!

Robert Macgregor.

SONNET CCVIII.

L' aura che 'l verde Lauro e l' aureo crine.

HE PRAYS THAT HE MAY DIE BEFORE LAURA.

The balmy gale, that, with its tender sigh,
Moves the green laurel and the golden hair,
Makes with its graceful visitings and rare
The gazer's spirit from his body fly.
A sweet and snow-white rose in hard thorns set!
Where in the world her fellow shall we find?
The glory of our age! Creator kind!
Grant that ere hers my death shall first be met.
So the great public loss I may not see,
The world without its sun, in darkness left,
And from my desolate eyes their sole light reft,
My mind with which no other thoughts agree,
Mine ears which by no other sound are stirr'd
Except her ever pure and gentle word.

Robert Macgregor.

SONNET CCIX.

Parrà forse ad alcun, che 'n lodar quella.

HE INVITES THOSE TO WHOM HIS PRAISES SEEM EXCESSIVE TO BEHOLD THE OBJECT OF THEM.

Haply my style to some may seem too free
In praise of her who holds my being's chain,
Queen of her sex describing her to reign,
Wise, winning, good, fair, noble, chaste to be:
To me it seems not so; I fear that she
My lays as low and trifling may disdain,
Worthy a higher and a better strain;
– Who thinks not with me let him come and see.
Then will he say, She whom his wishes seek
Is one indeed whose grace and worth might tire
The muses of all lands and either lyre.
But mortal tongue for state divine is weak,
And may not soar; by flattery and force,
As Fate not choice ordains, Love rules its course.

Robert Macgregor.

SONNET CCX.

Chi vuol veder quantunque può Natura.

WHOEVER BEHOLDS HER MUST ADMIT THAT HIS PRAISES CANNOT REACH HER PERFECTION.

Who wishes to behold the utmost might
Of Heaven and Nature, on her let him gaze,
Sole sun, not only in my partial lays,
But to the dark world, blind to virtue's light!
And let him haste to view; for death in spite
The guilty leaves, and on the virtuous preys;
For this loved angel heaven impatient stays;
And mortal charms are transient as they're bright!
Here shall he see, if timely he arrive,
Virtue and beauty, royalty of mind,
In one bless'd union join'd. Then shall he say
That vainly my weak rhymes to praise her strive,
Whose dazzling beams have struck my genius blind: –
He must for ever weep if he delay!

Lord Charlemont.

Stranger, whose curious glance delights to trace
What Heaven and Nature join'd to frame most rare;
Here view mine eyes' bright sun – a sight so fair,
That purblind worlds, like me, enamour'd gaze.
But speed thy step; for Death with rapid pace
Pursues the best, nor makes the bad his care:
Call'd to the skies through yon blue fields of air,
On buoyant plume the mortal grace obeys.
Then haste, and mark in one rich form combined
(And, for that dazzling lustre dimm'd mine eye,
Chide the weak efforts of my trembling lay)
Each charm of person, and each power of mind –
But, slowly if thy lingering foot comply,
Grief and repentant shame shall mourn the brief delay.

Francis Wrangham.

SONNET CCXI.

Qual paura ho, quando mi torna a mente.

MELANCHOLY RECOLLECTIONS AND PRESAGES.

O Laura! when my tortured mind
The sad remembrance bears
Of that ill-omen'd day,
When, victim to a thousand doubts and fears,
I left my soul behind,
That soul that could not from its partner stray;
In nightly visions to my longing eyes
Thy form oft seems to rise,
As ever thou wert seen,
Fair like the rose, 'midst paling flowers the queen,
But loosely in the wind,
Unbraided wave the ringlets of thy hair,
That late with studious care,
I saw with pearls and flowery garlands twined:
On thy wan lip, no cheerful smile appears;
Thy beauteous face a tender sadness wears;
Placid in pain thou seem'st, serene in grief,
As conscious of thy fate, and hopeless of relief!
Cease, cease, presaging heart! O angels, deign
To hear my fervent prayer, that all my fears be vain!

Lord Woodhouselee.

What dread I feel when I revolve the day
I left my mistress, sad, without repose,
My heart too with her: and my fond thought knows
Nought on which gladlier, oft'ner it can stay.
Again my fancy doth her form portray
Meek among beauty's train, like to some rose
Midst meaner flowers; nor joy nor grief she shows;
Not with misfortune prest but with dismay.
Then were thrown by her custom'd cheerfulness,
Her pearls, her chaplets, and her gay attire,
Her song, her laughter, and her mild address;
Thus doubtingly I quitted her I love:
Now dark ideas, dreams, and bodings dire
Raise terrors, which Heaven grant may groundless prove!

Dr Nott

SONNET CCXII.

Solea lontana in sonno consolarme.

SHE ANNOUNCES TO HIM, IN A VISION, THAT HE WILL NEVER SEE HER MORE.

To soothe me distant far, in days gone by,
With dreams of one whose glance all heaven combined,
Was mine; now fears and sorrow haunt my mind,
Nor can I from that grief, those terrors fly:
For oft in sleep I mark within her eye
Deep pity with o'erwhelming sadness join'd;
And oft I seem to hear on every wind
Accents, which from my breast chase peace and joy.
"That last dark eve," she cries, "remember'st thou,
When to those doting eyes I bade farewell,
Forced by the time's relentless tyranny?
I had not then the power, nor heart to tell,
What thou shalt find, alas! too surely true –
Hope not again on earth thy Laura's face to see."

Francis Wrangham.

SONNET CCXIII.

O misera ed orribil visione.

HE CANNOT BELIEVE IN HER DEATH, BUT IF TRUE, HE PRAYS GOD TO TAKE HIM ALSO FROM LIFE.

O misery! horror! can it, then, be true,
That the sweet light before its time is spent,
'Mid all its pains which could my life content,
And ever with fresh hopes of good renew?
If so, why sounds not other channels through,
Nor only from herself, the great event?
No! God and Nature could not thus consent,
And my dark fears are groundless and undue.
Still it delights my heart to hope once more
The welcome sight of that enchanting face,
The glory of our age, and life to me.
But if, to her eternal home to soar,
That heavenly spirit have left her earthly place,
Oh! then not distant may my last day be!

Robert Macgregor.

SONNET CCXIV.

In dubbio di mio stato, or piango, or canto.

TO HIS LONGING TO SEE HER AGAIN IS NOW ADDED THE FEAR OF SEEING HER NO MORE.

Uncertain of my state, I weep and sing,
I hope and tremble, and with rhymes and sighs
I ease my load, while Love his utmost tries
How worse my sore afflicted heart to sting.
Will her sweet seraph face again e'er bring
Their former light to these despairing eyes.
(What to expect, alas! or how advise)
Or must eternal grief my bosom wring?
For heaven, which justly it deserves to win,
It cares not what on earth may be their fate,
Whose sun it was, where centred their sole gaze.
Such terror, so perpetual warfare in,
Changed from my former self, I live of late
As one who midway doubts, and fears and strays.

Robert Macgregor.

SONNET CCXV.

O dolci sguardi, o parolette accorte.

HE SIGHS FOR THOSE GLANCES FROM WHICH, TO HIS GRIEF, FORTUNE EVER DELIGHTS TO WITHDRAW HIM.

O angel looks! O accents of the skies!
Shall I or see or hear you once again?
O golden tresses, which my heart enchain,
And lead it forth, Love's willing sacrifice!
O face of beauty given in anger's guise,
Which still I not enjoy, and still complain!
O dear delusion! O bewitching pain!
Transports, at once my punishment and prize!
If haply those soft eyes some kindly beam
(Eyes, where my soul and all my thoughts reside)
Vouchsafe, in tender pity to bestow;
Sudden, of all my joys the murtheress tried,
Fortune with steed or ship dispels the gleam;
Fortune, with stern behest still prompt to work my woe.

Francis Wrangham.

O gentle looks! O words of heavenly sound!
Shall I behold you, hear you once again?
O waving locks, that Love has made the chain,
In which this wretched ruin'd heart is bound!
O face divine! whose magic spells surround
My soul, distemper'd with unceasing pain:
O dear deceit! O loving errors vain!
To hug the dart and doat upon the wound!
Did those soft eyes, in whose angelic light
My life, my thoughts, a constant mansion find,
Ever impart a pure unmixed delight?
Or if they have one moment, then unkind
Fortune steps in, and sends me from their sight,
And gives my opening pleasures to the wind.

Dr Morehead.

SONNET CCXVI.

I' pur ascolto, e non odo novella.

HEARING NO TIDINGS OF HER, HE BEGINS TO DESPAIR.

Still do I wait to hear, in vain still wait,
Of that sweet enemy I love so well:
What now to think or say I cannot tell,
'Twixt hope and fear my feelings fluctuate:
The beautiful are still the marks of fate;
And sure her worth and beauty most excel:
What if her God have call'd her hence, to dwell
Where virtue finds a more congenial state?
If so, she will illuminate that sphere
Even as a sun: but I – 'tis done with me!
I then am nothing, have no business here!
O cruel absence! why not let me see
The worst? my little tale is told, I fear,
My scene is closed ere it accomplish'd be.

Dr Morehead.

No tidings yet – I listen, but in vain;
Of her, my beautiful belovèd foe,
What or to think or say I nothing know,
So thrills my heart, my fond hopes so sustain,
Danger to some has in their beauty lain;
Fairer and chaster she than others show;
God haply seeks to snatch from earth below
Virtue's best friend, that heaven a star may gain,
Or rather sun. If what I dread be nigh,
My life, its trials long, its brief repose
Are ended all. O cruel absence! why
Didst thou remove me from the menaced woes?
My short sad story is already done,
And midway in its course my vain race run.

Robert Macgregor.

SONNET CCXVII.

La sera desiar, odiar l' aurora.

CONTRARY TO THE WONT OF LOVERS, HE PREFERS MORN TO EVE.

Tranquil and happy loves in this agree,
The evening to desire and morning hate:
On me at eve redoubled sorrows wait –
Morning is still the happier hour for me.
For then my sun and Nature's oft I see
Opening at once the orient's rosy gate,
So match'd in beauty and in lustre great,
Heaven seems enamour'd of our earth to be!
As when in verdant leaf the dear boughs burst
Whose roots have since so centred in my core,
Another than myself is cherish'd more.
Thus the two hours contrast, day's last and first:
Reason it is who calms me to desire,
And fear and hate who fiercer feed my fire.

Robert Macgregor.

SONNET CCXVIII.

Far potess' io vendetta di colei.

HIS SOUL VISITS HER IN SLEEP.

Oh! that from her some vengeance I could wrest
With words and glances who my peace destroys,
And then abash'd, for my worse sorrow, flies,
Veiling her eyes so cruel, yet so blest;
Thus mine afflicted spirits and oppress'd
By sure degrees she sorely drains and dries,
And in my heart, as savage lion, cries
Even at night, when most I should have rest.
My soul, which sleep expels from his abode,
The body leaves, and, from its trammels free,
Seeks her whose mien so often menace show'd.
I marvel much, if heard its advent be,
That while to her it spake, and o'er her wept,
And round her clung, asleep she alway kept.

Robert Macgregor.

SONNET CCXIX.

In quel bel viso, ch' i' sospiro e bramo.

ON LAURA PUTTING HER HAND BEFORE HER EYES WHILE HE WAS GAZING ON HER.

On the fair face for which I long and sigh
Mine eyes were fasten'd with desire intense.
When, to my fond thoughts, Love, in best reply,
Her honour'd hand uplifting, shut me thence.
My heart there caught – as fish a fair hook by,
Or as a young bird on a limèd fence –
For good deeds follow from example high,
To truth directed not its busied sense.
But of its one desire my vision reft,
As dreamingly, soon oped itself a way,
Which closed, its bliss imperfect had been left:
My soul between those rival glories lay,
Fill'd with a heavenly and new delight,
Whose strange surpassing sweets engross'd it quite.

Robert Macgregor.

SONNET CCXX.

Vive faville uscian de' duo bei lumi.

A SMILING WELCOME, WHICH LAURA GAVE HIM UNEXPECTEDLY, ALMOST KILLS HIM WITH JOY.

Live sparks were glistening from her twin bright eyes,
So sweet on me whose lightning flashes beam'd,
And softly from a feeling heart and wise,
Of lofty eloquence a rich flood stream'd:
Even the memory serves to wake my sighs
When I recall that day so glad esteem'd,
And in my heart its sinking spirit dies
As some late grace her colder wont redeem'd.
My soul in pain and grief that most has been
(How great the power of constant habit is!)
Seems weakly 'neath its double joy to lean:
For at the sole taste of unusual bliss,
Trembling with fear, or thrill'd by idle hope,
Oft on the point I've been life's door to ope.

Robert Macgregor.

SONNET CCXXI.

Cercato ho sempre solitaria vita.

THINKING ALWAYS OF LAURA, IT PAINS HIM TO REMEMBER WHERE SHE IS LEFT.

Still have I sought a life of solitude;
The streams, the fields, the forests know my mind;
That I might 'scape the sordid and the blind,
Who paths forsake trod by the wise and good:
Fain would I leave, were mine own will pursued,
These Tuscan haunts, and these soft skies behind,
Sorga's thick-wooded hills again to find;
And sing and weep in concert with its flood.
But Fortune, ever my sore enemy,
Compels my steps, where I with sorrow see
Cast my fair treasure in a worthless soil:
Yet less a foe she justly deigns to prove,
For once, to me, to Laura, and to love;
Favouring my song, my passion, with her smile.

Dr Nott

Still have I sought a life of solitude –
This know the rivers, and each wood and plain –
That I might 'scape the blind and sordid train
Who from the path have flown of peace and good:
Could I my wish obtain, how vainly would
This cloudless climate woo me to remain;
Sorga's embowering woods I'd seek again,
And sing, weep, wander, by its friendly flood.
But, ah! my fortune, hostile still to me,
Compels me where I must, indignant, find
Amid the mire my fairest treasure thrown:
Yet to my hand, not all unworthy, she
Now proves herself, at least for once, more kind,
Since – but alone to Love and Laura be it known.

Robert Macgregor.

SONNET CCXXII.

In tale Stella duo begli occhi vidi.

THE BEAUTY OF LAURA IS PEERLESS.

In one fair star I saw two brilliant eyes,
With sweetness, modesty, so glistening o'er,
That soon those graceful nests of Love before
My worn heart learnt all others to despise:
Equall'd not her whoever won the prize
In ages gone on any foreign shore;
Not she to Greece whose wondrous beauty bore
Unnumber'd ills, to Troy death's anguish'd cries:
Not the fair Roman, who, with ruthless blade
Piercing her chaste and outraged bosom, fled
Dishonour worse than death, like charms display'd;
Such excellence should brightest glory shed
On Nature, as on me supreme delight,
But, ah! too lately come, too soon it takes its flight.

Robert Macgregor.

SONNET CCXXIII.

Qual donna attende a gloriosa fama.

THE EYES OF LAURA ARE THE SCHOOL OF VIRTUE.

Feels any fair the glorious wish to gain
Of sense, of worth, of courtesy, the praise?
On those bright eyes attentive let her gaze
Of her miscall'd my love, but sure my foe.
Honour to gain, with love of God to glow,
Virtue more bright how native grace displays,
May there be learn'd; and by what surest ways
To heaven, that for her coming pants, to go.
The converse sweet, beyond what poets write,
Is there; the winning silence, and the meek
And saint-like manners man would paint in vain.
The matchless beauty, dazzling to the sight,
Can ne'er be learn'd; for bootless 'twere to seek
By art, what by kind chance alone we gain.
Anonymous, Ox., 1795.

SONNET CCXXIV.

Cara la vita, e dopo lei mi pare.

HONOUR TO BE PREFERRED TO LIFE.

Methinks that life in lovely woman first,
And after life true honour should be dear;
Nay, wanting honour – of all wants the worst –
Friend! nought remains of loved or lovely here.
And who, alas! has honour's barrier burst,
Unsex'd and dead, though fair she yet appear,
Leads a vile life, in shame and torment curst,
A lingering death, where all is dark and drear.
To me no marvel was Lucretia's end,
Save that she needed, when that last disgrace
Alone sufficed to kill, a sword to die.
Sophists in vain the contrary defend:
Their arguments are feeble all and base,
And truth alone triumphant mounts on high!

Robert Macgregor.

SONNET CCXXV.

Arbor vittoriosa e trionfale.

HE EXTOLS THE VIRTUE OF LAURA.

Tree, victory's bright guerdon, wont to crown
Heroes and bards with thy triumphal leaf,
How many days of mingled joy and grief
Have I from thee through life's short passage known.
Lady, who, reckless of the world's renown,
Reapest in virtue's field fair honour's sheaf;
Nor fear'st Love's limed snares, "that subtle thief,"
While calm discretion on his wiles looks down.
The pride of birth, with all that here we deem
Most precious, gems and gold's resplendent grace.
Abject alike in thy regard appear:
Nay, even thine own unrivall'd beauties beam
No charm to thee – save as their circling blaze
Clasps fitly that chaste soul, which still thou hold'st most dear.

Francis Wrangham.

Blest laurel! fadeless and triumphant tree!
Of kings and poets thou the fondest pride!
How much of joy and sorrow's changing tide
In my short breath hath been awaked by thee!
Lady, the will's sweet sovereign! thou canst see
No bliss but virtue, where thou dost preside;
Love's chain, his snare, thou dost alike deride;
From man's deceit thy wisdom sets thee free.
Birth's native pride, and treasure's precious store,
(Whose bright possession we so fondly hail)
To thee as burthens valueless appear:
Thy beauty's excellence – (none viewed before)
Thy soul had wearied – but thou lov'st the veil,
That shrine of purity adorneth here.

Miss Wollaston.

CANZONE XXI.

I' vo pensando, e nel pensier m' assale.

SELF-CONFLICT.

Ceaseless I think, and in each wasting thought
So strong a pity for myself appears,
That often it has brought
My harass'd heart to new yet natural tears;
Seeing each day my end of life draw nigh,
Instant in prayer, I ask of God the wings
With which the spirit springs,
Freed from its mortal coil, to bliss on high;
But nothing, to this hour, prayer, tear, or sigh,
Whatever man could do, my hopes sustain:
And so indeed in justice should it be;
Able to stay, who went and fell, that he
Should prostrate, in his own despite, remain.
But, lo! the tender arms
In which I trust are open to me still,
Though fears my bosom fill
Of others' fate, and my own heart alarms,
Which worldly feelings spur, haply, to utmost ill.

One thought thus parleys with my troubled mind –
"What still do you desire, whence succour wait?
Ah! wherefore to this great,
This guilty loss of time so madly blind?
Take up at length, wisely take up your part:
Tear every root of pleasure from your heart,
Which ne'er can make it blest,
Nor lets it freely play, nor calmly rest.
If long ago with tedium and disgust
You view'd the false and fugitive delights
With which its tools a treacherous world requites,
Why longer then repose in it your trust,
Whence peace and firmness are in exile thrust?
While life and vigour stay,

The bridle of your thoughts is in your power:
Grasp, guide it while you may:
So clogg'd with doubt, so dangerous is delay,
The best for wise reform is still the present hour.

"Well known to you what rapture still has been
Shed on your eyes by the dear sight of her
Whom, for your peace it were
Better if she the light had never seen;
And you remember well (as well you ought)
Her image, when, as with one conquering bound,
Your heart in prey she caught,
Where flame from other light no entrance found.
She fired it, and if that fallacious heat
Lasted long years, expecting still one day,
Which for our safety came not, to repay,
It lifts you now to hope more blest and sweet,
Uplooking to that heaven around your head
Immortal, glorious spread;
If but a glance, a brief word, an old song,
Had here such power to charm
Your eager passion, glad of its own harm,
How far 'twill then exceed if now the joy so strong."

Another thought the while, severe and sweet,
Laborious, yet delectable in scope,
Takes in my heart its seat,
Filling with glory, feeding it with hope;
Till, bent alone on bright and deathless fame,
It feels not when I freeze, or burn in flame,
When I am pale or ill,
And if I crush it rises stronger still.
This, from my helpless cradle, day by day,
Has strengthen'd with my strength, grown with my growth,
Till haply now one tomb must cover both:
When from the flesh the soul has pass'd away,
No more this passion comrades it as here;
For fame – if, after death,
Learning speak aught of me – is but a breath:
Wherefore, because I fear
Hopes to indulge which the next hour may chase,

I would old error leave, and the one truth embrace.

But the third wish which fills and fires my heart
O'ershadows all the rest which near it spring:
Time, too, dispels a part,
While, but for her, self-reckless grown, I sing.
And then the rare light of those beauteous eyes,
Sweetly before whose gentle heat I melt,
As a fine curb is felt,
To combat which avails not wit or force;
What boots it, trammell'd by such adverse ties,
If still between the rocks must lie her course,
To trim my little bark to new emprize?
Ah! wilt Thou never, Lord, who yet dost keep
Me safe and free from common chains, which bind,
In different modes, mankind,
Deign also from my brow this shame to sweep?
For, as one sunk in sleep,
Methinks death ever present to my sight,
Yet when I would resist I have no arms to fight.

Full well I see my state, in nought deceived
By truth ill known, but rather forced by Love,
Who leaves not him to move
In honour, who too much his grace believed:
For o'er my heart from time to time I feel
A subtle scorn, a lively anguish, steal,
Whence every hidden thought,
Where all may see, upon my brow is writ.
For with such faith on mortal things to dote,
As unto God alone is just and fit,
Disgraces worst the prize who covets most:
Should reason, amid things of sense, be lost.
This loudly calls her to the proper track:
But, when she would obey
And home return, ill habits keep her back,
And to my view portray
Her who was only born my death to be,
Too lovely in herself, too loved, alas! by me.

I neither know, to me what term of life

Heaven destined when on earth I came at first
To suffer this sharp strife,
'Gainst my own peace which I myself have nursed,
Nor can I, for the veil my body throws,
Yet see the time when my sad life may close.
I feel my frame begin
To fail, and vary each desire within:
And now that I believe my parting day
Is near at hand, or else not distant lies,
Like one whom losses wary make and wise,
I travel back in thought, where first the way,
The right-hand way, I left, to peace which led.
While through me shame and grief,
Recalling the vain past on this side spread,
On that brings no relief,
Passion, whose strength I now from habit, feel,
So great that it would dare with death itself to deal.

Song! I am here, my heart the while more cold
With fear than frozen snow,
Feels in its certain core death's coming blow;
For thus, in weak self-communing, has roll'd
Of my vain life the better portion by:
Worse burden surely ne'er
Tried mortal man than that which now I bear;
Though death be seated nigh,
For future life still seeking councils new,
I know and love the good, yet, ah! the worse pursue.

Robert Macgregor.

SONNET CCXXVI.

Aspro core e selvaggio, e cruda voglia.

HOPE ALONE SUPPORTS HIM IN HIS MISERY.

Hard heart and cold, a stern will past belief,
In angel form of gentle sweet allure;
If thus her practised rigour long endure,
O'er me her triumph will be poor and brief.
For when or spring, or die, flower, herb, and leaf.
When day is brightest, night when most obscure,
Alway I weep. Great cause from Fortune sure,
From Love and Laura have I for my grief.
I live in hope alone, remembering still
How by long fall of small drops I have seen
Marble and solid stone that worn have been.
No heart there is so hard, so cold no will,
By true tears, fervent prayers, and faithful love
That will not deign at length to melt and move.

Robert Macgregor.

SONNET CCXXVII.

Signor mio caro, ogni pensier mi tira.

HE LAMENTS HIS ABSENCE FROM LAURA AND COLONNA, THE ONLY OBJECTS OF HIS AFFECTION.

My lord and friend! thoughts, wishes, all inclined
My heart to visit one so dear to me,
But Fortune – can she ever worse decree? –
Held me in hand, misled, or kept behind.
Since then the dear desire Love taught my mind
But leads me to a death I did not see,
And while my twin lights, wheresoe'er I be,
Are still denied, by day and night I've pined.
Affection for my lord, my lady's love,
The bonds have been wherewith in torments long
I have been bound, which round myself I wove.
A Laurel green, a Column fair and strong,
This for three lustres, that for three years more
In my fond breast, nor wish'd it free, I bore.

Robert Macgregor.

PART TWO

TO LAURA IN DEATH

SONNET I.

Oimè il bel viso! oimè il soave sguardo!

ON THE ANNOUNCEMENT OF THE DEATH OF LAURA.

Woe for the 'witching look of that fair face!
The port where ease with dignity combined!
Woe for those accents, that each savage mind
To softness tuned, to noblest thoughts the base!
And the sweet smile, from whence the dart I trace,
Which now leaves death my only hope behind!
Exalted soul, most fit on thrones to 've shined,
But that too late she came this earth to grace!
For you I still must burn, and breathe in you;
For I was ever yours; of you bereft,
Full little now I reck all other care.
With hope and with desire you thrill'd me through,
When last my only joy on earth I left: –
But caught by winds each word was lost in air.

Anonymous, Ox., 1795.

Alas! that touching glance, that beauteous face!
Alas! that dignity with sweetness fraught!
Alas! that speech which tamed the wildest thought!
That roused the coward, glory to embrace!
Alas! that smile which in me did encase
That fatal dart, whence here I hope for nought –
Oh! hadst thou earlier our regions sought,
The world had then confess'd thy sovereign grace!
In thee I breathed, life's flame was nursed by thee,
For I was thine; and since of thee bereaved,
Each other woe hath lost its venom'd sting:
My soul's blest joy! when last thy voice on me
In music fell, my heart sweet hope conceived;
Alas! thy words have sped on zephyrs' wings!

Miss Wollaston.

CANZONE I.

Che debb' io far? che mi consigli, Amore?

HE ASKS COUNSEL OF LOVE, WHETHER HE SHOULD FOLLOW LAURA, OR STILL ENDURE EXISTENCE.

What should I do? what, Love, dost thou advise?
Full time it is to die:
And longer than I wish have I delay'd.
My mistress is no more, and with her gone my heart;
To follow her, I must need
Break short the course of my afflictive years:
To view her here below
I ne'er can hope; and irksome 'tis to wait.
Since that my every joy
By her departure unto tears is turn'd,
Of all its sweets my life has been deprived.

Thou, Love, dost feel, therefore to thee I plain,
How grievous is my loss;
I know my sorrows grieve and weigh thee down,
E'en as our common cause: for on one rock
We both have wreck'd our bark;
And in one instant was its sun obscured.
What genius can with words
Rightly describe my lamentable state?
Ah, blind, ungrateful world!
Thou hast indeed just cause with me to mourn;
That beauty thou didst hold with her is fled!

Fall'n is thy glory, and thou seest it not;
Unworthy thou with her,
While here she dwelt, acquaintance to maintain.
Or to be trodden by her saintly feet;
For that, which is so fair,
Should with its presence decorate the skies
But I, a wretch who, reft
Of her, prize nor myself nor mortal life,

Recall her with my tears:
This only of my hope's vast sum remains;
And this alone doth still support me here.

Ah, me! her charming face is earth become,
Which wont unto our thought
To picture heaven and happiness above!
Her viewless form inhabits paradise,
Divested of that veil,
Which shadow'd while below her bloom of life,
Once more to put it on,
And never then to cast it off again;
When so much more divine,
And glorious render'd, 'twill by us be view'd,
As mortal beauty to eternal yields.

More bright than ever, and a lovelier fair,
Before me she appears,
Where most she's conscious that her sight will please
This is one pillar that sustains my life;
The other her dear name,
That to my heart sounds so delightfully.
But tracing in my mind,
That she who form'd my choicest hope is dead
E'en in her blossom'd prime;
Thou knowest, Love, full well what I become:
She I trust sees it too, who dwells with truth.

Ye sweet associates, who admired her charms,
Her life angelical,
And her demeanour heavenly upon earth
For me lament, and be by pity wrought
No wise for her, who, risen
To so much peace, me has in warfare left;
Such, that should any shut
The road to follow her, for some length of time,
What Love declares to me
Alone would check my cutting through the tie;
But in this guise he reasons from within:

"The mighty grief transporting thee restrain;

For passions uncontroll'd
Forfeit that heaven, to which thy soul aspires,
Where she is living whom some fancy dead;
While at her fair remains
She smiles herself, sighing for thee alone;
And that her fame, which lives
In many a clime hymn'd by thy tongue, may ne'er
Become extinct, she prays;
But that her name should harmonize thy voice;
If e'er her eyes were lovely held, and dear."
Fly the calm, green retreat;
And ne'er approach where song and laughter dwell,
O strain; but wail be thine!
It suits thee ill with the glad throng to stay,
Thou sorrowing widow wrapp'd in garb of woe.

Dr Nott

SONNET II.

Rotta è l' alta Colonna, e 'l verde Lauro.

HE BEWAILS HIS DOUBLE LOSS IN THE DEATHS OF LAURA, AND OF COLONNA.

Fall'n that proud Column, fall'n that Laurel tree,
Whose shelter once relieved my wearied mind;
I'm reft of what I ne'er again shall find,
Though ransack'd every shore and every sea:
Double the treasure death has torn from me,
In which life's pride was with its pleasure join'd;
Not eastern gems, nor the world's wealth combined,
Can give it back, nor land, nor royalty.
But, if so fate decrees, what can I more,
Than with unceasing tears these eyes bedew,
Abase my visage, and my lot deplore?
Ah, what is life, so lovely to the view!
How quickly in one little morn is lost
What years have won with labour and with cost!

Dr Nott

My laurell'd hope! and thou, Colonna proud!
Your broken strength can shelter me no more!
Nor Boreas, Auster, Indus, Afric's shore,
Can give me that, whose loss my soul hath bow'd:
My step exulting, and my joy avow'd,
Death now hath quench'd with ye, my heart's twin store;
Nor earth's high rule, nor gems, nor gold's bright ore,
Can e'er bring back what once my heart endow'd
But if this grief my destiny hath will'd,
What else can I oppose but tearful eyes,
A sorrowing bosom, and a spirit quell'd?
O life! whose vista seems so brightly fill'd,
A sunny breath, and that exhaling, dies
The hope, oft, many watchful years have swell'd.

Miss Wollaston.

CANZONE II.

Amor, se vuoi ch' i' torni al giogo antico.

UNLESS LOVE CAN RESTORE HER TO LIFE, HE WILL NEVER AGAIN BE HIS SLAVE.

If thou wouldst have me, Love, thy slave again,
One other proof, miraculous and new,
Must yet be wrought by you,
Ere, conquer'd, I resume my ancient chain –
Lift my dear love from earth which hides her now,
For whose sad loss thus beggar'd I remain;
Once more with warmth endow
That wise chaste heart where wont my life to dwell;
And if as some divine, thy influence so,
From highest heaven unto the depths of hell,
Prevail in sooth – for what its scope below,
'Mid us of common race,
Methinks each gentle breast may answer well –
Rob Death of his late triumph, and replace
Thy conquering ensign in her lovely face!

Relume on that fair brow the living light,
Which was my honour'd guide, and the sweet flame.
Though spent, which still the same
Kindles me now as when it burn'd most bright;
For thirsty hind with such desire did ne'er
Long for green pastures or the crystal brook,
As I for the dear look,
Whence I have borne so much, and – if aright
I read myself and passion – more must bear:
This makes me to one theme my thoughts thus bind,
An aimless wanderer where is pathway none,
With weak and wearied mind
Pursuing hopes which never can be won.
Hence to thy summons answer I disdain,
Thine is no power beyond thy proper reign.

Give me again that gentle voice to hear,
As in my heart are heard its echoes still,
Which had in song the skill
Hate to disarm, rage soften, sorrow cheer,
To tranquillize each tempest of the mind,
And from dark lowering clouds to keep it clear;
Which sweetly then refined
And raised my verse where now it may not soar.
And, with desire that hope may equal vie,
Since now my mind is waked in strength, restore
Their proper business to my ear and eye,
Awanting which life must
All tasteless be and harder than to die.
Vainly with me to your old power you trust,
While my first love is shrouded still in dust.

Give her dear glance again to bless my sight,
Which, as the sun on snow, beam'd still for me;
Open each window bright
Where pass'd my heart whence no return can be;
Resume thy golden shafts, prepare thy bow,
And let me once more drink with old delight
Of that dear voice the sound,
Whence what love is I first was taught to know.
And, for the lures, which still I covet so,
Were rifest, richest there my soul that bound,
Waken to life her tongue, and on the breeze
Let her light silken hair,
Loosen'd by Love's own fingers, float at ease;
Do this, and I thy willing yoke will bear,
Else thy hope faileth my free will to snare.

Oh! never my gone heart those links of gold,
Artlessly negligent, or curl'd with grace,
Nor her enchanting face,
Sweetly severe, can captive cease to hold;
These, night and day, the amorous wish in me
Kept, more than laurel or than myrtle, green,
When, doff'd or donn'd, we see
Of fields the grass, of woods their leafy screen.
And since that Death so haughty stands and stern

The bond now broken whence I fear'd to flee,
Nor thine the art, howe'er the world may turn,
To bind anew the chain,
What boots it, Love, old arts to try again?
Their day is pass'd: thy power, since lost the arms
Which were my terror once, no longer harms.

Thy arms were then her eyes, unrivall'd, whence
Live darts were freely shot of viewless flame;
No help from reason came,
For against Heaven avails not man's defence;
Thought, Silence, Feeling, Gaiety, Wit, Sense,
Modest demeanour, affable discourse,
In words of sweetest force
Whence every grosser nature gentle grew,
That angel air, humble to all and kind,
Whose praise, it needs not mine, from all we find;
Stood she, or sat, a grace which often threw
Doubt on the gazer's mind
To which the meed of highest praise was due –
O'er hardest hearts thy victory was sure,
With arms like these, which lost I am secure.

The minds which Heaven abandons to thy reign,
Haply are bound in many times and ways,
But mine one only chain,
Its wisdom shielding me from more, obeys;
Yet freedom brings no joy, though that he burst.
Rather I mournful ask, "Sweet pilgrim mine,
Alas! what doom divine
Me earliest bound to life yet frees thee first:
God, who has snatch'd thee from the world so soon,
Only to kindle our desires, the boon
Of virtue, so complete and lofty, gave
Now, Love, I may deride
Thy future wounds, nor fear to be thy slave;
In vain thy bow is bent, its bolts fall wide,
When closed her brilliant eyes their virtue died.

"Death from thy every law my heart has freed;
She who my lady was is pass'd on high,

Leaving me free to count dull hours drag by,
To solitude and sorrow still decreed."

Robert Macgregor.

SONNET III.

L' ardente nodo ov' io fui, d' ora in ora.

ON THE DEATH OF ANOTHER LADY.

That burning toil, in which I once was caught,
While twice ten years and one I counted o'er,
Death has unloosed: like burden I ne'er bore;
That grief ne'er fatal proves I now am taught.
But Love, who to entangle me still sought,
Spread in the treacherous grass his net once more,
So fed the fire with fuel as before,
That my escape I hardly could have wrought.
And, but that my first woes experience gave,
Snarèd long since and kindled I had been,
And all the more, as I'm become less green:
My freedom death again has come to save,
And break my bond; that flame now fades, and fails,
'Gainst which nor force nor intellect prevails.

Dr Nott

SONNET IV.

La vita fugge, e non s' arresta un' ora.

PAST, PRESENT, AND FUTURE ARE NOW ALIKE PAINFUL TO HIM.

Life passes quick, nor will a moment stay,
And death with hasty journeys still draws near;
And all the present joins my soul to tear,
With every past and every future day:
And to look back or forward, so does prey
On this distracted breast, that sure I swear,
Did I not to myself some pity bear,
I were e'en now from all these thoughts away.
Much do I muse on what of pleasures past
This woe-worn heart has known; meanwhile, t' oppose
My passage, loud the winds around me roar.
I see my bliss in port, and torn my mast
And sails, my pilot faint with toil, and those
Fair lights, that wont to guide me, now no more.

Anonymous, Ox., 1795.

Life ever flies with course that nought may stay,
Death follows after with gigantic stride;
Ills past and present on my spirit prey,
And future evils threat on every side:
Whether I backward look or forward fare,
A thousand ills my bosom's peace molest;
And were it not that pity bids me spare
My nobler part, I from these thoughts would rest.
If ever aught of sweet my heart has known,
Remembrance wakes its charms, while, tempest tost,
I mark the clouds that o'er my course still frown;
E'en in the port I see the storm afar;
Weary my pilot, mast and cable lost,
And set for ever my fair polar star.

Lady Dacre.

SONNET V.

Che fai? che pensi? che pur dietro guardi.

HE ENCOURAGES HIS SOUL TO LIFT ITSELF TO GOD, AND TO ABANDON THE VANITIES OF EARTH.

What dost thou? think'st thou? wherefore bend thine eye
Back on the time that never shall return?
The raging fire, where once 'twas thine to burn,
Why with fresh fuel, wretched soul, supply?
Those thrilling tones, those glances of the sky,
Which one by one thy fond verse strove to adorn,
Are fled; and – well thou knowest, poor forlorn! –
To seek them here were bootless industry.
Then toil not bliss so fleeting to renew;
To chase a thought so fair, so faithless, cease:
Thou rather that unwavering good pursue,
Which guides to heaven; since nought below can please.
Fatal for us that beauty's torturing view,
Living or dead alike which desolates our peace.

Francis Wrangham.

SONNET VI.

Datemi pace, o duri miei pensieri.

HE COMPARES HIMSELF TO A BESIEGED CITY, AND ACCUSES HIS OWN HEART OF TREASON.

O tyrant thoughts, vouchsafe me some repose!
Sufficeth not that Love, and Death, and Fate,
Make war all round me to my very gate,
But I must in me armèd hosts enclose?
And thou, my heart, to me alone that shows
Disloyal still, what cruel guides of late
In thee find shelter, now the chosen mate
Of my most mischievous and bitter foes?
Love his most secret embassies in thee,
In thee her worst results hard Fate explains,
And Death the memory of that blow, to me
Which shatters all that yet of hope remains;
In thee vague thoughts themselves with error arm,
And thee alone I blame for all my harm.

Robert Macgregor.

SONNET VII.

Occhi miei, oscurato è 'l nostro sole.

HE ENDEAVOURS TO FIND PEACE IN THE THOUGHT THAT SHE IS IN HEAVEN.

Mine eyes! our glorious sun is veil'd in night,
Or set to us, to rise 'mid realms of love;
There we may hail it still, and haply prove
It mourn'd that we delay'd our heavenward flight.
Mine ears! the music of her tones delight
Those, who its harmony can best approve;
My feet! who in her track so joy'd to move.
Ye cannot penetrate her regions bright!
But wherefore should your wrath on me descend?
No spell of mine hath hush'd for ye the joy
Of seeing, hearing, feeling, she was near:
Go, war with Death – yet, rather let us bend
To Him who can create – who can destroy –
And bids the ready smile succeed the tear.

Miss Wollaston.

O my sad eyes! our sun is overcast, –
Nay, rather borne to heaven, and there is shining,
Waiting our coming, and perchance repining
At our delay; there shall we meet at last:
And there, mine ears, her angel words float past,
Those who best understand their sweet divining;
Howe'er, my feet, unto the search inclining,
Ye cannot reach her in those regions vast.
Why, then, do ye torment me thus, for, oh!
It is no fault of mine, that ye no more
Behold, and hear, and welcome her below;
Blame Death, – or rather praise Him and adore,
Who binds and frees, restrains and letteth go,
And to the weeping one can joy restore.

Mrs Wrottesley.

SONNET VIII.

Poichè la vista angelica serena.

WITH HER, HIS ONLY SOLACE, IS TAKEN AWAY ALL HIS DESIRE OF LIFE.

Since her calm angel face, long beauty's fane,
My beggar'd soul by this brief parting throws
In darkest horrors and in deepest woes,
I seek by uttering to allay my pain.
Certes, just sorrow leads me to complain:
This she, who is its cause, and Love too shows;
No other remedy my poor heart knows
Against the troubles that in life obtain.
Death! thou hast snatch'd her hence with hand unkind,
And thou, glad Earth! that fair and kindly face
Now hidest from me in thy close embrace;
Why leave me here, disconsolate and blind,
Since she who of mine eyes the light has been,
Sweet, loving, bright, no more with me is seen?

Robert Macgregor.

SONNET IX.

S' Amor novo consiglio non n' apporta.

HE DESCRIBES HIS SAD STATE.

If Love to give new counsel still delay,
My life must change to other scenes than these;
My troubled spirit grief and terror freeze,
Desire augments while all my hopes decay.
Thus ever grows my life, by night and day,
Despondent, and dismay'd, and ill at ease,
Harass'd and helmless on tempestuous seas,
With no sure escort on a doubtful way.
Her path a sick imagination guides,
Its true light underneath – ah, no! on high,
Whence on my heart she beams more bright than eye,
Not on mine eyes; from them a dark veil hides
Those lovely orbs, and makes me, ere life's span
Is measured half, an old and broken man.

Robert Macgregor.

SONNET X.

Nell' età sua più bella e più fiorita.

HE DESIRES TO DIE, THAT HIS SOUL MAY BE WITH HER, AS HIS THOUGHTS ALREADY ARE.

E'en in youth's fairest flower, when Love's dear sway
Is wont with strongest power our hearts to bind,
Leaving on earth her fleshly veil behind,
My life, my Laura, pass'd from me away;
Living, and fair, and free from our vile clay,
From heaven she rules supreme my willing mind:
Alas! why left me in this mortal rind
That first of peace, of sin that latest day?
As my fond thoughts her heavenward path pursue,
So may my soul glad, light, and ready be
To follow her, and thus from troubles flee.
Whate'er delays me as worst loss I rue:
Time makes me to myself but heavier grow:
Death had been sweet to-day three years ago!

Robert Macgregor.

SONNET XI.

Se lamentar augelli, o Verdi fronde.

SHE IS EVER PRESENT TO HIM.

If the lorn bird complain, or rustling sweep
Soft summer airs o'er foliage waving slow,
Or the hoarse brook come murmuring down the steep,
Where on the enamell'd bank I sit below
With thoughts of love that bid my numbers flow;
'Tis then I see her, though in earth she sleep!
Her, form'd in heaven! I see, and hear, and know!
Responsive sighing, weeping as I weep:
"Alas," she pitying says, "ere yet the hour,
Why hurry life away with swifter flight?
Why from thy eyes this flood of sorrow pour?
No longer mourn my fate! through death my days
Become eternal! to eternal light
These eyes, which seem'd in darkness closed, I raise!"

Lady Dacre.

Where the green leaves exclude the summer beam,
And softly bend as balmy breezes blow,
And where with liquid lapse the lucid stream
Across the fretted rock is heard to flow,
Pensive I lay: when she whom earth conceals
As if still living to my eye appears;
And pitying Heaven her angel form reveals
To say, "Unhappy Petrarch, dry your tears.
Ah! why, sad lover, thus before your time
In grief and sadness should your life decay,
And, like a blighted flower, your manly prime
In vain and hopeless sorrow fade away?
Ah! yield not thus to culpable despair;
But raise thine eyes to heaven and think I wait thee there!"

Charlotte Smith.

Moved by the summer wind when all is still,
The light leaves quiver on the yielding spray;
Sighs from its flowery bank the lucid rill,
While the birds answer in their sweetest lay.
Vain to this sickening heart these scenes appear:
No form but hers can meet my tearful eyes;
In every passing gale her voice I hear;
It seems to tell me, "I have heard thy sighs.
But why," she cries, "in manhood's towering prime,
In grief's dark mist thy days, inglorious, hide?
Ah! dost thou murmur, that my span of time
Has join'd eternity's unchanging tide?
Yes, though I seem'd to shut mine eyes in night,
They only closed to wake in everlasting light!"

Anne Bannerman.

SONNET XII.

Mai non fu' in parte ove sì chiar' vedessi.

VAUCLUSE.

Nowhere before could I so well have seen
Her whom my soul most craves since lost to view;
Nowhere in so great freedom could have been
Breathing my amorous lays 'neath skies so blue;
Never with depths of shade so calm and green
A valley found for lover's sigh more true;
Methinks a spot so lovely and serene
Love not in Cyprus nor in Gnidos knew.
All breathes one spell, all prompts and prays that I
Like them should love – the clear sky, the calm hour,
Winds, waters, birds, the green bough, the gay flower –
But thou, beloved, who call'st me from on high,
By the sad memory of thine early fate,
Pray that I hold the world and these sweet snares in hate.

Robert Macgregor.

Never till now so clearly have I seen
Her whom my eyes desire, my soul still views;
Never enjoy'd a freedom thus serene;
Ne'er thus to heaven breathed my enamour'd muse,
As in this vale sequester'd, darkly green;
Where my soothed heart its pensive thought pursues,
And nought intrusively may intervene,
And all my sweetly-tender sighs renews.
To Love and meditation, faithful shade,
Receive the breathings of my grateful breast!
Love not in Cyprus found so sweet a nest
As this, by pine and arching laurel made!
The birds, breeze, water, branches, whisper love;
Herb, flower, and verdant path the lay symphonious move.

Capel Lofft.

SONNET XIII.

Quante fiate al mio dolce ricetto.

HER FORM STILL HAUNTS HIM IN SOLITUDE.

How oft, all lonely, to my sweet retreat
From man and from myself I strive to fly,
Bathing with dewy eyes each much-loved seat,
And swelling every blossom with a sigh!
How oft, deep musing on my woes complete,
Along the dark and silent glens I lie,
In thought again that dearest form to meet
By death possess'd, and therefore wish to die!
How oft I see her rising from the tide
Of Sorga, like some goddess of the flood;
Or pensive wander by the river's side;
Or tread the flowery mazes of the wood;
Bright as in life; while angel pity throws
O'er her fair face the impress of my woes.

J.H. Merivale.

SONNET XIV.

Alma felice, che sovente torni.

HE THANKS HER THAT FROM TIME TO TIME SHE RETURNS TO CONSOLE HIM WITH HER PRESENCE.

O blessed spirit! who dost oft return,
Ministering comfort to my nights of woe,
From eyes which Death, relenting in his blow,
Has lit with all the lustres of the morn:
How am I gladden'd, that thou dost not scorn
O'er my dark days thy radiant beam to throw!
Thus do I seem again to trace below
Thy beauties, hovering o'er their loved sojourn.
There now, thou seest, where long of thee had been
My sprightlier strain, of thee my plaint I swell –
Of thee! – oh, no! of mine own sorrows keen.
One only solace cheers the wretched scene:
By many a sign I know thy coming well –
Thy step, thy voice and look, and robe of favour'd green.

Francis Wrangham.

When welcome slumber locks my torpid frame,
I see thy spirit in the midnight dream;
Thine eyes that still in living lustre beam:
In all but frail mortality the same.
Ah! then, from earth and all its sorrows free,
Methinks I meet thee in each former scene:
Once the sweet shelter of a heart serene;
Now vocal only while I weep for thee.
For thee! – ah, no! From human ills secure.
Thy hallow'd soul exults in endless day;
'Tis I who linger on the toilsome way:
No balm relieves the anguish I endure;
Save the fond feeble hope that thou art near
To soothe my sufferings with an angel's tear.

Anne Bannerman.

SONNET XV.

Discolorato hai, Morte, il più bel volto.

HER PRESENCE IN VISIONS IS HIS ONLY CONSOLATION.

Death, thou of fairest face hast 'reft the hue,
And quench'd in deep thick night the brightest eyes,
And loosed from all its tenderest, closest ties
A spirit to faith and ardent virtue true.
In one short hour to all my bliss adieu!
Hush'd are those accents worthy of the skies,
Unearthly sounds, whose loss awakes my sighs;
And all I hear is grief, and all I view.
Yet oft, to soothe this lone and anguish'd heart,
By pity led, she comes my couch to seek,
Nor find I other solace here below:
And if her thrilling tones my strain could speak
And look divine, with Love's enkindling dart
Not man's sad breast alone, but fiercest beasts should glow.

Francis Wrangham.

Thou hast despoil'd the fairest face e'er seen –
Thou hast extinguish'd, Death, the brightest eyes,
And snapp'd the cord in sunder of the ties
Which bound that spirit brilliantly serene:
In one short moment all I love has been
Torn from me, and dark silence now supplies
Those gentle tones; my heart, which bursts with sighs,
Nor sight nor sound from weariness can screen:
Yet doth my lady, by compassion led,
Return to solace my unfailing woe;
Earth yields no other balm: – oh! could I tell
How bright she seems, and how her accents flow,
Not unto man alone Love's flames would spread,
But even bears and tigers share the spell.

Mrs Wrottesley.

SONNET XVI.

Sì breve è 'l tempo e 'l pensier sì veloce.

THE REMEMBRANCE OF HER CHASES SADNESS FROM HIS HEART.

So brief the time, so fugitive the thought
Which Laura yields to me, though dead, again,
Small medicine give they to my giant pain;
Still, as I look on her, afflicts me nought.
Love, on the rack who holds me as he brought,
Fears when he sees her thus my soul retain,
Where still the seraph face and sweet voice reign,
Which first his tyranny and triumph wrought.
As rules a mistress in her home of right,
From my dark heavy heart her placid brow
Dispels each anxious thought and omen drear.
My soul, which bears but ill such dazzling light,
Says with a sigh: "O blessed day! when thou
Didst ope with those dear eyes thy passage here!"

Robert Macgregor.

SONNET XVII.

Nè mai pietosa madre al caro figlio.

HER COUNSEL ALONE AFFORDS HIM RELIEF.

Ne'er did fond mother to her darling son,
Or zealous spouse to her belovèd mate,
Sage counsel give, in perilous estate,
With such kind caution, in such tender tone,
As gives that fair one, who, oft looking down
On my hard exile from her heavenly seat,
With wonted kindness bends upon my fate
Her brow, as friend or parent would have done:
Now chaste affection prompts her speech, now fear,
Instructive speech, that points what several ways
To seek or shun, while journeying here below;
Then all the ills of life she counts, and prays
My soul ere long may quit this terrene sphere:
And by her words alone I'm soothed and freed from woe.

Dr Nott

Ne'er to the son, in whom her age is blest,
The anxious mother – nor to her loved lord
The wedded dame, impending ill to ward,
With careful sighs so faithful counsel press'd,
As she, who, from her high eternal rest,
Bending – as though my exile she deplored –
With all her wonted tenderness restored,
And softer pity on her brow impress'd!
Now with a mother's fears, and now as one
Who loves with chaste affection, in her speech
She points what to pursue and what to shun!
Our years retracing of long, various grief,
Wooing my soul at higher good to reach,
And while she speaks, my bosom finds relief!

Lady Dacre.

SONNET XVIII.

Se quell' aura soave de' sospiri.

SHE RETURNS IN PITY TO COMFORT HIM WITH HER ADVICE.

If that soft breath of sighs, which, from above,
I hear of her so long my lady here,
Who, now in heaven, yet seems, as of our sphere,
To breathe, and move, to feel, and live, and love,
I could but paint, my passionate verse should move
Warmest desires; so jealous, yet so dear
O'er me she bends and breathes, without a fear,
That on the way I tire, or turn, or rove.
She points the path on high: and I who know
Her chaste anxiety and earnest prayer,
In whispers sweet, affectionate, and low,
Train, at her will, my acts and wishes there:
And find such sweetness in her words alone
As with their power should melt the hardest stone.

Robert Macgregor.

SONNET XIX.

Sennuccio mio, benchè doglioso e solo.

ON THE DEATH OF HIS FRIEND SENNUCCIO.

O friend! though left a wretched pilgrim here,
By thee though left in solitude to roam,
Yet can I mourn that thou hast found thy home,
On angel pinions borne, in bright career?
Now thou behold'st the ever-turning sphere,
And stars that journey round the concave dome;
Now thou behold'st how short of truth we come,
How blind our judgment, and thine own how clear!
That thou art happy soothes my soul oppress'd.
O friend! salute from me the laurell'd band,
Guitton and Cino, Dante, and the rest:
And tell my Laura, friend, that here I stand,
Wasting in tears, scarce of myself possess'd,
While her blest beauties all my thoughts command.

Dr Morehead.

Sennuccio mine! I yet myself console,
Though thou hast left me, mournful and alone,
For eagerly to heaven thy spirit has flown,
Free from the flesh which did so late enrol;
Thence, at one view, commands it either pole,
The planets and their wondrous courses known,
And human sight how brief and doubtful shown;
Thus with thy bliss my sorrow I control.
One favour – in the third of those bright spheres.
Guido and Dante, Cino, too, salute,
With Franceschin and all that tuneful train,
And tell my lady how I live, in tears,
(Savage and lonely as some forest brute)
Her sweet face and fair works when memory brings again.

Robert Macgregor.

SONNET XX.

I' ho pien di sospir quest' aer tutto.

VAUCLUSE HAS BECOME TO HIM A SCENE OF PAIN.

To every sound, save sighs, this air is mute,
When from rude rocks, I view the smiling land
Where she was born, who held my life in hand
From its first bud till blossoms turn'd to fruit:
To heaven she's gone, and I'm left destitute
To mourn her loss, and cast around in pain
These wearied eyes, which, seeking her in vain
Where'er they turn, o'erflow with grief acute;
There's not a root or stone amongst these hills,
Nor branch nor verdant leaf 'midst these soft glades,
Nor in the valley flowery herbage grows,
Nor liquid drop the sparkling fount distils,
Nor savage beast that shelters in these shades,
But knows how sharp my grief – how deep my woes.

Mrs Wrottesley.

SONNET XXI.

L' alma mia fiamma oltra le belle bella.

HE ACKNOWLEDGES THE WISDOM OF HER PAST COLDNESS TO HIM.

My noble flame – more fair than fairest are
Whom kind Heaven here has e'er in favour shown –
Before her time, alas for me! has flown
To her celestial home and parent star.
I seem but now to wake; wherein a bar
She placed on passion 'twas for good alone,
As, with a gentle coldness all her own,
She waged with my hot wishes virtuous war.
My thanks on her for such wise care I press,
That with her lovely face and sweet disdain
She check'd my love and taught me peace to gain.
O graceful artifice! deserved success!
I with my fond verse, with her bright eyes she,
Glory in her, she virtue got in me.

Robert Macgregor.

SONNET XXII.

Come va 'l mondo! or mi diletta e piace.

HE BLESSES LAURA FOR HER VIRTUE.

How goes the world! now please me and delight
What most displeased me: now I see and feel
My trials were vouchsafed me for my weal,
That peace eternal should brief war requite.
O hopes and wishes, ever fond and slight,
In lovers most, which oftener harm than heal!
Worse had she yielded to my warm appeal
Whom Heaven has welcomed from the grave's dark night.
But blind love and my dull mind so misled,
I sought to trespass even by main force
Where to have won my precious soul were dead.
Blessèd be she who shaped mine erring course
To better port, by turns who curb'd and lured
My bold and passionate will where safety was secured.

Robert Macgregor.

Alas! this changing world! my present joy
Was once my grief's dark source, and now I feel
My sufferings pass'd were but my soul to heal
Its fearful warfare – peace's soft decoy.
Poor human wishes! Hope, thou fragile toy
To lovers oft! my woe had met its seal,
Had she but hearken'd to my love's appeal,
Who, throned in heaven, hath fled this world's alloy.
My blinded love, and yet more stubborn mind,
Resistless urged me to my bosom's shame,
And where my soul's destruction I had met:
But blessèd she who bade life's current find
A holier course, who still'd my spirit's flame
With gentle hope that soul might triumph yet.

Miss Wollaston.

SONNET XXIII.

Quand' io veggio dal ciel scender l' Aurora.

MORN RENDERS HIS GRIEF MORE POIGNANT.

When from the heavens I see Aurora beam,
With rosy-tinctured cheek and golden hair,
Love bids my face the hue of sadness wear:
"There Laura dwells!" I with a sigh exclaim.
Thou knowest well the hour that shall redeem,
Happy Tithonus, thy much-valued fair;
But not to her I love can I repair,
Till death extinguishes this vital flame.
Yet need'st thou not thy separation mourn;
Certain at evening's close is the return
Of her, who doth not thy hoar locks despise;
But my nights sad, my days are render'd drear,
By her, who bore my thoughts to yonder skies,
And only a remember'd name left here.

Dr Nott

When from the east appears the purple ray
Of morn arising, and salutes the eyes
That wear the night in watching for the day,
Thus speaks my heart: "In yonder opening skies,
In yonder fields of bliss, my Laura lies!"
Thou sun, that know'st to wheel thy burning car,
Each eve, to the still surface of the deep,
And there within thy Thetis' bosom sleep;
Oh! could I thus my Laura's presence share,
How would my patient heart its sorrows bear!
Adored in life, and honour'd in the dust,
She that in this fond breast for ever reigns
Has pass'd the gulph of death! – To deck that bust,
No trace of her but the sad name remains.

Lord Woodhouselee.

SONNET XXIV.

Gli occhi di ch' io parlai sì caldamente.

HIS LYRE IS NOW ATTUNED ONLY TO WOE.

The eyes, the face, the limbs of heavenly mould,
So long the theme of my impassion'd lay,
Charms which so stole me from myself away,
That strange to other men the course I hold;
The crispèd locks of pure and lucid gold,
The lightning of the angelic smile, whose ray
To earth could all of paradise convey,
A little dust are now! – to feeling cold!
And yet I live! – but that I live bewail,
Sunk the loved light that through the tempest led
My shatter'd bark, bereft of mast and sail:
Hush'd be for aye the song that breathed love's fire!
Lost is the theme on which my fancy fed,
And turn'd to mourning my once tuneful lyre.

Lady Dacre.

The eyes, the arms, the hands, the feet, the face,
Which made my thoughts and words so warm and wild,
That I was almost from myself exiled,
And render'd strange to all the human race;
The lucid locks that curl'd in golden grace,
The lightening beam that, when my angel smiled,
Diffused o'er earth an Eden heavenly mild;
What are they now? Dust, lifeless dust, alas!
And I live on, a melancholy slave,
Toss'd by the tempest in a shatter'd bark,
Reft of the lovely light that cheer'd the wave.
The flame of genius, too, extinct and dark,
Here let my lays of love conclusion have;
Mute be the lyre: tears best my sorrows mark.

Dr Morehead.

Those eyes whose living lustre shed the heat
Of bright meridian day; the heavenly mould
Of that angelic form; the hands, the feet,
The taper arms, the crispèd locks of gold;
Charms that the sweets of paradise enfold;
The radiant lightning of her angel-smile,
And every grace that could the sense beguile
Are now a pile of ashes, deadly cold!
And yet I bear to drag this cumbrous chain,
That weighs my soul to earth – to bliss or pain
Alike insensible: – her anchor lost,
The frail dismantled bark, all tempest-toss'd,
Surveys no port of comfort – closed the scene
Of life's delusive joys; – and dry the Muse's vein.

Lord Woodhouselee.

Those eyes, sweet subject of my rapturous strain!
The arms, the hands, the feet, that lovely face,
By which I from myself divided was,
And parted from the vulgar and the vain;
Those crispèd locks, pure gold unknown to stain!
Of that angelic smile the lightening grace,
Which wont to make this earth a heavenly place!
Dissolved to senseless ashes now remain!
And yet I live, to endless grief a prey,
'Reft of that star, my loved, my certain guide,
Disarm'd my bark, while tempests round me blow!
Stop, then, my verse – dry is the fountain's tide.
That fed my genius! Cease, my amorous lay!
Changed is my lyre, attuned to endless woe!

Lord Charlemont.

SONNET XXV.

S' io avessi pensato che sì care.

HIS POEMS WERE WRITTEN ONLY TO SOOTHE HIS OWN GRIEF: OTHERWISE HE WOULD HAVE LABOURED TO MAKE THEM MORE DESERVING OF THE FAME THEY HAVE ACQUIRED.

Had I e'er thought that to the world so dear
The echo of my sighs would be in rhyme,
I would have made them in my sorrow's prime
Rarer in style, in number more appear.
Since she is dead my muse who prompted here,
First in my thoughts and feelings at all time,
All power is lost of tender or sublime
My rough dark verse to render soft and clear.
And certes, my sole study and desire
Was but – I knew not how – in those long years
To unburthen my sad heart, not fame acquire.
I wept, but wish'd no honour in my tears.
Fain would I now taste joy; but that high fair,
Silent and weary, calls me to her there.

Robert Macgregor.

Oh! had I deem'd my sighs, in numbers rung,
Could e'er have gain'd the world's approving smile,
I had awoke my rhymes in choicer style,
My sorrow's birth more tunefully had sung:
But she is gone whose inspiration hung
On all my words, and did my thoughts beguile;
My numbers harsh seem'd melody awhile,
Now she is mute who o'er them music flung.
Nor fame, nor other incense, then I sought,
But how to quell my heart's o'erwhelming grief;
I wept, but sought no honour in my tear:
But could the world's fair suffrage now be bought,
'Twere joy to gain, but that my hour is brief,
Her lofty spirit waves me to her bier.

Miss Wollaston.

SONNET XXVI.

Soleasi nel mio cor star bella e viva.

SINCE HER DEATH, NOTHING IS LEFT TO HIM BUT GRIEF.

She stood within my heart, warm, young, alone,
As in a humble home a lady bright;
By her last flight not merely am I grown
Mortal, but dead, and she an angel quite.
A soul whence every bliss and hope is flown,
Love shorn and naked of its own glad light,
Might melt with pity e'en a heart of stone:
But none there is to tell their grief or write;
These plead within, where deaf is every ear
Except mine own, whose power its griefs so mar
That nought is left me save to suffer here.
Verily we but dust and shadows are!
Verily blind and evil is our will!
Verily human hopes deceive us still!

Robert Macgregor.

'Mid life's bright glow she dwelt within my soul,
The sovereign tenant of a humble cell,
But when for heaven she bade the world farewell,
Death seem'd to grasp me in his fierce control:
My wither'd love torn from its brightening goal –
My soul without its treasure doom'd to dwell –
Could I but trace their grief, their sorrow tell,
A stone might wake, and fain with them condole.
They inly mourn, where none can hear their woe
Save I alone, who too with grief oppress'd,
Can only soothe my anguish by my sighs:
Life is indeed a shadowy dream below;
Our blind desires by Reason's chain unbless'd,
Whilst Hope in treacherous wither'd fragments lies.

Miss Wollaston.

SONNET XXVII.

Soleano i miei pensier soavemente.

HE COMFORTS HIMSELF WITH THE HOPE THAT SHE HEARS HIM.

My thoughts in fair alliance and array
Hold converse on the theme which most endears:
Pity approaches and repents delay:
E'en now she speaks of us, or hopes, or fears.
Since the last day, the terrible hour when Fate
This present life of her fair being reft,
From heaven she sees, and hears, and feels our state:
No other hope than this to me is left.
O fairest miracle! most fortunate mind!
O unexampled beauty, stately, rare!
Whence lent too late, too soon, alas! rejoin'd.
Hers is the crown and palm of good deeds there,
Who to the world so eminent and clear
Made her great virtue and my passion here.

Robert Macgregor.

My thoughts were wont with sentiment so sweet
To meditate their object in my breast –
Perhaps her sympathies my wishes meet
With gentlest pity, seeing me distress'd:
Nor when removed to that her sacred rest
The present life changed for that blest retreat,
Vanish'd in air my former visions fleet,
My hopes, my tears, in vain to her address'd.
O lovely miracle! O favour'd mind!
Beauty beyond example high and rare,
So soon return'd from us to whence it came!
There the immortal wreaths her temples bind;
The sacred palm is hers: on earth so fair
Who shone by her own virtues and my flame.

Capel Lofft.

SONNET XXVIII.

I' mi soglio accusare, ed or mi scuso.

HE GLORIES IN HIS LOVE.

I now excuse myself who wont to blame,
Nay, more, I prize and even hold me dear,
For this fair prison, this sweet-bitter shame,
Which I have borne conceal'd so many a year.
O envious Fates! that rare and golden frame
Rudely ye broke, where lightly twined and clear,
Yarn of my bonds, the threads of world-wide fame
Which lovely 'gainst his wont made Death appear.
For not a soul was ever in its days
Of joy, of liberty, of life so fond,
That would not change for her its natural ways,
Preferring thus to suffer and despond,
Than, fed by hope, to sing in others' praise,
Content to die, or live in such a bond.

Robert Macgregor.

SONNET XXIX.

Due gran nemiche insieme erano aggiunte.

THE UNION OF BEAUTY AND VIRTUE IS DISSOLVED BY HER DEATH.

Two mortal foes in one fair breast combined,
Beauty and Virtue, in such peace allied
That ne'er rebellion ruffled that pure mind,
But in rare union dwelt they side by side;
By Death they now are shatter'd and disjoin'd;
One is in heaven, its glory and its pride,
One under earth, her brilliant eyes now blind,
Whence stings of love once issued far and wide.
That winning air, that rare discourse and meek,
Surely from heaven inspired, that gentle glance
Which wounded my poor heart, and wins it still,
Are gone; if I am slow her road to seek,
I hope her fair and graceful name perchance
To consecrate with this worn weary quill.

Robert Macgregor.

Within one mortal shrine two foes had met –
Beauty and Virtue – yet they dwelt so bright,
That ne'er within the soul did they excite
Rebellious thought, their union might beget:
But, parted to fulfil great nature's debt,
One blooms in heaven, exulting in its height;
Its twin on earth doth rest, from whose veil'd night
No more those eyes of love man's soul can fret.
That speech by Heaven inspired, so humbly wise –
That graceful air – her look so winning, meek,
That woke and kindles still my bosom's pain –
They all have fled; but if to gain her skies
I tardy seem, my weary pen would seek
For her blest name a consecrated reign!

Miss Wollaston.

SONNET XXX.

Quand' io mi volgo indietro a mirar gli anni.

THE REMEMBRANCE OF THE PAST ENHANCES HIS MISERY.

When I look back upon the many years
Which in their flight my best thoughts have entomb'd,
And spent the fire, that, spite her ice, consumed,
And finish'd the repose so full of tears,
Broken the faith which Love's young dream endears,
And the two parts of all my blessing doom'd,
This low in earth, while heaven has that resumed,
And lost the guerdon of my pains and fears,
I wake, and feel me to the bitter wind
So bare, I envy the worst lot I see;
Self-terror and heart-grief on me so wait.
O Death, O Fate, O Fortune, stars unkind!
O day for ever dark and drear to me!
How have ye sunk me in this abject state!

Robert Macgregor.

When memory turns to gaze on time gone by
(Which in its flight hath arm'd e'en thought with wings),
And to my troubled rest a period brings,
Quells, too, the flame which long could ice defy;
And when I mark Love's promise wither'd lie,
That treasure parted which my bosom wrings
(For she in heaven, her shrine to nature clings),
Whilst thus my toils' reward she doth deny; –
I then awake and feel bereaved indeed!
The darkest fate on earth seems bliss to mine –
So much I fear myself, and dread its woe!
O Fortune! – Death! O star! O fate decreed!
O bitter day! that yet must sweetly shine,
Alas! too surely thou hast laid me low!

Miss Wollaston.

SONNET XXXI.

Ov' è la fronte che con picciol cenno.

HE ENUMERATES AND EULOGISES THE GRACES OF LAURA.

Where is the brow whose gentlest beckonings led
My raptured heart at will, now here, now there?
Where the twin stars, lights of this lower sphere,
Which o'er my darkling path their radiance shed?
Where is true worth, and wit, and wisdom fled?
The courteous phrase, the melting accent, where?
Where, group'd in one rich form, the beauties rare,
Which long their magic influence o'er me shed?
Where is the shade, within whose sweet recess
My wearied spirit still forgot its sighs,
And all my thoughts their constant record found?
Where, where is she, my life's sole arbitress? –
Ah, wretched world! and wretched ye, mine eyes
(Of her pure light bereft) which aye with tears are drown'd.

Francis Wrangham.

Where is that face, whose slightest air could move
My trembling heart, and strike the springs of love?
That heaven, where two fair stars, with genial ray,
Shed their kind influence on life's dim way?
Where are that science, sense, and worth confess'd?
That speech by virtue, by the graces dress'd?
Where are those beauties, where those charms combined,
That caused this long captivity of mind?
Where the dear shade of all that once was fair,
The source, the solace, of each amorous care –
My heart's sole sovereign, Nature's only boast?
– Lost to the world, to me for ever lost!

Langhorne.

SONNET XXXII.

Quanta invidia ti porto, avara terra.

HE ENVIES EARTH, HEAVEN, AND DEATH THEIR POSSESSION OF HIS TREASURE.

O earth, whose clay-cold mantle shrouds that face,
And veils those eyes that late so brightly shone,
Whence all that gave delight on earth was known,
How much I envy thee that harsh embrace!
O heaven, that in thy airy courts confined
That purest spirit, when from earth she fled,
And sought the mansions of the righteous dead;
How envious, thus to leave my panting soul behind!
O angels, that in your seraphic choir
Received her sister-soul, and now enjoy
Still present, those delights without alloy,
Which my fond heart must still in vain desire!
In her I lived – in her my life decays;
Yet envious Fate denies to end my hapless days.

Lord Woodhouselee.

What envy of the greedy earth I bear,
That holds from me within its cold embrace
The light, the meaning, of that angel face,
On which to gaze could soften e'en despair.
What envy of the saints, in realms so fair,
Who eager seem'd, from that bright form of grace
The spirit pure to summon to its place,
Amidst those joys, which few can hope to share;
What envy of the blest in heaven above,
With whom she dwells in sympathies divine
Denied to me on earth, though sought in sighs;
And oh! what envy of stern Death I prove,
That with her life has ta'en the light of mine,
Yet calls me not, – though fixed and cold those eyes.

Mrs Wrottesley.

SONNET XXXIII.

Valle che d' lamenti miei se' piena.

ON HIS RETURN TO VAUCLUSE AFTER LAURA'S DEATH.

Valley, which long hast echoed with my cries;
Stream, which my flowing tears have often fed;
Beasts, fluttering birds, and ye who in the bed
Of Cabrieres' wave display your speckled dyes;
Air, hush'd to rest and soften'd by my sighs;
Dear path, whose mazes lone and sad I tread;
Hill of delight – though now delight is fled –
To rove whose haunts Love still my foot decoys;
Well I retain your old unchanging face!
Myself how changed! in whom, for joy's light throng,
Infinite woes their constant mansion find!
Here bloom'd my bliss: and I your tracks retrace,
To mark whence upward to her heaven she sprung,
Leaving her beauteous spoil, her robe of flesh behind!

Francis Wrangham.

Ye vales, made vocal by my plaintive lay;
Ye streams, embitter'd with the tears of love;
Ye tenants of the sweet melodious grove;
Ye tribes that in the grass fringed streamlet play;
Ye tepid gales, to which my sighs convey
A softer warmth; ye flowery plains, that move
Reflection sad; ye hills, where yet I rove,
Since Laura there first taught my steps to stray; –
You, you are still the same! How changed, alas,
Am I! who, from a state of life so blest,
Am now the gloomy dwelling-place of woe!
'Twas here I saw my love: here still I trace
Her parting steps, when she her mortal vest
Cast to the earth, and left these scenes below.

Anonymous

SONNET XXXIV.

Levommi il mio pensier in parte ov' era.

SOARING IN IMAGINATION TO HEAVEN, HE MEETS LAURA, AND IS HAPPY.

Fond fancy raised me to the spot, where strays
She, whom I seek but find on earth no more:
There, fairer still and humbler than before,
I saw her, in the third heaven's blessèd maze.
She took me by the hand, and "Thou shalt trace,
If hope not errs," she said, "this happy shore:
I, I am she, thy breast with slights who tore,
And ere its evening closed my day's brief space.
What human heart conceives, my joys exceed;
Thee only I expect, and (what remain
Below) the charms, once objects of thy love."
Why ceased she? Ah! my captive hand why freed?
Such of her soft and hallow'd tones the chain,
From that delightful heaven my soul could scarcely move.

Francis Wrangham.

Thither my ecstatic thought had rapt me, where
She dwells, whom still on earth I seek in vain;
And there, with those whom the third heavens contain,
I saw her, much more kind, and much more fair.
My hand she took, and said: "Within this sphere,
If hope deceive me not, thou shalt again
With me reside: who caused thy mortal pain
Am I, and even in summer closed my year.
My bliss no human thought can understand:
Thee only I await; and, that erewhile
You held so dear, the veil I left behind." –
She ceased – ah why? Why did she loose my hand?
For oh! her hallow'd words, her roseate smile
In heaven had well nigh fix'd my ravish'd mind!

Lord Charlemont.

SONNET XXXV.

Amor che meco al buon tempo ti stavi.

HE VENTS HIS SORROW TO ALL WHO WITNESSED HIS FORMER FELICITY.

Love, that in happier days wouldst meet me here
Along these meads that nursed our kindred strains;
And that old debt to clear which still remains,
Sweet converse with the stream and me wouldst share:
Ye flowers, leaves, grass, woods, grots, rills, gentle air,
Low valleys, lofty hills, and sunny plains:
The harbour where I stored my love-sick pains,
And all my various chance, my racking care:
Ye playful inmates of the greenwood shade;
Ye nymphs, and ye that in the waves pursue
That life its cool and grassy bottom lends: –
My days were once so fair; now dark and dread
As death that makes them so. Thus the world through
On each as soon as born his fate attends.

Anonymous, Ox., 1795.

On these green banks in happier days I stray'd
With Love, who whisper'd many a tender tale;
And the glad waters, winding through the dale,
Heard the sweet eloquence fond Love display'd.
You, purpled plain, cool grot, and arching glade;
Ye hills, ye streams, where plays the silken gale;
Ye pathless wilds, you rock-encircled vale
Which oft have beard the tender plaints I made;
Ye blue-hair'd nymphs, who ceaseless revel keep,
In the cool bosom of the crystal deep;
Ye woodland maids who climb the mountain's brow;
Ye mark'd how joy once wing'd each hour so gay;
Ah, mark how sad each hour now wears away!
So fate with human bliss blends human woe!

Anonymous 1777.

SONNET XXXVI.

Mentre che 'l cor dagli amorosi vermi.

HAD SHE NOT DIED SO EARLY, HE WOULD HAVE LEARNED TO PRAISE HER MORE WORTHILY.

While on my heart the worms consuming prey'd
Of Love, and I with all his fire was caught;
The steps of my fair wild one still I sought
To trace o'er desert mountains as she stray'd;
And much I dared in bitter strains to upbraid
Both Love and her, whom I so cruel thought;
But rude was then my genius, and untaught
My rhymes, while weak and new the ideas play'd.
Dead is that fire; and cold its ashes lie
In one small tomb; which had it still grown on
E'en to old age, as oft by others felt,
Arm'd with the power of rhyme, which wretched I
E'en now disclaim, my riper strains had won
E'en stones to burst, and in soft sorrows melt.

Anonymous, Ox., 1795.

SONNET XXXVII.

Anima bella, da quel nodo sciolta.

HE PRAYS LAURA TO LOOK DOWN UPON HIM FROM HEAVEN.

Bright spirit, from those earthly bonds released,
The loveliest ever wove in Nature's loom,
From thy bright skies compassionate the gloom
Shrouding my life that once of joy could taste!
Each false suggestion of thy heart has ceased,
That whilom bade thee stem disdain assume;
Now, all secure, heaven's habitant become,
List to my sighs, thy looks upon me cast.
Mark the huge rock, whence Sorga's waters rise;
And see amidst its waves and borders stray
One fed by grief and memory that ne'er dies
But from that spot, oh! turn thy sight away
Where I first loved, where thy late dwelling lies;
That in thy friends thou nought ungrateful may'st survey!

Dr Nott

Blest soul, that, loosen'd from those bands, art flown –
Bands than which Nature never form'd more fair,
Look down and mark how changed to carking care
From gladdest thoughts I pass my days unknown.
Each false opinion from my heart is gone,
That once to me made thy sweet sight appear
Most harsh and bitter; now secure from fear
Here turn thine eyes, and listen to my moan.
Turn to this rock whence Sorga's waters rise,
And mark, where through the mead its waters flow,
One who of thee still mindful ceaseless sighs:
But leave me there unsought for, where to glow
Our flames began, and where thy mansion lies,
Lest thou in thine shouldst see what grieved thee so.

Anonymous, Ox., 1795.

SONNET XXXVIII.

Quel sol che mi mostrava il cammin destro.

LOVE AND HE SEEK LAURA, BUT FIND NO TRACES OF HER EXCEPT IN THE SKY.

That sun, which ever signall'd the right road,
Where flash'd her own bright feet, to heaven to fly,
Returning to the Eternal Sun on high,
Has quench'd my light, and cast her earthly load;
Thus, lone and weary, my oft steps have trode,
As some wild animal, the sere woods by,
Fleeing with heavy heart and downcast eye
The world which since to me a blank has show'd.
Still with fond search each well-known spot I pace
Where once I saw her: Love, who grieves me so,
My only guide, directs me where to go.
I find her not: her every sainted trace
Seeks, in bright realms above, her parent star
From grisly Styx and black Avernus far.

Robert Macgregor.

SONNET XXXIX.

Io pensava assai destro esser sull' ale.

UNWORTHY TO HAVE LOOKED UPON HER, HE IS STILL MORE SO TO ATTEMPT HER PRAISES.

I thought me apt and firm of wing to rise
(Not of myself, but him who trains us all)
In song, to numbers fitting the fair thrall
Which Love once fasten'd and which Death unties.
Slow now and frail, the task too sorely tries,
As a great weight upon a sucker small:
"Who leaps," I said, "too high may midway fall:
Man ill accomplishes what Heaven denies."
So far the wing of genius ne'er could fly –
Poor style like mine and faltering tongue much less –
As Nature rose, in that rare fabric, high.
Love follow'd Nature with such full success
In gracing her, no claim could I advance
Even to look, and yet was bless'd by chance.

Robert Macgregor.

SONNET XL.

Quella per cui con Sorga ho cangiat' Arno.

HE ATTEMPTS TO PAINT HER BEAUTIES, BUT NOT HER VIRTUES.

She, for whose sake fair Arno I resign,
And for free poverty court-affluence spurn,
Has known to sour the precious sweets to turn
On which I lived, for which I burn and pine.
Though since, the vain attempt has oft been mine
That future ages from my song should learn
Her heavenly beauties, and like me should burn,
My poor verse fails her sweet face to define.
The gifts, though all her own, which others share,
Which were but stars her bright sky scatter'd o'er,
Haply of these to sing e'en I might dare;
But when to the diviner part I soar,
To the dull world a brief and brilliant light,
Courage and wit and art are baffled quite.

Robert Macgregor.

SONNET XLI.

L' alto e novo miracol ch' a dì nostri.

IT IS IMPOSSIBLE FOR HIM TO DESCRIBE HER EXCELLENCES.

The wonder, high and new, that, in our days,
Dawn'd on the world, yet would not there remain,
Which heaven but show'd to us to snatch again
Better to blazon its own starry ways;
That to far times I her should paint and praise
Love wills, who prompted first my passionate strain;
But now wit, leisure, pen, page, ink in vain
To the fond task a thousand times he sways.
My slow rhymes struggle not to life the while;
I feel it, and whoe'er to-day below,
Or speak or write of love will prove it so.
Who justly deems the truth beyond all style,
Here silent let him muse, and sighing say,
Blessèd the eyes who saw her living day!

Robert Macgregor.

SONNET XLII.

Zefiro torna, e 'l bel tempo rimena.

RETURNING SPRING BRINGS TO HIM ONLY INCREASE OF GRIEF.

Zephyr returns; and in his jocund train
Brings verdure, flowers, and days serenely clear;
Brings Progne's twitter, Philomel's lorn strain,
With every bloom that paints the vernal year;
Cloudless the skies, and smiling every plain;
With joyance flush'd, Jove views his daughter dear;
Love's genial power pervades earth, air, and main;
All beings join'd in fond accord appear.
But nought to me returns save sorrowing sighs,
Forced from my inmost heart by her who bore
Those keys which govern'd it unto the skies:
The blossom'd meads, the choristers of air,
Sweet courteous damsels can delight no more;
Each face looks savage, and each prospect drear.

Dr Nott

The spring returns, with all her smiling train;
The wanton Zephyrs breathe along the bowers,
The glistening dew-drops hang on bending flowers,
And tender green light-shadows o'er the plain:
And thou, sweet Philomel, renew'st thy strain,
Breathing thy wild notes to the midnight grove:
All nature feels the kindling fire of love,
The vital force of spring's returning reign.
But not to me returns the cheerful spring!
O heart! that know'st no period to thy grief,
Nor Nature's smiles to thee impart relief,
Nor change of mind the varying seasons bring:
She, she is gone! All that e'er pleased before,
Adieu! ye birds ye flowers, ye fields, that charm no more!

Lord Woodhouselee.

Returning Zephyr the sweet season brings,
With flowers and herbs his breathing train among,
And Progne twitters, Philomela sings,
Leading the many-colour'd spring along;
Serene the sky, and fair the laughing field,
Jove views his daughter with complacent brow;
Earth, sea, and air, to Love's sweet influence yield,
And creatures all his magic power avow:
But nought, alas! for me the season brings,
Save heavier sighs, from my sad bosom drawn
By her who can from heaven unlock its springs;
And warbling birds and flower-bespangled lawn,
And fairest acts of ladies fair and mild,
A desert seem, and its brute tenants wild.

Lady Dacre.

Zephyr returns and winter's rage restrains,
With herbs, with flowers, his blooming progeny!
Now Progne prattles, Philomel complains,
And spring assumes her robe of various dye;
The meadows smile, heaven glows, nor Jove disdains
To view his daughter with delighted eye;
While Love through universal nature reigns,
And life is fill'd with amorous sympathy!
But grief, not joy, returns to me forlorn,
And sighs, which from my inmost heart proceed
For her, by whom to heaven its keys were borne.
The song of birds, the flower-enamell'd mead,
And graceful acts, which most the fair adorn,
A desert seem, and beasts of savage prey!

Lord Charlemont.

SONNET XLIII.

Quel rosignuol che sì soave piagne.

THE SONG OF THE NIGHTINGALE REMINDS HIM OF HIS UNHAPPY LOT.

Yon nightingale, whose bursts of thrilling tone,
Pour'd in soft sorrow from her tuneful throat,
Haply her mate or infant brood bemoan,
Filling the fields and skies with pity's note;
Here lingering till the long long night is gone,
Awakes the memory of my cruel lot –
But I my wretched self must wail alone:
Fool, who secure from death an angel thought!
O easy duped, who thus on hope relies!
Who would have deem'd the darkness, which appears,
From orbs more brilliant than the sun should rise?
Now know I, made by sad experience wise,
That Fate would teach me by a life of tears,
On wings how fleeting fast all earthly rapture flies!

Francis Wrangham.

Yon nightingale, whose strain so sweetly flows,
Mourning her ravish'd young or much-loved mate,
A soothing charm o'er all the valleys throws
And skies, with notes well tuned to her sad state:
And all the night she seems my kindred woes
With me to weep and on my sorrows wait;
Sorrows that from my own fond fancy rose,
Who deem'd a goddess could not yield to fate.
How easy to deceive who sleeps secure!
Who could have thought that to dull earth would turn
Those eyes that as the sun shone bright and pure?
Ah! now what Fortune wills I see full sure:
That loathing life, yet living I should see
How few its joys, how little they endure!

Anonymous, Ox., 1795.

That nightingale, who now melodious mourns
Perhaps his children or his consort dear,
The heavens with sweetness fills; the distant bourns
Resound his notes, so piteous and so clear;
With me all night he weeps, and seems by turns
To upbraid me with my fault and fortune drear,
Whose fond and foolish heart, where grief sojourns,
A goddess deem'd exempt from mortal fear.
Security, how easy to betray!
The radiance of those eyes who could have thought
Should e'er become a senseless clod of clay?
Living, and weeping, late I've learn'd to say
That here below – Oh, knowledge dearly bought! –
Whate'er delights will scarcely last a day!

Lord Charlemont.

SONNET XLIV.

Nè per sereno cielo ir vaghe stelle.

NOTHING THAT NATURE OFFERS CAN AFFORD HIM CONSOLATION.

Not skies serene, with glittering stars inlaid,
Nor gallant ships o'er tranquil ocean dancing,
Nor gay careering knights in arms advancing,
Nor wild herds bounding through the forest glade,
Nor tidings new of happiness delay'd,
Nor poesie, Love's witchery enhancing,
Nor lady's song beside clear fountain glancing,
In beauty's pride, with chastity array'd;
Nor aught of lovely, aught of gay in show,
Shall touch my heart, now cold within her tomb
Who was erewhile my life and light below!
So heavy – tedious – sad – my days unblest,
That I, with strong desire, invoke Death's gloom,
Her to behold, whom ne'er to have seen were best!

Lady Dacre.

Nor stars bright glittering through the cool still air,
Nor proud ships riding on the tranquil main,
Nor armed knights light pricking o'er the plain,
Nor deer in glades disporting void of care,
Nor tidings hoped by recent messenger,
Nor tales of love in high and gorgeous strain,
Nor by clear stream, green mead, or shady lane
Sweet-chaunted roundelay of lady fair;
Nor aught beside my heart shall e'er engage –
Sepulchred, as 'tis henceforth doom'd to be,
With her, my eyes' sole mirror, beam, and bliss.
Oh! how I long this weary pilgrimage
To close; that I again that form may see,
Which never to have seen had been my happiness!

Francis Wrangham.

SONNET XLV.

Passato è 'l tempo omai, lasso! che tanto.

HIS ONLY DESIRE IS AGAIN TO BE WITH HER.

Fled – fled, alas! for ever – is the day,
Which to my flame some soothing whilom brought;
And fled is she of whom I wept and wrote:
Yet still the pang, the tear, prolong their stay!
And fled that angel vision far away;
But flying, with soft glance my heart it smote
('Twas then my own) which straight, divided, sought
Her, who had wrapp'd it in her robe of clay.
Part shares her tomb, part to her heaven is sped;
Where now, with laurel wreathed, in triumph's car
She reaps the meed of matchless holiness:
So might I, of this flesh discumberèd,
Which holds me prisoner here, from sorrow far
With her expatiate free 'midst realms of endless bliss!

Francis Wrangham.

Ah! gone for ever are the happy years
That soothed my soul amid Love's fiercest fire,
And she for whom I wept and tuned my lyre
Has gone, alas! – But left my lyre, my tears:
Gone is that face, whose holy look endears;
But in my heart, ere yet it did retire,
Left the sweet radiance of its eyes, entire; –
My heart? Ah; no! not mine! for to the spheres
Of light she bore it captive, soaring high,
In angel robe triumphant, and now stands
Crown'd with the laurel wreath of chastity:
Oh! could I throw aside these earthly bands
That tie me down where wretched mortals sigh, –
To join blest spirits in celestial lands!

Dr Morehead.

SONNET XLVI.

Mente mia che presaga de' tuoi danni.

HE RECALLS WITH GRIEF THEIR LAST MEETING.

My mind! prophetic of my coming fate,
Pensive and gloomy while yet joy was lent,
On the loved lineaments still fix'd, intent
To seek dark bodings, ere thy sorrow's date!
From her sweet acts, her words, her looks, her gait,
From her unwonted pity with sadness blent,
Thou might'st have said, hadst thou been prescient,
"I taste my last of bliss in this low state!"
My wretched soul! the poison, oh, how sweet!
That through my eyes instill'd the burning smart,
Gazing on hers, no more on earth to meet!
To them – my bosom's wealth! condemn'd to part
On a far journey – as to friends discreet,
All my fond thoughts I left, and lingering heart.

Lady Dacre.

SONNET XLVII.

Tutta la mia fiorita e verde etade.

JUST WHEN HE MIGHT FAIRLY HOPE SOME RETURN OF AFFECTION, ENVIOUS DEATH CARRIES HER OFF.

All my green years and golden prime of man
Had pass'd away, and with attemper'd sighs
My bosom heaved – ere yet the days arise
When life declines, contracting its brief span.
Already my loved enemy began
To lull suspicion, and in sportive guise,
With timid confidence, though playful, wise,
In gentle mockery my long pains to scan:
The hour was near when Love, at length, may mate
With Chastity; and, by the dear one's side,
The lover's thoughts and words may freely flow:
Death saw, with envy, my too happy state,
E'en its fair promise – and, with fatal pride,
Strode in the midway forth, an armèd foe!

Lady Dacre.

Now of my life each gay and greener year
Pass'd by, and cooler grew each hour the flame
With which I burn'd: and to that point we came
Whence life descends, as to its end more near;
Now 'gan my lovely foe each virtuous fear
Gently to lay aside, as safe from blame;
And though with saint-like virtue still the same,
Mock'd my sweet pains indeed, but deign'd to hear
Nigh drew the time when Love delights to dwell
With Chastity; and lovers with their mate
Can fearless sit, and all they muse of tell.
Death envied me the joys of such a state;
Nay, e'en the hopes I form'd: and on them fell
E'en in midway, like some arm'd foe in wait.

Anonymous, Ox., 1795.

SONNET XLVIII.

Tempo era omai da trovar pace o tregua.

HE CONSOLES HIMSELF WITH THE BELIEF THAT SHE NOW AT LAST SYMPATHISES WITH HIM.

'Twas time at last from so long war to find
Some peace or truce, and, haply, both were nigh,
But Death their welcome feet has turn'd behind,
Who levels all distinctions, low as high;
And as a cloud dissolves before the wind,
So she, who led me with her lustrous eye,
Whom ever I pursue with faithful mind,
Her fair life briefly ending, sought the sky.
Had she but stay'd, as I grew changed and old
Her tone had changed, and no distrust had been
To parley with me on my cherish'd ill:
With what frank sighs and fond I then had told
My lifelong toils, which now from heaven, I ween,
She sees, and with me sympathises still.

Robert Macgregor.

My life's long warfare seem'd about to cease,
Peace had my spirit's contest well nigh freed;
But levelling Death, who doth to all concede
An equal doom, clipp'd Time's blest wings of peace:
As zephyrs chase the clouds of gathering fleece,
So did her life from this world's breath recede,
Their vision'd light could once my footsteps lead,
But now my all, save thought, she doth release.
Oh! would that she her flight awhile had stay'd,
For Time had stamp'd on me his warning hand,
And calmer I had told my storied love:
To her in virtue's tone I had convey'd
My heart's long grief – now, she doth understand,
And sympathises with that grief above.

Miss Wollaston.

SONNET XLIX.

Tranquillo porto avea mostrato Amore.

DEATH HAS ROBBED HIM IN ONE MOMENT OF THE FRUIT OF HIS LIFE.

From life's long storm of trouble and of tears
Love show'd a tranquil haven and fair end
'Mid better thoughts which riper age attend,
That vice lays bare and virtue clothes and cheers.
She saw my true heart, free from doubts and fears,
And its high faith which could no more offend;
Ah, cruel Death! how quick wert thou to rend
In so few hours the fruit of many years!
A longer life the time had surely brought
When in her chaste ear my full heart had laid
The ancient burthen of its dearest thought;
And she, perchance, might then have answer made,
Forth-sighing some blest words, whilst white and few
Our locks became, and wan our cheeks in hue.

Robert Macgregor.

SONNET L.

Al cader d' una pianta che si svelse.

UNDER THE ALLEGORY OF A LAUREL HE AGAIN DEPLORES HER DEATH.

As a fair plant, uprooted by oft blows
Of trenchant spade, or which the blast upheaves,
Scatters on earth its green and lofty leaves,
And its bare roots to the broad sunlight shows;
Love such another for my object chose,
Of whom for me the Muse a subject weaves,
Who in my captured heart her home achieves,
As on some wall or tree the ivy grows
That living laurel – where their chosen nest
My high thoughts made, where sigh'd mine ardent grief,
Yet never stirr'd of its fair boughs a leaf –
To heaven translated, in my heart, her rest,
Left deep its roots, whence ever with sad cry
I call on her, who ne'er vouchsafes reply.

Robert Macgregor.

SONNET LI.

I dì miei più leggier che nessun cervo.

HIS PASSION FINDS ITS ONLY CONSOLATION IN CONTEMPLATING HER IN HEAVEN.

My days more swiftly than the forest hind
Have fled like shadows, and no pleasure seen
Save for a moment, and few hours serene,
Whose bitter-sweet I treasure in true mind.
O wretched world, unstable, wayward! Blind
Whose hopes in thee alone have centred been;
In thee my heart was captived by her mien
Who bore it with her when she earth rejoin'd:
Her better spirit, now a deathless flower,
And in the highest heaven that still shall be,
Each day inflames me with its beauties more.
Alone, though frailer, fonder every hour,
I muse on her – Now what, and where is she,
And what the lovely veil which here she wore?

Robert Macgregor.

Oh! swifter than the hart my life hath fled,
A shadow'd dream; one winged glance hath seen
Its only good; its hours (how few serene!)
The sweet and bitter tide of thought have fed:
Ephemeral world! in pride and sorrow bred,
Who hope in thee, are blind as I have been;
I hoped in thee, and thus my heart's loved queen
Hath borne it mid her nerveless, kindred dead.
Her form decay'd – its beauty still survives,
For in high heaven that soul will ever bloom,
With which each day I more enamour'd grow:
Thus though my locks are blanch'd, my hope revives
In thinking on her home – her soul's high doom:
Alas! how changed the shrine she left below!

Miss Wollaston.

SONNET LII.

Sente l' aura mia antica, e i dolci colli.

HE REVISITS VAUCLUSE.

I feel the well-known gale; the hills I spy
So pleasant, whence my fair her being drew,
Which made these eyes, while Heaven was willing, shew
Wishful, and gay; now sad, and never dry.
O feeble hopes! O thoughts of vanity!
Wither'd the grass, the rills of turbid hue;
And void and cheerless is that dwelling too,
In which I live, in which I wish'd to die;
Hoping its mistress might at length afford
Some respite to my woes by plaintive sighs,
And sorrows pour'd from her once-burning eyes.
I've served a cruel and ungrateful lord:
While lived my beauteous flame, my heart be fired;
And o'er its ashes now I weep expired.

Dr Nott

Once more, ye balmy gales, I feel you blow;
Again, sweet hills, I mark the morning beams
Gild your green summits; while your silver streams
Through vales of fragrance undulating flow.
But you, ye dreams of bliss, no longer here
Give life and beauty to the glowing scene:
For stern remembrance stands where you have been,
And blasts the verdure of the blooming year.
O Laura! Laura! in the dust with thee,
Would I could find a refuge from despair!
Is this thy boasted triumph. Love, to tear
A heart thy coward malice dares not free;
And bid it live, while every hope is fled,
To weep, among the ashes of the dead?

Anne Bannerman.

SONNET LIII.

E questo 'l nido in che la mia Fenice.

THE SIGHT OF LAURA'S HOUSE REMINDS HIM OF HIS MISERY.

Is this the nest in which my phœnix first
Her plumage donn'd of purple and of gold,
Beneath her wings who knew my heart to hold,
For whom e'en yet its sighs and wishes burst?
Prime root in which my cherish'd ill had birth,
Where is the fair face whence that bright light came.
Alive and glad which kept me in my flame?
Now bless'd in heaven as then alone on earth;
Wretched and lonely thou hast left me here,
Fond lingering by the scenes, with sorrows drown'd,
To thee which consecrate I still revere.
Watching the hills as dark night gathers round,
Whence its last flight to heaven thy soul did take,
And where my day those bright eyes wont to make.

Robert Macgregor.

Is this the nest in which her wings of gold,
Of gold and purple plume, my phœnix laid?
How flutter'd my fond heart beneath their shade!
But now its sighs proclaim that dwelling cold:
Sweet source! from which my bliss, my bane, have roll'd,
Where is that face, in living light array'd,
That burn'd me, yet my sole enjoyment made?
Unparallel'd on earth, the heavens now hold
Thee bless'd! – but I am left wretched, alone!
Yet ever in my grief return to see
And honour this sweet place, though thou art gone.
A black night veils the hills, whence rising free
Thou took'st thy heavenward flight! Ah! when they shone
In morning radiance, it was all from thee!

Dr Morehead.

SONNET LIV.

Mai non vedranno le mie luci asciutte.

TO THE MEMORY OF GIACOMO COLONNA, WHO DIED BEFORE PETRARCH COULD REPLY TO A LETTER OF HIS.

Ne'er shall I see again with eyes unwet,
Or with the sure powers of a tranquil mind,
Those characters where Love so brightly shined,
And his own hand affection seem'd to set;
Spirit! amid earth's strifes unconquer'd yet,
Breathing such sweets from heaven which now has shrined,
As once more to my wandering verse has join'd
The style which Death had led me to forget.
Another work, than my young leaves more bright,
I thought to show: what envying evil star
Snatch'd thee, my noble treasure, thus from me?
So soon who hides thee from my fond heart's sight,
And from thy praise my loving tongue would bar?
My soul has rest, sweet sigh! alone in thee.

Robert Macgregor.

Oh! ne'er shall I behold with tearless eye
Or tranquil soul those characters of thine,
In which affection doth so brightly shine,
And charity's own hand I can descry!
Blest soul! that could this earthly strife defy,
Thy sweets instilling from thy home divine,
Thou wakest in me the tone which once was mine,
To sing my rhymes Death's power did long deny.
With these, my brow's young leaves, I fondly dream'd
Another work than this had greeted thee:
What iron planet envied thus our love?
My treasure! veil'd ere age had darkly gleam'd;
Thou – whom my song records – my heart doth see;
Thou wakest my sigh, and sighing, rest I prove.

Miss Wollaston.

CANZONE III.

Standomi un giorno solo alla finestra.

UNDER VARIOUS ALLEGORIES HE PAINTS THE VIRTUE, BEAUTY, AND UNTIMELY DEATH OF LAURA.

While at my window late I stood alone,
So new and many things there cross'd my sight,
To view them I had almost weary grown.
A dappled hind appear'd upon the right,
In aspect gentle, yet of stately stride,
By two swift greyhounds chased, a black and white,
Who tore in the poor side
Of that fair creature wounds so deep and wide,
That soon they forced her where ravine and rock
The onward passage block:
Then triumph'd Death her matchless beauties o'er,
And left me lonely there her sad fate to deplore.

Upon the summer wave a gay ship danced,
Her cordage was of silk, of gold her sails,
Her sides with ivory and ebon glanced,
The sea was tranquil, favouring were the gales,
And heaven as when no cloud its azure veils.
A rich and goodly merchandise is hers;
But soon the tempest wakes,
And wind and wave to such mad fury stirs,
That, driven on the rocks, in twain she breaks;
My heart with pity aches,
That a short hour should whelm, a small space hide,
Riches for which the world no equal had beside.

In a fair grove a bright young laurel made
– Surely to Paradise the plant belongs! –
Of sacred boughs a pleasant summer shade,
From whose green depths there issued so sweet songs
Of various birds, and many a rare delight
Of eye and ear, what marvel from the world

They stole my senses quite!
While still I gazed, the heavens grew black around,
The fatal lightning flash'd, and sudden hurl'd,
Uprooted to the ground,
That blessed birth. Alas! for it laid low,
And its dear shade whose like we ne'er again shall know.

A crystal fountain in that very grove
Gush'd from a rock, whose waters fresh and clear
Shed coolness round and softly murmur'd love;
Never that leafy screen and mossy seat
Drew browsing flock or whistling rustic near
But nymphs and muses danced to music sweet.
There as I sat and drank
With infinite delight their carols gay,
And mark'd their sport, thc carth before me sank
And bore with it away
The fountain and the scene, to my great grief,
Who now in memory find a sole and scant relief.

A lovely and rare bird within the wood,
Whose crest with gold, whose wings with purple gleam'd,
Alone, but proudly soaring, next I view'd,
Of heavenly and immortal birth which seem'd,
Flitting now here, now there, until it stood
Where buried fount and broken laurel lay,
And sadly seeing there
The fallen trunk, the boughs all stripp'd and bare,
The channel dried – for all things to decay
So tend – it turn'd away
As if in angry scorn, and instant fled,
While through me for her loss new love and pity spread.

At length along the flowery sward I saw
So sweet and fair a lady pensive move
That her mere thought inspires a tender awe;
Meek in herself, but haughty against Love,
Flow'd from her waist a robe so fair and fine
Seem'd gold and snow together there to join:
But, ah! each charm above
Was veil'd from sight in an unfriendly cloud:

Stung by a lurking snake, as flowers that pine
Her head she gently bow'd,
And joyful pass'd on high, perchance secure:
Alas! that in the world grief only should endure.

My song! in each sad change,
These visions, as they rise, sweet, solemn, strange,
But show how deeply in thy master's breast
The fond desire abides to die and be at rest.

Robert Macgregor.

BALLATA I.

Amor, quando fioria.

HIS GRIEF AT SURVIVING HER IS MITIGATED BY THE CONSCIOUSNESS THAT SHE NOW KNOWS HIS HEART.

Yes, Love, at that propitious time
When hope was in its bloomy prime,
And when I vainly fancied nigh
The meed of all my constancy;
Then sudden she, of whom I sought
Compassion, from my sight was caught.
O ruthless Death! O life severe!
The one has sunk me deep in care,
And darken'd cruelly my day,
That shone with hope's enlivening ray:
The other, adverse to my will,
Doth here on earth detain me still;
And interdicts me to pursue
Her, who from all its scenes withdrew:
Yet in my heart resides the fair,
For ever, ever present there;
Who well perceives the ills that wait
Upon my wretched, mortal state.

Dr Nott

Yes, Love, while hope still bloom'd with me in pride,
While seem'd of all my faith the guerdon nigh,
She, upon whom for mercy I relied,
Was ravish'd from my doting desolate eye.
O ruthless Death! O life unwelcome! this
Plunged me in deepest woe,
And rudely crush'd my every hope of bliss;
Against my will that keeps me here below,
Who else would yearn to go,
And join the sainted fair who left us late;
Yet present every hour
In my heart's core there wields she her old power,
And knows, whate'er my life, its every state!

Robert Macgregor.

CANZONE IV.

Tacer non posso, e temo non adopre.

HE RECALLS HER MANY GRACES.

Fain would I speak – too long has silence seal'd
Lips that would gladly with my full heart move
With one consent, and yield
Homage to her who listens from above;
Yet how can I, without thy prompting, Love,
With mortal words e'er equal things divine,
And picture faithfully
The high humility whose chosen shrine
Was that fair prison whence she now is free?
Which held, erewhile, her gentle spirit, when
So in my conscious heart her power began.
That, instantly, I ran,
– Alike o' th' year and me 'twas April then –
From these gay meadows round sweet flowers to bind,
Hoping rich pleasure at her eyes to find.

The walls were alabaster, the roof gold,
Ivory the doors, the sapphire windows lent
Whence on my heart of old
Its earliest sigh, as shall my last, was sent;
In arrowy jets of fire thence came and went
Arm'd messengers of love, whereof to think
As then they were, with awe
– Though now for them with laurel crown'd – I shrink
Of one rare diamond, square, without a flaw,
High in the midst a stately throne was placed
Where sat the lovely lady all alone:
In front a column shone
Of crystal, and thereon each thought was traced
In characters so clear, and quick, and true,
By turns it gladden'd me and grieved to view.

To weapons such as these, sharp, burning, bright,

To the green glorious banner waved above,
– 'Gainst which would fail in fight
Mars, Polypheme, Apollo, mighty Jove –
While still my sorrow fresh and verdant throve,
I stood defenceless, doom'd; her easy prey
She led me as she chose
Whence to escape I knew nor art nor way;
But, as a friend, who, haply, grieves yet goes,
Sees something still to lure his eyes and heart,
Just so on her, for whom I am in thrall,
Sole perfect work of all
That graced her age, unable to depart,
With such desire my rapt regards I set,
As soon myself and misery to forget.

On earth myself, my heart in Eden dwelt,
Lost in sweet Lethe every other care,
As my live frame I felt
To marble turn, watching that wonder rare;
When old in years, but youthful still in air,
A lady briefly, quietly drew nigh,
And thus beholding me,
With reverent aspect and admiring eye,
Kind offer made my counsellor to be:
"My power," she said, "is more than mortals know –
Lighter than air, I, in an instant, make
Their hearts exult or ache,
I loose and bind whate'er is seen below;
Thine eyes, upon that sun, as eagles', bend,
But to my words with willing ears attend.

"The day when she was born, the stars that win
Prosperity for man shone bright above;
Their high glad homes within
Each on the other smiled with gratulant love;
Fair Venus, and, with gentle aspect, Jove
The beautiful and lordly mansions held:
Seem'd as each adverse light
Throughout all heaven was darken'd and dispell'd,
The sun ne'er look'd upon a day so bright;
The air and earth rejoiced; the waves had rest

By lake and river, and o'er ocean green:
'Mid the enchanting scene
One distant cloud alone my thought distress'd,
Lest sometime it might be of tears the source
Unless kind Heaven should elsewhere turn its course.

"When first she enter'd on this life below,
Which, to say sooth, not worthy was to hold,
'Twas strange to see her so
Angelical and dear in baby mould;
A snowy pearl she seem'd in finest gold;
Next as she crawl'd, or totter'd with short pace,
Wood, water, earth, and stone
Grew green, and clear, and soft; with livelier grace
The sward beneath her feet and fingers shone;
With flowers the champain to her bright eyes smiled;
At her sweet voice, babbling through lips that yet
From Love's own fount were wet,
The hoarse wind silent grew, the tempest mild:
Thus clearly showing to the dull blind world
How much in her was heaven's own light unfurl'd.

"At length, her life's third flowery epoch won,
She, year by year, so grew in charms and worth,
That ne'er, methinks, the sun
Such gracefulness and beauty saw on earth;
Her eyes so full of modesty and mirth,
Music and welcome on her words so hung,
That mute in her high praise,
Which thine alone may sound, is every tongue:
So bright her countenance with heavenly rays,
Not long thy dazzled vision there may rest;
From this her fair and fleshly tenement
Such fire through thine is sent
(Though gentler never kindled human breast),
That yet I fear her sudden flight may be
Too soon the cause of bitter grief to thee."

This said, she turn'd her to the rapid wheel
Whereon she winds of mortal life the thread;
Too true did she reveal

The doom of woe which darken'd o'er my head!
A few brief years flew by,
When she, for whom I so desire to die,
By black and pitiless Death, who could not slay
A fairer form than hers, was snatch'd away!

Robert Macgregor.

SONNET LV.

Or hai fatto l' estremo di tua possa.

DEATH MAY DEPRIVE HIM OF THE SIGHT OF HER BEAUTIES, BUT NOT OF THE MEMORY OF HER VIRTUES.

Now hast thou shown, fell Death! thine utmost might.
Through Love's bright realm hast want and darkness spread,
Hast now cropp'd beauty's flower, its heavenly light
Quench'd, and enclosed in the grave's narrow bed;
Now hast thou life despoil'd of all delight,
Its ornament and sovereign honour shed:
But fame and worth it is not thine to blight;
These mock thy power, and sleep not with the dead.
Be thine the mortal part; heaven holds the best,
And, glorying in its brightness, brighter glows,
While memory still records the great and good.
O thou, in thine high triumph, angel blest!
Let thy heart yield to pity of my woes,
E'en as thy beauty here my soul subdued.

Lady Dacre.

Now hast thou shown the utmost of thy might,
O cruel Death! Love's kingdom hast thou rent,
And made it poor; in narrow grave hast pent
The blooming flower of beauty and its light!
Our wretched life thou hast despoil'd outright
Of every honour, every ornament!
But then her fame, her worth, by thee unblent,
Shall still survive! – her dust is all thy right;
The rest heaven holds, proud of her charms divine
As of a brighter sun. Nor dies she here –
Her memory lasts, to good men ever dear!
O angel new, in thy celestial sphere
Let pity now thy sainted heart incline,
As here below thy beauty vanquish'd mine!

Lord Charlemont.

SONNET LVI.

L' aura e l' odore e 'l refrigerio e l' ombra.

HER OWN VIRTUES IMMORTALISE HER IN HEAVEN, AND HIS PRAISES ON EARTH.

The air and scent, the comfort and the shade
Of my sweet laurel, and its flowery sight,
That to my weary life gave rest and light,
Death, spoiler of the world, has lowly laid.
As when the moon our sun's eclipse has made,
My lofty light has vanish'd so in night;
For aid against himself I Death invite;
With thoughts so dark does Love my breast invade.
Thou didst but sleep, bright lady, a brief sleep,
In bliss amid the chosen spirits to wake,
Who gaze upon their God, distinct and near:
And if my verse shall any value keep,
Preserved and praised 'mid noble minds to make
Thy name, its memory shall be deathless here.

Robert Macgregor.

The fragrant gale, and the refreshing shade
Of my sweet laurel, and its verdant form,
That were my shelter in life's weary storm,
Have felt the power that makes all nature fade:
Now has my light been lost in gloomy shade,
E'en as the sun behind his sister's form:
I call for Death to free me from Death's storm,
But Love descends and brings me better aid!
He tells me, lady, that one moment's sleep
Alone was thine, and then thou didst awake
Among the elect, and in thy Maker's arms:
And if my verse oblivion's power can keep
Aloof, thy name its place on earth-will take
Where Genius still will dote upon thy charms!

Dr Morehead.

SONNET LVII.

L' ultimo, lasso! de' miei giorni allegri.

HE REVERTS TO THEIR LAST MEETING.

The last, alas! of my bright days and glad
– Few have been mine in this brief life below –
Had come; I felt my heart as tepid snow,
Presage, perchance, of days both dark and sad.
As one in nerves, and pulse, and spirits bad,
Who of some frequent fever waits the blow,
E'en so I felt – for how could I foreknow
Such near end of the half-joys I have had?
Her beauteous eyes, in heaven now bright and bless'd
With the pure light whence health and life descends,
(Wretched and beggar'd leaving me behind,)
With chaste and soul-lit beams our grief address'd:
"Tarry ye here in peace, beloved friends,
Though here no more, we yet shall there be join'd."

Robert Macgregor.

Ah me! the last of all my happy days
(Not many happy days my years can show)
Was come! I felt my heart as turn'd to snow,
Presage, perhaps, that happiness decays!
E'en as the man whose shivering frame betrays,
And fluttering pulse, the ague's coming blow;
'Twas thus I felt! – but could I therefore know
How soon would end the bliss that never stays?
Those eyes that now, in heaven's delicious light,
Drink in pure beams which life and glory rain,
Just as they left mine, blinded, sunk in night,
Seem'd thus to say, sparkling unwonted bright, –
"Awhile, beloved friends, in peace remain,
Oh, we shall yet elsewhere exchange fond looks again!"

Dr Morehead.

SONNET LVIII.

O giorno, o ora, o ultimo momento.

HE MOURNS HIS WANT OF PERCEPTION AT THAT MEETING.

O Day, O hour, O moment sweetest, last,
O stars conspired to make me poor indeed!
O look too true, in which I seem'd to read.
At parting, that my happiness was past;
Now my full loss I know, I feel at last:
Then I believed (ah! weak and idle creed!)
'Twas but a part alone I lost; instead,
Was there a hope that flew not with the blast?
For, even then, it was in heaven ordain'd
That the sweet light of all my life should die:
'Twas written in her sadly-pensive eye!
But mine unconscious of the truth remain'd;
Or, what it would not see, to see refrain'd,
That I might sink in sudden misery!

Dr Morehead.

Dark hour, last moment of that fatal day!
Stars which to beggar me of bliss combined!
O faithful glance, too well which seem'dst to say
Farewell to me, farewell to peace of mind!
Awaken'd now, my losses I survey:
Alas! I fondly thought – thoughts weak and blind! –
That absence would take part, not all, away;
How many hopes it scatter'd to the wind.
Heaven had already doom'd it otherwise,
To quench for ever my life's genial light,
And in her sad sweet face 'twas written so.
Surely a veil was placed around mine eyes,
That blinded me to all before my sight,
And sank at once my life in deepest woe.

Robert Macgregor.

SONNET LIX.

Quel vago, dolce, caro, onesto sguardo.

HE SHOULD HAVE FORESEEN HIS LOSS IN THE UNUSUAL LUSTRE OF HER EYES.

That glance of hers, pure, tender, clear, and sweet,
Methought it said, "Take what thou canst while nigh;
For here no more thou'lt see me, till on high
From earth have mounted thy slow-moving feet."
O intellect than forest pard more fleet!
Yet slow and dull thy sorrow to descry,
How didst thou fail to see in her bright eye
What since befell, whence I my ruin meet.
Silently shining with a fire sublime,
They said, "O friendly lights, which long have been
Mirrors to us where gladly we were seen,
Heaven waits for you, as ye shall know in time;
Who bound us to the earth dissolves our bond,
But wills in your despite that you shall live beyond."

Robert Macgregor.

CANZONE V.

Solea dalla fontana di mia vita.

MEMORY IS HIS ONLY SOLACE AND SUPPORT.

I who was wont from life's best fountain far
So long to wander, searching land and sea,
Pursuing not my pleasure, but my star,
And alway, as Love knows who strengthen'd me,
Ready in bitter exile to depart,
For hope and memory both then fed my heart;
Alas! now wring my hands, and to unkind
And angry Fortune, which away has reft
That so sweet hope, my armour have resign'd;
And, memory only left,
I feed my great desire on that alone,
Whence frail and famish'd is my spirit grown.

As haply by the way, if want of food
Compel the traveller to relax his speed,
Losing that strength which first his steps endued,
So feeling, for my weary life, the need
Of that dear nourishment Death rudely stole,
Leaving the world all bare, and sad my soul,
From time to time fair pleasures pall, my sweet
To bitter turns, fear rises, and hopes fail,
My course, though brief, that I shall e'er complete:
Cloudlike before the gale,
To win some resting-place from rest I flee,
– If such indeed my doom, so let it be.

Never to mortal life could I incline,
– Be witness, Love, with whom I parley oft –
Except for her who was its light and mine.
And since, below extinguish'd, shines aloft
The life in which I lived, if lawful 'twere,
My chief desire would be to follow her:
But mine is ample cause of grief, for I

To see my future fate was ill supplied;
This Love reveal'd within her beauteous eye
Elsewhere my hopes to guide:
Too late he dies, disconsolate and sad,
Whom death a little earlier had made glad.

In those bright eyes, where wont my heart to dwell,
Until by envy my hard fortune stirr'd
Rose from so rich a temple to expel,
Love with his proper hand had character'd
In lines of pity what, ere long, I ween
The issue of my old desire had been.
Dying alone, and not my life with me,
Comely and sweet it then had been to die,
Leaving my life's best part unscathed and free;
But now my fond hopes lie
Dead in her silent dust: a secret chill
Shoots through me when I think that I live still.

If my poor intellect had but the force
To help my need, and if no other lure
Had led it from the plain and proper course,
Upon my lady's brow 'twere easy sure
To have read this truth, "Here all thy pleasure dies,
And hence thy lifelong trial dates its rise."
My spirit then had gently pass'd away
In her dear presence from all mortal care;
Freed from this troublesome and heavy clay,
Mounting, before her, where
Angels and saints prepared on high her place,
Whom I but follow now with slow sad pace.

My song! if one there be
Who in his love finds happiness and rest,
Tell him this truth from me,
"Die, while thou still art bless'd,
For death betimes is comfort, not dismay,
And who can rightly die needs no delay."

Robert Macgregor.

SESTINA I.

Mia benigna fortuna e 'l viver lieto.

IN HIS MISERY HE DESIRES DEATH THE MORE HE REMEMBERS HIS PAST CONTENTMENT AND COMFORT.

My favouring fortune and my life of joy,
My days so cloudless, and my tranquil nights,
The tender sigh, the pleasing power of song,
Which gently wont to sound in verse and rhyme,
Suddenly darken'd into grief and tears,
Make me hate life and inly pray for death!

O cruel, grim, inexorable Death!
How hast thou dried my every source of joy,
And left me to drag on a life of tears,
Through darkling days and melancholy nights.
My heavy sighs no longer meet in rhyme,
And my hard martyrdom exceeds all song!

Where now is vanish'd my once amorous song?
To talk of anger and to treat with death;
Where the fond verses, where the happy rhyme
Welcomed by gentle hearts with pensive joy?
Where now Love's communings that cheer'd my nights?
My sole theme, my one thought, is now but tears!

Erewhile to my desire so sweet were tears
Their tenderness refined my else rude song,
And made me wake and watch the livelong nights;
But sorrow now to me is worse than death,
Since lost for aye that look of modest joy,
The lofty subject of my lowly rhyme!

Love in those bright eyes to my ready rhyme
Gave a fair theme, now changed, alas! to tears;
With grief remembering that time of joy,
My changed thoughts issue find in other song,

Evermore thee beseeching, pallid Death,
To snatch and save me from these painful nights!

Sleep has departed from my anguish'd nights,
Music is absent from my rugged rhyme,
Which knows not now to sound of aught but death;
Its notes, so thrilling once, all turn'd to tears,
Love knows not in his reign such varied song,
As full of sadness now as then of joy!

Man lived not then so crown'd as I with joy,
Man lives not now such wretched days and nights;
And my full festering grief but swells the song
Which from my bosom draws the mournful rhyme;
I lived in hope, who now live but in tears,
Nor against death have other hope save death!

Me Death in her has kill'd; and only Death
Can to my sight restore that face of joy,
Which pleasant made to me e'en sighs and tears,
Balmy the air, and dewy soft the nights,
Wherein my choicest thoughts I gave to rhyme
While Love inspirited my feeble song!

Would that such power as erst graced Orpheus' song
Were mine to win my Laura back from death,
As he Eurydice without a rhyme;
Then would I live in best excess of joy;
Or, that denied me, soon may some sad night
Close for me ever these twin founts of tears!

Love! I have told with late and early tears,
My grievous injuries in doleful song;
Not that I hope from thee less cruel nights;
And therefore am I urged to pray for death,
Which hence would take me but to crown with joy,
Where lives she whom I sing in this sad rhyme!

If so high may aspire my weary rhyme,
To her now shelter'd safe from rage and tears,
Whose beauties fill e'en heaven with livelier joy,

Well would she recognise my alter'd song,
Which haply pleased her once, ere yet by death
Her days were cloudless made and dark my nights!

O ye, who fondly sigh for better nights,
Who listen to love's will, or sing in rhyme,
Pray that for me be no delay in death,
The port of misery, the goal of tears,
But let him change for me his ancient song,
Since what makes others sad fills me with joy!

Ay! for such joy, in one or in few nights,
I pray in rude song and in anguish'd rhyme,
That soon my tears may ended be in death!

Robert Macgregor.

SONNET LX.

Ite, rime dolenti, al duro sasso.

HE PRAYS THAT SHE WILL BE NEAR HIM AT HIS DEATH, WHICH HE FEELS APPROACHING.

Go, plaintive verse, to the cold marble go,
Which hides in earth my treasure from these eyes;
There call on her who answers from yon skies,
Although the mortal part dwells dark and low.
Of life how I am wearied make her know,
Of stemming these dread waves that round me rise:
But, copying all her virtues I so prize,
Her track I follow, yet my steps are slow.
I sing of her, living, or dead, alone;
(Dead, did I say? She is immortal made!)
That by the world she should be loved, and known.
Oh! in my passage hence may she be near,
To greet my coming that's not long delay'd;
And may I hold in heaven the rank herself holds there!

Dr Nott

Go, melancholy rhymes! your tribute bring
To that cold stone, which holds the dear remains
Of all that earth held precious; – uttering,
If heaven should deign to hear them, earthly strains.
Tell her, that sport of tempests, fit no more
To stem the troublous ocean, – here at last
Her votary treads the solitary shore;
His only pleasure to recall the past.
Tell her, that she who living ruled his fate,
In death still holds her empire: all his care,
So grant the Muse her aid, – to celebrate
Her every word, and thought, and action fair.
Be this my meed, that in the hour of death
Her kindred spirit may hail, and bless my parting breath!

Lord Woodhouselee.

SONNET LXI.

S' onesto amor può meritar mercede.

HE PRAYS THAT, IN REWARD FOR HIS LONG AND VIRTUOUS ATTACHMENT, SHE WILL VISIT HIM IN DEATH.

If Mercy e'er rewardeth virtuous love,
If Pity still can do, as she has done,
I shall have rest, for clearer than the sun
My lady and the world my faith approve.
Who fear'd me once, now knows, yet scarce believes
I am the same who wont her love to seek,
Who seek it still; where she but heard me speak,
Or saw my face, she now my soul perceives.
Wherefore I hope that e'en in heaven she mourns
My heavy anguish, and on me the while
Her sweet face eloquent of pity turns,
And that when shuffled off this mortal coil,
Her way to me with that fair band she'll wend,
True follower of Christ and virtue's friend.

Robert Macgregor.

If virtuous love doth merit recompense –
If pity still maintain its wonted sway –
I that reward shall win, for bright as day
To earth and Laura breathes my faith's incense.
She fear'd me once – now heavenly confidence
Reveals my heart's first hope's unchanging stay;
A word, a look, could this alone convey,
My heart she reads now, stripp'd of earth's defence.
And thus I hope, she for my heavy sighs
To heaven complains, to me she pity shows
By sympathetic visits in my dream:
And when this mortal temple breathless lies,
Oh! may she greet my soul, enclosed by those
Whom heaven and virtue love – our friends supreme.

Miss Wollaston.

SONNET LXII.

Vidi fra mille donne una già tale.

BEAUTY SHOWED ITSELF IN, AND DISAPPEARED WITH, LAURA.

'Mid many fair one such by me was seen
That amorous fears my heart did instant seize,
Beholding her – nor false the images –
Equal to angels in her heavenly mien.
Nothing in her was mortal or terrene,
As one whom nothing short of heaven can please;
My soul well train'd for her to burn and freeze
Sought in her wake to mount the blue serene.
But ah! too high for earthly wings to rise
Her pitch, and soon she wholly pass'd from sight:
The very thought still makes me cold and numb;
O beautiful and high and lustrous eyes,
Where Death, who fills the world with grief and fright,
Found entrance in so fair a form to come.

Robert Macgregor.

SONNET LXIII.

Tornami a mente, anzi v' è dentro quella.

SHE IS SO FIXED IN HIS HEART THAT AT TIMES HE BELIEVES HER STILL ALIVE, AND IS FORCED TO RECALL THE DATE OF HER DEATH.

Oh! to my soul for ever she returns;
Or rather Lethe could not blot her thence,
Such as she was when first she struck my sense,
In that bright blushing age when beauty burns:
So still I see her, bashful as she turns
Retired into herself, as from offence:
I cry – "'Tis she! she still has life and sense:
Oh, speak to me, my love!" – Sometimes she spurns
My call; sometimes she seems to answer straight:
Then, starting from my waking dream, I say, –
"Alas! poor wretch, thou art of mind bereft!
Forget'st thou the first hour of the sixth day
Of April, the three hundred, forty eight,
And thousandth year, – when she her earthly mansion left?"

Dr Morehead.

My mind recalls her; nay, her home is there,
Nor can Lethean draught drive thence her form,
I see that star's pure ray her spirit warm,
Whose grace and spring-time beauty she doth wear.
As thus my vision paints her charms so rare,
That none to such perfection may conform,
I cry, "'Tis she! death doth to life transform!"
And then to hear that voice, I wake my prayer.
She now replies, and now doth mute appear,
Like one whose tottering mind regains its power;
I speak my heart: "Thou must this cheat resign;
The thirteen hundred, eight and fortieth year,
The sixth of April's suns, his first bright hour,
Thou know'st that soul celestial fled its shrine!"

Miss Wollaston.

SONNET LXIV.

Questo nostro caduco e fragil bene.

NATURE DISPLAYED IN HER EVERY CHARM, BUT SOON WITHDREW HER FROM SIGHT.

This gift of beauty which a good men name,
Frail, fleeting, fancied, false, a wind, a shade,
Ne'er yet with all its spells one fair array'd,
Save in this age when for my cost it came.
Not such is Nature's duty, nor her aim,
One to enrich if others poor are made,
But now on one is all her wealth display'd,
– Ladies, your pardon let my boldness claim.
Like loveliness ne'er lived, or old or new,
Nor ever shall, I ween, but hid so strange,
Scarce did our erring world its marvel view,
So soon it fled; thus too my soul must change
The little light vouchsafed me from the skies
Only for pleasure of her sainted eyes.

Robert Macgregor.

SONNET LXV.

O tempo, o ciel volubil che fuggendo.

HE NO LONGER CONTEMPLATES THE MORTAL, BUT THE IMMORTAL BEAUTIES OF LAURA.

O Time! O heavens! whose flying changes frame
Errors and snares for mortals poor and blind;
O days more swift than arrows or the wind,
Experienced now, I know your treacherous aim.
You I excuse, myself alone I blame,
For Nature for your flight who wings design'd
To me gave eyes which still I have inclined
To mine own ill, whence follow grief and shame.
An hour will come, haply e'en now is pass'd,
Their sight to turn on my diviner part
And so this infinite anguish end at last.
Rejects not your long yoke, O Love, my heart,
But its own ill by study, sufferings vast:
Virtue is not of chance, but painful art.

Robert Macgregor.

O Time! O circling heavens! in your flight
Us mortals ye deceive – so poor and blind;
O days! more fleeting than the shaft or wind,
Experience brings your treachery to my sight!
But mine the error – ye yourselves are right;
Your flight fulfils but that your wings design'd:
My eyes were Nature's gift, yet ne'er could find
But one blest light – and hence their present blight.
It now is time (perchance the hour is pass'd)
That they a safer dwelling should select,
And thus repose might soothe my grief acute:
Love's yoke the spirit may not from it cast,
(With oh what pain!) it may its ill eject;
But virtue is attain'd but by pursuit!

Miss Wollaston.

SONNET LXVI.

Quel, che d' odore e di color vincea.

THE LAUREL, IN WHOM HE PLACED ALL HIS JOY HAS BEEN TAKEN FROM HIM TO ADORN HEAVEN.

That which in fragrance and in hue defied
The odoriferous and lucid East,
Fruits, flowers and herbs and leaves, and whence the West
Of all rare excellence obtain'd the prize,
My laurel sweet, which every beauty graced,
Where every glowing virtue loved to dwell,
Beheld beneath its fair and friendly shade
My Lord, and by his side my Goddess sit.
Still have I placed in that beloved plant
My home of choicest thoughts: in fire, in frost
Shivering or burning, still I have been bless'd.
The world was of her perfect honours full
When God, his own bright heaven therewith to grace,
Reclaim'd her for Himself, for she was his.

Robert Macgregor.

SONNET LXVII.

Lasciato hai, Morte, senza sole il mondo.

HER TRUE WORTH WAS KNOWN ONLY TO HIM AND TO HEAVEN.

Death, thou the world, since that dire arrow sped,
Sunless and cold hast left; Love weak and blind;
Beauty and grace their brilliance have resign'd,
And from my heavy heart all joy is fled;
Honour is sunk, and softness banishèd.
I weep alone the woes which all my kind
Should weep – for virtue's fairest flower has pined
Beneath thy touch: what second blooms instead?
Let earth, sea, air, with common wail bemoan
Man's hapless race; which now, since Laura died,
A flowerless mead, a gemless ring appears.
The world possess'd, nor knew her worth, till flown!
I knew it well, who here in grief abide;
And heaven too knows, which decks its forehead with my tears.

Francis Wrangham.

Thou, Death, hast left this world's dark cheerless way
Without a sun: Love blind and stripp'd of arms;
Left mirth despoil'd; beauty bereaved of charms;
And me self-wearied, to myself a prey;
Left vanish'd, sunk, whate'er was courteous, gay:
I only weep, yet all must feel alarms:
If beauty's bud the hand of rapine harms
It dies, and not a second views the day!
Let air, earth, ocean weep for human kind;
For human kind, deprived of Laura, seems
A flowerless mead, a ring whose gem is lost.
None knew her worth while to this orb confined,
Save me her bard, whose sorrow ceaseless streams,
And heaven, that's made more beauteous at my cost.

Dr Nott

SONNET LXVIII.

Conobbi, quanto il ciel gli occhi m' aperse.

HER PRAISES ARE, COMPARED WITH HER DESERTS, BUT AS A DROP TO THE OCEAN.

So far as to mine eyes its light heaven show'd,
So far as love and study train'd my wings,
Novel and beautiful but mortal things
From every star I found on her bestow'd:
So many forms in rare and varied mode
Of heavenly beauty from immortal springs
My panting intellect before me brings,
Sunk my weak sight before their dazzling load.
Hence, whatsoe'er I spoke of her or wrote,
Who, at God's right, returns me now her prayers,
Is in that infinite abyss a mote:
For style beyond the genius never dares;
Thus, though upon the sun man fix his sight,
He seeth less as fiercer burns its light.

Robert Macgregor.

SONNET LXIX.

Dolce mio caro e prezioso pegno.

HE PRAYS HER TO APPEAR BEFORE HIM IN A VISION.

Dear precious pledge, by Nature snatch'd away,
But yet reserved for me in realms undying;
O thou on whom my life is aye relying,
Why tarry thus, when for thine aid I pray?
Time was, when sleep could to mine eyes convey
Sweet visions, worthy thee; – why is my sighing
Unheeded now? – who keeps thee from replying?
Surely contempt in heaven cannot stay:
Often on earth the gentlest heart is fain
To feed and banquet on another's woe
(Thus love is conquer'd in his own domain),
But thou, who seest through me, and dost know
All that I feel, – thou, who canst soothe my pain,
Oh! let thy blessed shade its peace bestow.

Mrs Wrottesley.

SONNET LXX.

Deh qual pietà, qual angel fu sì presto.

HIS PRAYER IS HEARD.

What angel of compassion, hovering near,
Heard, and to heaven my heart grief instant bore,
Whence now I feel descending as of yore
My lady, in that bearing chaste and dear,
My lone and melancholy heart to cheer,
So free from pride, of humbleness such store,
In fine, so perfect, though at death's own door,
I live, and life no more is dull and drear.
Blessèd is she who so can others bless
With her fair sight, or with that tender speech
To whose full meaning love alone can reach.
"Dear friend," she says, "thy pangs my soul distress;
But for our good I did thy homage shun" –
In sweetest tones which might arrest the sun.

Robert Macgregor.

SONNET LXXI.

Del cibo onde 'l signor mio sempre abbonda.

HE DESCRIBES THE APPARITION OF LAURA.

Food wherewithal my lord is well supplied,
With tears and grief my weary heart I've fed;
As fears within and paleness o'er me spread,
Oft thinking on its fatal wound and wide:
But in her time with whom no other vied,
Equal or second, to my suffering bed
Comes she to look on whom I almost dread,
And takes her seat in pity by my side.
With that fair hand, so long desired in vain,
She check'd my tears, while at her accents crept
A sweetness to my soul, intense, divine.
"Is this thy wisdom, to parade thy pain?
No longer weep! hast thou not amply wept?
Would that such life were thine as death is mine!"

Robert Macgregor.

With grief and tears (my soul's proud sovereign's food)
I ever nourish still my aching heart;
I feel my blanching cheek, and oft I start
As on Love's sharp engraven wound I brood.
But she, who e'er on earth unrivall'd stood,
Flits o'er my couch, when prostrate by his dart
I lie; and there her presence doth impart.
Whilst scarce my eyes dare meet their vision'd good,
With that fair hand in life I so desired,
She stays my eyes' sad tide; her voice's tone
Awakes the balm earth ne'er to man can give:
And thus she speaks: – "Oh! vain hath wisdom fired
The hopeless mourner's breast; no more bemoan,
I am not dead – would thou like me couldst live!"

Miss Wollaston.

SONNET LXXII.

Ripensando a quel ch' oggi il ciel onora.

HE WOULD DIE OF GRIEF WERE SHE NOT SOMETIMES TO CONSOLE HIM BY HER PRESENCE.

To that soft look which now adorns the skies,
The graceful bending of the radiant head,
The face, the sweet angelic accents fled,
That soothed me once, but now awake my sighs
Oh! when to these imagination flies,
I wonder that I am not long since dead!
'Tis she supports me, for her heavenly tread
Is round my couch when morning visions rise!
In every attitude how holy, chaste!
How tenderly she seems to hear the tale
Of my long woes, and their relief to seek!
But when day breaks she then appears in haste
The well-known heavenward path again to scale,
With moisten'd eye, and soft expressive cheek!

Dr Morehead.

'Tis sweet, though sad, my trembling thoughts to raise,
As memory dwells upon that form so dear,
And think that now e'en angels join to praise
The gentle virtues that adorn'd her here;
That face, that look, in fancy to behold –
To hear that voice that did with music vie –
The bending head, crown'd with its locks of gold –
All, all that charm'd, now but sad thoughts supply.
How had I lived her bitter loss to weep,
If that pure spirit, pitying my woe,
Had not appear'd to bless my troubled sleep,
Ere memory broke upon the world below?
What pure, what gentle greetings then were mine!
In what attention wrapt she paused to hear
My life's sad course, of which she bade me speak!
But as the dawn from forth the East did shine
Back to that heaven to which her way was clear,
She fled, – while falling tears bedew'd each cheek.

Mrs Wrottesley.

SONNET LXXIII.

Fu forse un tempo dolce cosa amore.

HE COMPLAINS OF HIS SUFFERINGS, WHICH ADMIT OF NO RELIEF.

Love, haply, was erewhile a sweet relief;
I scarce know when; but now it bitter grows
Beyond all else. Who learns from life well knows,
As I have learnt to know from heavy grief;
She, of our age, who was its honour chief,
Who now in heaven with brighter lustre glows,
Has robb'd my being of the sole repose
It knew in life, though that was rare and brief.
Pitiless Death my every good has ta'en!
Not the great bliss of her fair spirit freed
Can aught console the adverse life I lead.
I wept and sang; who now can wake no strain,
But day and night the pent griefs of my soul
From eyes and tongue in tears and verses roll.

Robert Macgregor.

SONNET LXXIV.

Spinse amor e dolor ove ir non debbe.

REFLECTING THAT LAURA IS IN HEAVEN, HE REPENTS HIS EXCESSIVE GRIEF, AND IS CONSOLED.

Sorrow and Love encouraged my poor tongue,
Discreet in sadness, where it should not go,
To speak of her for whom I burn'd and sung,
What, even were it true, 'twere wrong to show.
That blessèd saint my miserable state
Might surely soothe, and ease my spirit's strife,
Since she in heaven is now domesticate
With Him who ever ruled her heart in life.
Wherefore I am contented and consoled,
Nor would again in life her form behold;
Nay, I prefer to die, and live alone.
Fairer than ever to my mental eye,
I see her soaring with the angels high,
Before our Lord, her maker and my own.

Robert Macgregor.

My love and grief compell'd me to proclaim
My heart's lament, and urged me to convey
That, were it true, of her I should not say
Who woke alike my song and bosom's flame.
For I should comfort find, 'mid this world's shame,
To mark her soul's beatified array,
To think that He who here had own'd its sway,
Doth now within his home its presence claim.
And true I comfort find – myself resign'd,
I would not woo her back to earthly gloom;
Oh! rather let me die, or live still lone!
My mental eye, that holds her there enshrined,
Now paints her wing'd, bright with celestial bloom,
Prostrate beneath our mutual Heaven's throne.

Miss Wollaston.

SONNET LXXV.

Gli angeli eletti e l' anime beate.

HE DIRECTS ALL HIS THOUGHTS TO HEAVEN, WHERE LAURA AWAITS AND BECKONS HIM.

The elect angels and the souls in bliss,
The citizens of heaven, when, that first day,
My lady passed from me and went their way,
Of marvel and pity full, did round her press.
"What light is this, and what new loveliness?"
They said among them; "for such sweet display
Did never mount, that from the earth did stray
To this high dwelling, all this age, we guess!"[4]
She, well content her lodging chang"d to find,
Shows perfect, by her peers most perfect placed;
And now and then half turning looks behind
To see if I walk in the way she traced:
Hence I lift heavenward all my heart and mind
Because I hear her pray me to make haste.

George Macdonald

4 Footnote by George Macdonald: Pure English of Petrarch's time.

The chosen angels, and the spirits blest,
Celestial tenants, on that glorious day
My Lady join'd them, throng'd in bright array
Around her, with amaze and awe imprest.
"What splendour, what new beauty stands confest
Unto our sight?" – among themselves they say;
"No soul, in this vile age, from sinful clay
To our high realms has risen so fair a guest."
Delighted to have changed her mortal state,
She ranks amid the purest of her kind;
And ever and anon she looks behind,
To mark my progress and my coming wait;
Now my whole thought, my wish to heaven I cast;
'Tis Laura's voice I hear, and hence she bids me haste.

Dr Nott

The chosen angels, and the blest above,
Heaven's citizens! – the day when Laura ceased
To adorn the world, about her thronging press'd,
Replete with wonder and with holy love.
"What sight is this? – what will this beauty prove?"
Said they; "for sure no form in charms so dress'd,
From yonder globe to this high place of rest,
In all the latter age, did e'er remove!"
She, pleased and happy with her mansion new,
Compares herself with the most perfect there;
And now and then she casts a glance to view
If yet I come, and seems to wish me near.
Rise then, my thoughts, to heaven! – vain world, adieu!
My Laura calls! her quickening voice I hear!

Lord Charlemont.

SONNET LXXVI.

Donna che lieta col Principio nostro.

HE CONJURES LAURA, BY THE PURE LOVE HE EVER BORE HER, TO OBTAIN FOR HIM A SPEEDY ADMISSION TO HER IN HEAVEN.

Lady, in bliss who, by our Maker's feet,
As suited for thine excellent life alone,
Art now enthroned in high and glorious seat,
Adorn'd with charms nor pearls nor purple own;
O model high and rare of ladies sweet!
Now in his face to whom all things are known,
Look on my love, with that pure faith replete,
As long my verse and truest tears have shown,
And know at last my heart on earth to thee
Was still as now in heaven, nor wish'd in life
More than beneath thine eyes' bright sun to be:
Wherefore, to recompense the tedious strife,
Which turn'd my liege heart from the world away,
Pray that I soon may come with thee to stay.

Robert Macgregor.

Lady! whose gentle virtues have obtain'd
For thee a dwelling with thy Maker blest,
To sit enthroned above, in angels' vest
(Whose lustre gold nor purple had attain'd):
Ah! thou who here the most exalted reign'd,
Now through the eyes of Him who knows each breast,
That heart's pure faith and love thou canst attest,
Which both my pen and tears alike sustain'd.
Thou, knowest, too, my heart was thine on earth,
As now it is in heaven; no wish was there
But to avow thine eyes, its only shrine:
Thus to reward the strife which owes its birth
To thee, who won my each affection'd care,
Pray God to waft me to his home and thine!

Miss Wollaston.

SONNET LXXVII.

Da' più begli occhi e dal più chiaro viso.

HIS ONLY COMFORT IS THE EXPECTATION OF MEETING HER AGAIN IN HEAVEN.

The brightest eyes, the most resplendent face
That ever shone; and the most radiant hair,
With which nor gold nor sunbeam could compare;
The sweetest accent, and a smile all grace;
Hands, arms, that would e'en motionless abase
Those who to Love the most rebellious were;
Fine, nimble feet; a form that would appear
Like that of her who first did Eden trace;
These fann'd life's spark: now heaven, and all its choir
Of angel hosts those kindred charms admire;
While lone and darkling I on earth remain.
Yet is not comfort fled; she, who can read
Each secret of my soul, shall intercede;
And I her sainted form behold again.

Dr Nott

Yes, from those finest eyes, that face most sweet
That ever shone, and from that loveliest hair,
With which nor gold nor sunbeam may compare,
That speech with love, that smile with grace replete,
From those soft hands, those white arms which defeat.
Themselves unmoved, the stoutest hearts that e'er
To Love were rebels; from those feet so fair,
From her whole form, for Eden only meet,
My spirit took its life – now these delight
The King of Heaven and his angelic train,
While, blind and naked, I am left in night.
One only balm expect I 'mid my pain –
That she, mine every thought who now can see,
May win this grace – that I with her may be.

Robert Macgregor.

SONNET LXXVIII.

E' mi par d' or in ora udire il messo.

HE FEELS THAT THE DAY OF THEIR REUNION IS AT HAND.

Methinks from hour to hour her voice I hear:
My Lady calls me! I would fain obey;
Within, without, I feel myself decay;
And am so alter'd – not with many a year –
That to myself a stranger I appear;
All my old usual life is put away –
Could I but know how long I have to stay!
Grant, Heaven, the long-wish'd summons may be near!
Oh, blest the day when from this earthly gaol
I shall be freed, when burst and broken lies
This mortal guise, so heavy yet so frail,
When from this black night my saved spirit flies,
Soaring up, up, above the bright serene,
Where with my Lord my Lady shall be seen.

Robert Macgregor.

SONNET LXXIX.

L' aura mia sacra al mio stanco riposo.

HE TELLS HER IN SLEEP OF HIS SUFFERINGS, AND, OVERCOME BY HER SYMPATHY, AWAKES.

On my oft-troubled sleep my sacred air
So softly breathes, at last I courage take,
To tell her of my past and present ache,
Which never in her life my heart did dare.
I first that glance so full of love declare
Which served my lifelong torment to awake,
Next, how, content and wretched for her sake,
Love day by day my tost heart knew to tear.
She speaks not, but, with pity's dewy trace,
Intently looks on me, and gently sighs,
While pure and lustrous tears begem her face;
My spirit, which her sorrow fiercely tries,
So to behold her weep with anger burns,
And freed from slumber to itself returns.

Robert Macgregor.

SONNET LXXX.

Ogni giorno mi par più di mill' anni.

FAR FROM FEARING, HE PRAYS FOR DEATH.

Each day to me seems as a thousand years,
That I my dear and faithful star pursue,
Who guided me on earth, and guides me too
By a sure path to life without its tears.
For in the world, familiar now, appears
No snare to tempt; so rare a light and true
Shines e'en from heaven my secret conscience through,
Of lost time and loved sin the glass it rears.
Not that I need the threats of death to dread,
(Which He who loved us bore with greater pain)
That, firm and constant, I his path should tread:
'Tis but a brief while since in every vein
Of her he enter'd who my fate has been,
Yet troubled not the least her brow serene.

Robert Macgregor.

SONNET LXXXI.

Non può far morte il dolce viso amaro.

SINCE HER DEATH HE HAS CEASED TO LIVE.

Death cannot make that beauteous face less fair,
But that sweet face may lend to death a grace;
My spirit's guide! from her each good I trace;
Who learns to die, may seek his lesson there.
That holy one! who not his blood would spare,
But did the dark Tartarean bolts unbrace;
He, too, doth from my soul death's terrors chase:
Then welcome, death! thy impress I would wear.
And linger not! 'tis time that I had fled;
Alas! my stay hath little here avail'd,
Since she, my Laura blest, resign'd her breath:
Life's spring in me hath since that hour lain dead,
In her I lived, my life in hers exhaled,
The hour she died I felt within me death!
Miss Wollaston.

CANZONE VI.

Quando il suave mio fido conforto.

SHE APPEARS TO HIM, AND, WITH MORE THAN WONTED AFFECTION, ENDEAVOURS TO CONSOLE HIM.

When she, the faithful soother of my pain,
This life's long weary pilgrimage to cheer,
Vouchsafes beside my nightly couch to appear,
With her sweet speech attempering reason's strain;
O'ercome by tenderness, and terror vain,
I cry, "Whence comest thou, O spirit blest?"
She from her beauteous breast
A branch of laurel and of palm displays,
And, answering, thus she says.
"From th' empyrean seat of holy love
Alone thy sorrows to console I move."

In actions, and in words, in humble guise
I speak my thanks, and ask, "How may it be
That thou shouldst know my wretched state?" and she
"Thy floods of tears perpetual, and thy sighs
Breathed forth unceasing, to high heaven arise.
And there disturb thy blissful state serene;
So grievous hath it been,
That freed from this poor being, I at last
To a better life have pass'd,
Which should have joy'd thee hadst thou loved as well
As thy sad brow, and sadder numbers tell."

"Oh! not thy ills, I but deplore my own,
In darkness, and in grief remaining here,
Certain that thou hast reach'd the highest sphere,
As of a thing that man hath seen and known.
Would God and Nature to the world have shown
Such virtue in a young and gentle breast,
Were not eternal rest
The appointed guerdon of a life so fair?

Thou! of the spirits rare,
Who, from a course unspotted, pure and high,
Are suddenly translated to the sky.

"But I! how can I cease to weep? forlorn,
Without thee nothing, wretched, desolate!
Oh, in the cradle had I met my fate,
Or at the breast! and not to love been born!"
And she: "Why by consuming grief thus worn?
Were it not better spread aloft thy wings,
And now all mortal things,
With these thy sweet and idle fantasies,
At their just value prize,
And follow me, if true thy tender vows,
Gathering henceforth with me these honour'd boughs?"

Then answering her: – "Fain would I thou shouldst say
What these two verdant branches signify."
"Methinks," she says, "thou may'st thyself reply,
Whose pen has graced the one by many a lay.
The palm shows victory; and in youth's bright day
I overcame the world, and my weak heart:
The triumph mine in part,
Glory to Him who made my weakness strength!
And thou, yet turn at length!
'Gainst other powers his gracious aid implore,
That we may be with Him thy trial o'er!"

"Are these the crisped locks, and links of gold
That bind me still? And these the radiant eyes.
To me the Sun?" "Err not with the unwise,
Nor think," she says, "as they are wont. Behold
In me a spirit, among the blest enroll'd;
Thou seek'st what hath long been earth again:
Yet to relieve thy pain
'Tis given me thus to appear, ere I resume
That beauty from the tomb,
More loved, that I, severe in pity, win
Thy soul with mine to Heaven, from death and sin."

I weep; and she my cheek,

Soft sighing, with her own fair hand will dry;
And, gently chiding, speak
In tones of power to rive hard rocks in twain;
Then vanishing, sleep follows in her train.

Lady Dacre.

CANZONE VII.

Quell' antiquo mio dolce empio signore.

LOVE, SUMMONED BY THE POET TO THE TRIBUNAL OF REASON, PASSES A SPLENDID EULOGIUM ON LAURA.

Long had I suffer'd, till – to combat more
In strength, in hope too sunk – at last before
Impartial Reason's seat,
Whence she presides our nobler nature o'er,
I summon'd my old tyrant, stern and sweet;
There, groaning 'neath a weary weight of grief,
With fear and horror stung,
Like one who dreads to die and prays relief,
My plea I open'd thus: "When life was young,
I, weakly, placed my peace within his power,
And nothing from that hour
Save wrong I've met; so many and so great
The torments I have borne,
That my once infinite patience is outworn,
And my life worthless grown is held in very hate!

"Thus sadly has my time till now dragg'd by
In flames and anguish: I have left each way
Of honour, use, and joy,
This my most cruel flatterer to obey.
What wit so rare such language to employ
That yet may free me from this wretched thrall.
Or even my complaint,
So great and just, against this ingrate paint?
O little sweet! much bitterness and gall!
How have you changed my life, so tranquil, ere
With the false witchery blind,
That alone lured me to his amorous snare!
If right I judge, a mind
I boasted once with higher feelings rife,
– But he destroy'd my peace, he plunged me in this strife!

"Less for myself to care, through him I've grown.
And less my God to honour than I ought:
Through him my every thought
On a frail beauty blindly have I thrown;
In this my counsellor he stood alone,
Still prompt with cruel aid so to provoke
My young desire, that I
Hoped respite from his harsh and heavy yoke.
But, ah! what boots – though changing time sweep by,
If from this changeless passion nought can save –
A genius proud and high?
Or what Heaven's other envied gifts to have,
If still I groan the slave
Of the fierce despot whom I here accuse,
Who turns e'en my sad life to his triumphant use?

"'Twas he who made me desert countries seek,
Wild tribes and nations dangerous, manners rude,
My path with thorns he strew'd,
And every error that betrays the weak.
Valley and mountain, marsh, and stream, and sea,
On every side his snares were set for me.
In June December came,
With present peril and sharp toil the same;
Alone they left me never, neither he,
Nor she, whom I so fled, my other foe:
Untimely in my tomb,
If by some painful death not yet laid low.
My safety from such doom
Heaven's gracious pity, not this tyrant, deigns,
Who feeds upon my grief, and profits in my pains!

"No quiet hour, since first I own'd his reign,
I've known, nor hope to know: repose is fled
From my unfriendly bed,
Nor herb nor spells can bring it back again.
By fraud and force he gain'd and guards his power
O'er every sense; soundeth from steeple near,
By day, by night, the hour,
I feel his hand in every stroke I hear.
Never did cankerworm fair tree devour,

As he my heart, wherein he, gnawing, lurks,
And, there, my ruin works.
Hence my past martyrdom and tears arise,
My present speech, these sighs,
Which tear and tire myself, and haply thee,
– Judge then between us both, thou knowest him and me!"

With fierce reproach my adversary rose:
"Lady," he spoke, "the rebel to a close
Is heard at last, the truth
Receive from me which he has shrunk to tell:
Big words to bandy, specious lies to sell,
He plies right well the vile trade of his youth,
Freed from whose shame, to share
My easy pleasures, by my friendly care,
From each false passion which had work'd him ill,
Kept safe and pure, laments he, graceless, still
The sweet life he has gain'd?
And, blindly, thus his fortune dares he blame,
Who owes his very fame
To me, his genius who sublimed, sustain'd,
In the proud flight to which he, else, had dared not aim?

"Well knows he how, in history's every page,
The laurell'd chief, the monarch on his throne,
The poet and the sage,
Favourites of fortune, or for virtue known,
Were cursed by evil stars, in loves debased,
Soulless and vile, their hearts, their fame, to waste:
While I, for him alone,
From all the lovely ladies of the earth,
Chose one, so graced with beauty and with worth,
The eternal sun her equal ne'er beheld.
Such charm was in her life,
Such virtue in her speech with music rife,
Their wondrous power dispell'd
Each vain and vicious fancy from his heart,
– A foe I am indeed, if this a foeman's part!

"Such was my anger, these my hate and slights,
Than all which others could bestow more sweet;

Evil for good I meet,
If thus ingratitude my grace requites.
So high, upon my wings, he soar'd in fame,
To hear his song, fair dames and gentle knights
In throngs delighted came.
Among the gifted spirits of our time
His name conspicuous shines; in every clime
Admired, approved, his strains an echo find.
Such is he, but for me
A mere court flatterer who was doom'd to be,
Unmark'd amid his kind,
Till, in my school, exalted and made known
By her, who, of her sex, stood peerless and alone!

"If my great service more there need to tell,
I have so fenced and fortified him well,
That his pure mind on nought
Of gross or grovelling now can brook to dwell;
Modest and sensitive, in deed, word, thought,
Her captive from his youth, she so her fair
And virtuous image press'd
Upon his heart, it left its likeness there:
Whate'er his life has shown of good or great,
In aim or action, he from us possess'd.
Never was midnight dream
So full of error as to us his hate!
For Heaven's and man's esteem
If still he keep, the praise is due to us,
Whom in its thankless pride his blind rage censures thus!

"In fine, 'twas I, my past love to exceed,
Who heavenward fix'd his hope, who gave him wings
To fly from mortal things,
Which to eternal bliss the path impede;
With his own sense, that, seeing how in her
Virtues and charms so great and rare combined,
A holy pride might stir
And to the Great First Cause exalt his mind,
(In his own verse confess'd this truth we see,)
While that dear lady whom I sent to be
The grace, the guard, and guide

Of his vain life" – But here a heart-deep groan
I sudden gave, and cried,
"Yes! sent and snatch'd her from me." He replied,
"Not I, but Heaven above, which will'd her for its own!"

At length before that high tribunal each –
With anxious trembling I, while in his mien
Was conscious triumph seen –
With earnest prayer concluded thus his speech:
"Speak, noble lady! we thy judgment wait."
She then with equal air:
"It glads me to have heard your keen debate,
But in a cause so great,
More time and thought it needs just verdict to declare!"

Robert Macgregor.

I cited once t' appear before the noble queen,
That ought to guide each mortal life that in this world is seen,
That pleasant cruel foe that robbeth hearts of ease,
And now doth frown, and then doth fawn, and can both grieve and
please;
And there, as gold in fire full fined to each intent,
Charged with fear, and terror eke I did myself present,
As one that doubted death, and yet did justice crave,
And thus began t' unfold my cause in hope some help to have.

"Madam, in tender youth I enter'd first this reign,
Where other sweet I never felt, than grief and great disdain;
And eke so sundry kinds of torments did endure.
As life I loathed, and death desired my cursèd case to cure;
And thus my woeful days unto this hour have pass'd
In smoky sighs and scalding tears, my wearied life to waste;
O Lord! what graces great I fled, and eke refused
To serve this cruel crafty Sire that doubtless trust abused."

"What wit can use such words to argue and debate,
What tongue express the full effect of mine unhappy state;
What hand with pen can paint t' uncipher this deceit;
What heart so hard that would not yield that once hath seen his bate;
What great and grievous wrongs, what threats of ill success,
What single sweet, mingled with mass of double bitterness.
With what unpleasant pangs, with what an hoard of pains,
Hath he acquainted my green years by his false pleasant trains."

"Who by resistless power hath forced me sue his dance,
That if I be not much abused had found much better
And when I most resolved to lead most quiet life, chance;
He spoil'd me of discordless state, and thrust me in truceless strife.
He hath bewitch'd me so that God the less I served,
And due respect unto myself the further from me swerv'd;
He hath the love of one so painted in my thought,
That other thing I can none mind, nor care for as I ought.
And all this comes from him, both counsel and the cause.
That whet my young desire so much to th' honour of his laws."

John Harington MS. (Only parts of the *canzone* are translated).

SONNET LXXXII.

Dicemi spesso il mio fidato speglio.

HE AWAKES TO A CONVICTION OF THE NEAR APPROACH OF DEATH.

My faithful mirror oft to me has told –
My weary spirit and my shrivell'd skin
My failing powers to prove it all begin –
"Deceive thyself no longer, thou art old."
Man is in all by Nature best controll'd,
And if with her we struggle, time creeps in;
At the sad truth, on fire as waters win,
A long and heavy sleep is off me roll'd;
And I see clearly our vain life depart,
That more than once our being cannot be:
Her voice sounds ever in my inmost heart.
Who now from her fair earthly frame is free:
She walk'd the world so peerless and alone,
Its fame and lustre all with her are flown.

Robert Macgregor.

The mirror'd friend – my changing form hath read.
My every power's incipient decay –
My wearied soul – alike, in warning say
"Thyself no more deceive, thy youth hath fled."
'Tis ever best to be by Nature led,
We strive with her, and Death makes us his prey;
At that dread thought, as flames the waters stay,
The dream is gone my life hath sadly fed.
I wake to feel how soon existence flies:
Once known, 'tis gone, and never to return.
Still vibrates in my heart the thrilling tone
Of her, who now her beauteous shrine defies:
But she, who here to rival, none could learn,
Hath robb'd her sex, and with its fame hath flown.

Miss Wollaston.

SONNET LXXXIII.

Volo con l' ali de' pensieri al cielo.

HE SEEMS TO BE WITH HER IN HEAVEN.

So often on the wings of thought I fly
Up to heaven's blissful seats, that I appear
As one of those whose treasure is lodged there,
The rent veil of mortality thrown by.
A pleasing chillness thrills my heart, while I
Listen to her voice, who bids me paleness wear –
"Ah! now, my friend, I love thee, now revere,
For changed thy face, thy manners," doth she cry.
She leads me to her Lord: and then I bow,
Preferring humble prayer, He would allow
That I his glorious face, and hers might see.
Thus He replies: "Thy destiny's secure;
To stay some twenty, or some ten years more,
Is but a little space, though long it seems to thee."

Dr Nott

SONNET LXXXIV.

Morte ha spento quel Sol ch' abbagliar suolmi.

WEARY OF LIFE, NOW THAT SHE IS NO LONGER WITH HIM, HE DEVOTES HIMSELF TO GOD.

Death has the bright sun quench'd which wont to burn;
Her pure and constant eyes his dark realms hold:
She now is dust, who dealt me heat and cold;
To common trees my chosen laurels turn;
Hence I at once my bliss and bane discern.
None now there is my feelings who can mould
From fire to frost, from timorous to bold,
In grief to languish or with hope to yearn.
Out of his tyrant hands who harms and heals,
Erewhile who made in it such havoc sore,
My heart the bitter-sweet of freedom feels.
And to the Lord whom, thankful, I adore,
The heavens who ruleth merely with his brow,
I turn life-weary, if not satiate, now.

Robert Macgregor.

SONNET LXXXV.

Tennemi Amor anni ventuno ardendo.

HE CONFESSES AND REGRETS HIS SINS, AND PRAYS GOD TO SAVE HIM FROM ETERNAL DEATH.

Love held me one and twenty years enchain'd,
His flame was joy – for hope was in my grief!
For ten more years I wept without relief,
When Laura with my heart, to heaven attain'd.
Now weary grown, my life I had arraign'd
That in its error, check'd (to my belief)
Blest virtue's seeds – now, in my yellow leaf,
I grieve the misspent years, existence stain'd.
Alas! it might have sought a brighter goal,
In flying troublous thoughts, and winning peace;
O Father! I repentant seek thy throne:
Thou, in this temple hast enshrined my soul,
Oh, bless me yet, and grant its safe release!
Unjustified – my sin I humbly own.

Miss Wollaston.

SONNET LXXXVI.

I' vo piangendo i miei passati tempi.

HE HUMBLY CONFESSES THE ERRORS OF HIS PAST LIFE, AND PRAYS FOR DIVINE GRACE.

Weeping, I still revolve the seasons flown
In vain idolatry of mortal things;
Not soaring heavenward; though my soul had wings
Which might, perchance, a glorious flight have shown.
O Thou, discerner of the guilt I own,
Giver of life immortal, King of Kings,
Heal Thou the wounded heart which conscience stings:
It looks for refuge only to thy throne.
Thus, although life was warfare and unrest,
Be death the haven of peace; and if my day
Was vain – yet make the parting moment blest!
Through this brief remnant of my earthly way,
And in death's billows, be thy hand confess'd;
Full well Thou know'st, this hope is all my stay!

W. Sheppard.

Still do I mourn the years for aye gone by,
Which on a mortal love I lavishèd,
Nor e'er to soar my pinions balancèd,
Though wing'd perchance no humble height to fly.
Thou, Dread Invisible, who from on high
Look'st down upon this suffering erring head,
Oh, be thy succour to my frailty sped,
And with thy grace my indigence supply!
My life in storms and warfare doom'd to spend,
Harbour'd in peace that life may I resign:
It's course though idle, pious be its end!
Oh, for the few brief days, which yet are mine,
And for their close, thy guiding hand extend!
Thou know'st on Thee alone my heart's firm hopes recline.

Francis Wrangham.

SONNET LXXXVII.

Dolci durezze e placide repulse.

HE OWES HIS OWN SALVATION TO THE VIRTUOUS CONDUCT OF LAURA.

O sweet severity, repulses mild,
With chasten'd love, and tender pity fraught;
Graceful rebukes, that to mad passion taught
Becoming mastery o'er its wishes wild;
Speech dignified, in which, united, smiled
All courtesy, with purity of thought;
Virtue and beauty, that uprooted aught
Of baser temper had my heart defiled:
Eyes, in whose glance man is beatified –
Awful, in pride of virtue, to restrain
Aspiring hopes that justly are denied,
Then prompt the drooping spirit to sustain!
These, beautiful in every change, supplied
Health to my soul, that else were sought in vain.

Lady Dacre.

SONNET LXXXVIII.

Spirto felice, che sì dolcemente.

BEHOLDING IN FANCY THE SHADE OF LAURA, HE TELLS HER THE LOSS THAT THE WORLD SUSTAINED IN HER DEPARTURE.

Blest spirit, that with beams so sweetly clear
Those eyes didst bend on me, than stars more bright,
And sighs didst breathe, and words which could delight
Despair; and which in fancy still I hear; –
I see thee now, radiant from thy pure sphere
O'er the soft grass, and violet's purple light,
Move, as an angel to my wondering sight;
More present than earth gave thee to appear.
Yet to the Cause Supreme thou art return'd:
And left, here to dissolve, that beauteous veil
In which indulgent Heaven invested thee.
Th' impoverish'd world at thy departure mourn'd:
For love departed, and the sun grew pale,
And death then seem'd our sole felicity.

Capel Lofft.

O blessed Spirit! who those sun-like eyes
So sweetly didst inform and brightly fill,
Who the apt words didst frame and tender sighs
Which in my fond heart have their echo still.
Erewhile I saw thee, glowing with chaste flame,
Thy feet 'mid violets and verdure set,
Moving in angel not in mortal frame,
Life-like and light, before me present yet!
Her, when returning with thy God to dwell,
Thou didst relinquish and that fair veil given
For purpose high by fortune's grace to thee:
Love at thy parting bade the world farewell;
Courtesy died; the sun abandon'd heaven,
And Death himself our best friend 'gan to be.

Robert Macgregor.

SONNET LXXXIX.

Deh porgi mano all' affannato ingegno.

HE BEGS LOVE TO ASSIST HIM, THAT HE MAY WORTHILY CELEBRATE HER.

Ah, Love! some succour to my weak mind deign,
Lend to my frail and weary style thine aid,
To sing of her who is immortal made,
A citizen of the celestial reign.
And grant, Lord, that my verse the height may gain
Of her great praises, else in vain essay'd,
Whose peer in worth or beauty never stay'd
In this our world, unworthy to retain.
Love answers: "In myself and Heaven what lay,
By conversation pure and counsel wise,
All was in her whom death has snatch'd away.
Since the first morn when Adam oped his eyes,
Like form was ne'er – suffice it this to say,
Write down with tears what scarce I tell for sighs."

Robert Macgregor.

SONNET XC.

Vago augelletto che cantando vai.

THE PLAINTIVE SONG OF A BIRD RECALLS TO HIM HIS OWN KEENER SORROW.

Poor solitary bird, that pour'st thy lay;
Or haply mournest the sweet season gone:
As chilly night and winter hurry on,
And day-light fades and summer flies away;
If as the cares that swell thy little throat
Thou knew'st alike the woes that wound my rest.
Ah, thou wouldst house thee in this kindred breast,
And mix with mine thy melancholy note.
Yet little know I ours are kindred ills:
She still may live the object of thy song:
Not so for me stern death or Heaven wills!
But the sad season, and less grateful hour,
And of past joy and sorrow thoughts that throng
Prompt my full heart this idle lay to pour.

Lady Dacre.

Sweet bird, that singest on thy airy way,
Or else bewailest pleasures that are past;
What time the night draws nigh, and wintry blast;
Leaving behind each merry month, and day;
Oh, couldst thou, as thine own, my state survey,
With the same gloom of misery o'ercast;
Unto my bosom thou mightst surely haste
And, by partaking, my sad griefs allay.
Yet would thy share of woe not equal mine,
Since the loved mate thou weep'st doth haply live,
While death, and heaven, me of my fair deprive:
But hours less gay, the season's drear decline;
With thoughts on many a sad, and pleasant year,
Tempt me to ask thy piteous presence here.

Dr Nott

CANZONE VIII.

Vergine bella che di sol vestita.

TO THE VIRGIN MARY.

Beautiful Virgin! clothed with the sun,
Crown'd with the stars, who so the Eternal Sun
Well pleasedst that in thine his light he hid;
Love pricks me on to utter speech of thee,
And – feeble to commence without thy aid –
Of Him who on thy bosom rests in love.
Her I invoke who gracious still replies
To all who ask in faith,
Virgin! if ever yet
The misery of man and mortal things
To mercy moved thee, to my prayer incline;
Help me in this my strife,
Though I am but of dust, and thou heaven's radiant Queen!

Wise Virgin! of that lovely number one
Of Virgins blest and wise,
Even the first and with the brightest lamp:
O solid buckler of afflicted hearts!
'Neath which against the blows of Fate and Death,
Not mere deliverance but great victory is;
Relief from the blind ardour which consumes
Vain mortals here below!
Virgin! those lustrous eyes,
Which tearfully beheld the cruel prints
In the fair limbs of thy beloved Son,
Ah! turn on my sad doubt,
Who friendless, helpless thus, for counsel come to thee!

O Virgin! pure and perfect in each part,
Maiden or Mother, from thy honour'd birth,
This life to lighten and the next adorn;
O bright and lofty gate of open'd heaven!
By thee, thy Son and His, the Almighty Sire,

In our worst need to save us came below:
And, from amid all other earthly seats,
Thou only wert elect,
Virgin supremely blest!
The tears of Eve who turnedst into joy;
Make me, thou canst, yet worthy of his grace,
O happy without end,
Who art in highest heaven a saint immortal shrined.

O holy Virgin! full of every good,
Who, in humility most deep and true,
To heaven art mounted, thence my prayers to hear,
That fountain thou of pity didst produce,
That sun of justice light, which calms and clears
Our age, else clogg'd with errors dark and foul.
Three sweet and precious names in thee combine,
Of mother, daughter, wife,
Virgin! with glory crown'd,
Queen of that King who has unloosed our bonds,
And free and happy made the world again,
By whose most sacred wounds,
I pray my heart to fix where true joys only are!

Virgin! of all unparallel'd, alone,
Who with thy beauties hast enamour'd Heaven,
Whose like has never been, nor e'er shall be;
For holy thoughts with chaste and pious acts
To the true God a sacred living shrine
In thy fecund virginity have made:
By thee, dear Mary, yet my life may be
Happy, if to thy prayers,
O Virgin meek and mild!
Where sin abounded grace shall more abound!
With bended knee and broken heart I pray
That thou my guide wouldst be,
And to such prosperous end direct my faltering way.

Bright Virgin! and immutable as bright,
O'er life's tempestuous ocean the sure star
Each trusting mariner that truly guides,
Look down, and see amid this dreadful storm

How I am tost at random and alone,
And how already my last shriek is near,
Yet still in thee, sinful although and vile,
My soul keeps all her trust;
Virgin! I thee implore
Let not thy foe have triumph in my fall;
Remember that our sin made God himself,
To free us from its chain,
Within thy virgin womb our image on Him take!

Virgin! what tears already have I shed,
Cherish'd what dreams and breathed what prayers in vain
But for my own worse penance and sure loss;
Since first on Arno's shore I saw the light
Till now, whate'er I sought, wherever turn'd,
My life has pass'd in torment and in tears,
For mortal loveliness in air, act, speech,
Has seized and soil'd my soul:
O Virgin! pure and good,
Delay not till I reach my life's last year;
Swifter than shaft and shuttle are, my days
'Mid misery and sin
Have vanish'd all, and now Death only is behind!

Virgin! She now is dust, who, living, held
My heart in grief, and plunged it since in gloom;
She knew not of my many ills this one,
And had she known, what since befell me still
Had been the same, for every other wish
Was death to me and ill renown for her;
But, Queen of Heaven, our Goddess – if to thee
Such homage be not sin –
Virgin! of matchless mind,
Thou knowest now the whole; and that, which else
No other can, is nought to thy great power:
Deign then my grief to end,
Thus honour shall be thine, and safe my peace at last!

Virgin! in whom I fix my every hope,
Who canst and will'st assist me in great need,
Forsake me not in this my worst extreme,

Regard not me but Him who made me thus;
Let his high image stamp'd on my poor worth
Towards one so low and lost thy pity move:
Medusa spells have made me as a rock
Distilling a vain flood;
Virgin! my harass'd heart
With pure and pious tears do thou fulfil,
That its last sigh at least may be devout,
And free from earthly taint,
As was my earliest vow ere madness fill'd my veins!

Virgin! benevolent, and foe of pride,
Ah! let the love of our one Author win,
Some mercy for a contrite humble heart:
For, if her poor frail mortal dust I loved
With loyalty so wonderful and long,
Much more my faith and gratitude for thee.
From this my present sad and sunken state
If by thy help I rise,
Virgin! to thy dear name
I consecrate and cleanse my thoughts, speech, pen,
My mind, and heart with all its tears and sighs;
Point then that better path,
And with complacence view my changed desires at last.

The day must come, nor distant far its date,
Time flies so swift and sure,
O peerless and alone!
When death my heart, now conscience struck, shall seize:
Commend me, Virgin! then to thy dear Son,
True God and Very Man,
That my last sigh in peace may, in his arms, be breathed!

Robert Macgregor.

SONNET FOUND IN LAURA'S TOMB.

Qui reposan quei caste e felice ossa.

Here peaceful sleeps the chaste, the happy shade
Of that pure spirit, which adorn'd this earth:
Pure fame, true beauty, and transcendent worth,
Rude stone! beneath thy rugged breast are laid.
Death sudden snatch'd the dear lamented maid!
Who first to all my tender woes gave birth,
Woes! that estranged my sorrowing soul to mirth,
While full four lustres time completely made.
Sweet plant! that nursed on Avignon's sweet soil,
There bloom'd, there died; when soon the weeping Muse
Threw by the lute, forsook her wonted toil.
Bright spark of beauty, that still fires my breast!
What pitying mortal shall a prayer refuse,
That Heaven may number thee amid the blest?

Anonymous 1777.

Here rest the chaste, the dear, the blest remains
Of her most lovely; peerless while on earth:
What late was beauty, spotless honour, worth,
Stern marble, here thy chill embrace retains.
The freshness of the laurel Death disdains;
And hath its root thus wither'd. – Such the dearth
O'ertakes me. Here I bury ease and mirth,
And hope from twenty years of cares and pains.
This happy plant Avignon lonely fed
With Life, and saw it die. – And with it lies
My pen, my verse, my reason; – useless, dead.
O graceful form! – Fire, which consuming flies
Through all my frame! – For blessings on thy head
Oh, may continual prayers to heaven rise!

Capel Lofft.

Here now repose those chaste, those blest remains
Of that most gentle spirit, sole in earth!
Harsh monumental stone, that here confinest
True honour, fame, and beauty, all o'erthrown!
Death has destroy'd that Laurel green, and torn
Its tender roots; and all the noble meed
Of my long warfare, passing (if aright
My melancholy reckoning holds) four lustres.
O happy plant! Avignon's favour'd soil
Has seen thee spring and die; – and here with thee
Thy poet's pen, and muse, and genius lies.
O lovely, beauteous limbs! O vivid fire,
That even in death hast power to melt the soul!
Heaven be thy portion, peace with God on high!

Lord Woodhouselee.

CRESCENT MOON PUBLISHING

web: www.crmoon.com e-mail: cresmopub@yahoo.co.uk

ARTS, PAINTING, SCULPTURE

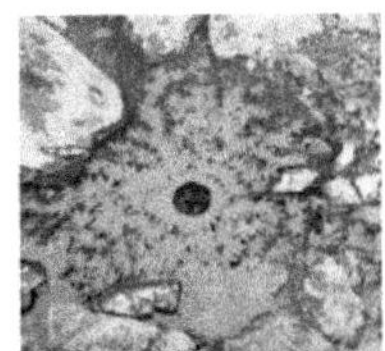

The Art of Andy Goldsworthy
Andy Goldsworthy: Touching Nature
Andy Goldsworthy in Close-Up
Andy Goldsworthy: Pocket Guide
Andy Goldsworthy In America
Land Art: A Complete Guide
The Art of Richard Long
Richard Long: Pocket Guide
Land Art In the UK
Land Art in Close-Up
Land Art In the U.S.A.
Land Art: Pocket Guide
Installation Art in Close-Up
Minimal Art and Artists In the 1960s and After
Colourfield Painting
Land Art DVD, TV documentary
Andy Goldsworthy DVD, TV documentary
The Erotic Object: Sexuality in Sculpture From Prehistory to the Present Day
Sex in Art: Pornography and Pleasure in Painting and Sculpture
Postwar Art
Sacred Gardens: The Garden in Myth, Religion and Art
Glorification: Religious Abstraction in Renaissance and 20th Century Art
Early Netherlandish Painting
Leonardo da Vinci
Piero della Francesca
Giovanni Bellini
Fra Angelico: Art and Religion in the Renaissance
Mark Rothko: The Art of Transcendence
Frank Stella: American Abstract Artist
Jasper Johns
Brice Marden
Alison Wilding: The Embrace of Sculpture
Vincent van Gogh: Visionary Landscapes
Eric Gill: Nuptials of God
Constantin Brancusi: Sculpting the Essence of Things
Max Beckmann
Caravaggio
Gustave Moreau
Egon Schiele: Sex and Death In Purple Stockings
Delizioso Fotografico Fervore: Works In Process I
Sacro Cuore: Works In Process 2
The Light Eternal: J.M.W. Turner
The Madonna Glorified: Karen Arthurs

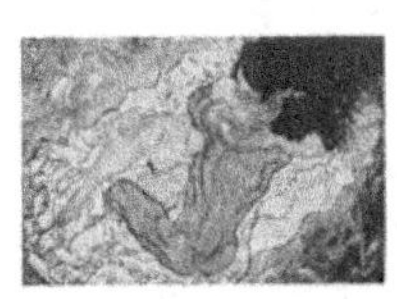

LITERATURE

J.R.R. Tolkien: The Books, The Films, The Whole Cultural Phenomenon
J.R.R. Tolkien: Pocket Guide
Tolkien's Heroic Quest
The *Earthsea* Books of Ursula Le Guin
Beauties, Beasts and Enchantment: Classic French Fairy Tales
German Popular Stories by the Brothers Grimm
Philip Pullman and *His Dark Materials*
Sexing Hardy: Thomas Hardy and Feminism
Thomas Hardy's *Tess of the d'Urbervilles*
Thomas Hardy's *Jude the Obscure*
Thomas Hardy: The Tragic Novels
Love and Tragedy: Thomas Hardy
The Poetry of Landscape in Hardy
Wessex Revisited: Thomas Hardy and John Cowper Powys
Wolfgang Iser: Essays and Interviews
Petrarch, Dante and the Troubadours
Maurice Sendak and the Art of Children's Book Illustration
Andrea Dworkin
Cixous, Irigaray, Kristeva: The *Jouissance* of French Feminism
Julia Kristeva: Art, Love, Melancholy, Philosophy, Semiotics and Psychoanalysis
Hélene Cixous I Love You: The *Jouissance* of Writing
Luce Irigaray: Lips, Kissing, and the Politics of Sexual Difference
Peter Redgrove: Here Comes the Flood
Peter Redgrove: Sex-Magic-Poetry-Cornwall
Lawrence Durrell: Between Love and Death, East and West
Love, Culture & Poetry: Lawrence Durrell
Cavafy: Anatomy of a Soul
German Romantic Poetry: Goethe, Novalis, Heine, Hölderlin
Feminism and Shakespeare
Shakespeare: Love, Poetry & Magic
The Passion of D.H. Lawrence
D.H. Lawrence: Symbolic Landscapes
D.H. Lawrence: Infinite Sensual Violence
Rimbaud: Arthur Rimbaud and the Magic of Poetry
The Ecstasies of John Cowper Powys
Sensualism and Mythology: The Wessex Novels of John Cowper Powys
Amorous Life: John Cowper Powys and the Manifestation of Affectivity (H.W. Fawkner)
Postmodern Powys: New Essays on John Cowper Powys (Joe Boulter)
Rethinking Powys: Critical Essays on John Cowper Powys
Paul Bowles & Bernardo Bertolucci
Rainer Maria Rilke
Joseph Conrad: *Heart of Darkness*
In the Dim Void: Samuel Beckett
Samuel Beckett Goes into the Silence
André Gide: Fiction and Fervour
Jackie Collins and the Blockbuster Novel
Blinded By Her Light: The Love-Poetry of Robert Graves
The Passion of Colours: Travels In Mediterranean Lands
Poetic Forms

MEDIA, CINEMA, FEMINISM and CULTURAL STUDIES

J.R.R. Tolkien: The Books, The Films, The Whole Cultural Phenomenon
J.R.R. Tolkien: Pocket Guide
The *Lord of the Rings* Movies: Pocket Guide
The Cinema of Hayao Miyazaki
Hayao Miyazaki: *Princess Mononoke*: Pocket Movie Guide
Hayao Miyazaki: *Spirited Away*: Pocket Movie Guide
Tim Burton : Hallowe'en For Hollywood
Ken Russell
Ken Russell: *Tommy*: Pocket Movie Guide
The Ghost Dance: The Origins of Religion
The Peyote Cult
Cixous, Irigaray, Kristeva: The *Jouissance* of French Feminism
Julia Kristeva: Art, Love, Melancholy, Philosophy, Semiotics and Psychoanalysis
Luce Irigaray: Lips, Kissing, and the Politics of Sexual Difference
Hélene Cixous I Love You: The *Jouissance* of Writing
Andrea Dworkin
'Cosmo Woman': The World of Women's Magazines
Women in Pop Music
HomeGround: The Kate Bush Anthology

Discovering the Goddess (Geoffrey Ashe)
The Poetry of Cinema
The Sacred Cinema of Andrei Tarkovsky
Andrei Tarkovsky: Pocket Guide
Andrei Tarkovsky: *Mirror*: Pocket Movie Guide
Andrei Tarkovsky: *The Sacrifice*: Pocket Movie Guide
Walerian Borowczyk: Cinema of Erotic Dreams

Jean-Luc Godard: The Passion of Cinema
Jean-Luc Godard: *Hail Mary*: Pocket Movie Guide
Jean-Luc Godard: *Contempt*: Pocket Movie Guide
Jean-Luc Godard: *Pierrot le Fou*: Pocket Movie Guide
John Hughes and Eighties Cinema
Ferris Bueller's Day Off: Pocket Movie Guide
Jean-Luc Godard: Pocket Guide

The Cinema of Richard Linklater
Liv Tyler: Star In Ascendance
Blade Runner and the Films of Philip K. Dick
Paul Bowles and Bernardo Bertolucci
Media Hell: Radio, TV and the Press
An Open Letter to the BBC
Detonation Britain: Nuclear War in the UK

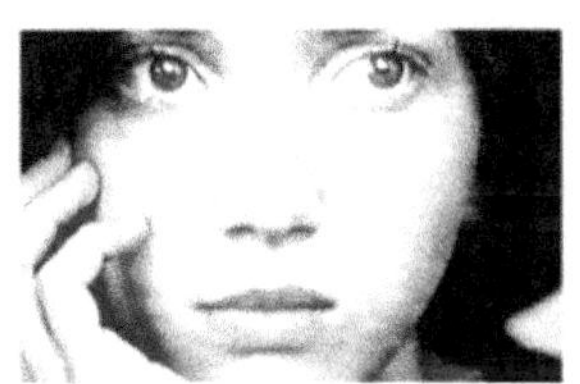

Feminism and Shakespeare
Wild Zones: Pornography, Art and Feminism
Sex in Art: Pornography and Pleasure in Painting and Sculpture
Sexing Hardy: Thomas Hardy and Feminism

The Light Eternal is a model monograph, an exemplary job. The subject matter of the book is beautifully organised and dead on beam. (Lawrence Durrell)
It is amazing for me to see my work treated with such passion and respect. (Andrea Dworkin)

CRESCENT MOON PUBLISHING
P.O. Box 1312, Maidstone, Kent, ME14 5XU, Great Britain. www.crmoon.com

cresmopub@yahoo.co.uk www.crescentmoon.org.uk

www.ingramcontent.com/pod-product-compliance
Lightning Source LLC
LaVergne TN
LVHW020501100826
845148LV00003B/684
9781861715999